~The

GREAT MUGHALS

Farhat Nasreen is a professor of History at Jamia Millia Islamia, New Delhi. Her work, *Kashful Baghaavat Gorakhpur*, presents an extremely rare eyewitness account of the Revolt of 1857. She has authored several monographs and articles on historical themes, including the much acclaimed, *If History Has Taught Us Anything*.

The
GREAT
MUGHALS

Farhat Nasreen

RUPA

Published by
Rupa Publications India Pvt. Ltd 2021
7/16, Ansari Road, Daryaganj
New Delhi 110002

Sales Centres:
Allahabad Bengaluru Chennai
Hyderabad Jaipur Kathmandu
Kolkata Mumbai

ISBN: 978-93-90260-12-6

First impression 2021

10 9 8 7 6 5 4 3 2 1

Printed at Thomson Press India Ltd, Faridabad

CONTENTS

INTRODUCTION

Contemporaries of the Mughal Empire called it the *Sultanate-i Mughalia*. In terms of the area and the time period that it covered, the empire was gigantic. It played the double role of being a modern version of an ancient state, and an ancient version of the modern one. To assign it its precise place in history can be tricky. Generally speaking, it was a continuous whole, but the people and policies involved in its sustenance changed. This change steered it away from the blanket module. But it can't be called a patchwork either, due to the continuities. Perhaps comparing it to a Rubik's cube might be a good idea. Such a cube is made up of multicoloured squares, which a player attempts to twist and turn so that all the squares on each face are of the same colour. Likewise, the first six of the Mughal emperors negotiated political, military and cultural twists and turns, to give an even tone to all fronts of their empire. They usually found a way of getting themselves out of tight corners.

Babur, the founder of the empire, drew legitimacy and enthusiasm from his Timurid-Mongol blood. However, he disapproved of the blind following of any tradition whatsoever. His successors also kept the doors open for revamping. Customs were selected or rejected on their own merit, like absorbing the good from a talk irrespective of who the speaker is. Links to the policies of local non-Muslim rulers and predecessor like Alauddin Khalji, Muhammad bin Tughlaq and Sher Shah are easily noticeable in the methods of the Mughals. They wisely used these linkages as substructures to build superstructures of their own. A super symmetry was achieved. *Jharokha-darshan* (the emperor giving an audience to the commonest of his subjects) and *Tula-daan* (items equal to the emperor's weight being distributed among the needy) were popular adaptations of customs from the non-Muslim rulers' courts. Alauddin Khalji's and Sher Shah's systems of land revenue assessment, tax collection, maintenance of records and currency, etc. were used as guidelines. The precedents of branding of horses, maintenance of muster books, nurturing of spy networks, and the conscious building of a centralized despotic state were also adopted. Of course these were refashioned and refined. For example, their *Mansabdari* system took cues from earlier practices, but was in itself unique. The Khaljis (1290–1320) were pioneers of merit-based appointments. They broke the Turkish racial monopoly on high offices. Exclusive religious monopolies were challenged by Muhammad bin Tughlaq. He personally interacted with Hindu mendicants and is known to have played Holi (an ancient Hindu festival). The Mughals insisted on religious equality; their personal beliefs, piety or impiety notwithstanding. Instead of religion, they made a great play of spirituality. Raw power supported their sovereignty, but only just.

The Mughals celebrated their blue blood, flowing from the exalted bloodline of Chingiz Khan and Timur. This facilitated their collaboration with indigenous royals who were proud of their own lineages. Thus their personal networking with other influential families, Muslims or non-Muslims, became high, wide and handsome. However, when it came to winning the confidence of the commoners, the Timurid blood would hardly have helped their case in Hindustan. Thus, Akbar heightened the strains of inclusiveness. His policy of *Sulh-i-kul* (universal peace/absolute peace) became the ultimate equilibrial *mantra*. Mughal blood and Rajput blood were mixed, through marital alliances. Inclusion of non-Muslim women in the Mughal harem changed the latter's role and character. It promoted something more than passive toleration. Perhaps, it advocated mutual respect and happy coexistence. The sociopolitical gains were immeasurable. Many cultures were subsumed under Mughal culture. For example, Mughal architecture was a mix of many styles, and so were the paintings. Sanskrit texts were translated into Persian with amazing zealousness. Mughal culture became a concoction of Indian, Persian and Central Asian styles. Besides, there was a curiosity about Western thought and actions as well.

The Divine Right Theory of Kingship may not have suited their multireligious empire. Thus the Mughals claimed a kind of spiritual authority, where sovereignty was a ray of light from the divine Sun. Since unifying the Hindustanis at a physical/ritualistic level was difficult, they tried to unify them at a mental/intellectual level. Common goals were professed before personal agendas. They used a prototype of the Social Contract Theory to rationalize their absoluteness. In a chapter from the *Ain-i-Akbari* titled, *Rawa-i rozi*, it is explained that the individual subject owed taxes and loyalty to the emperor because the latter protected him. The halo around the dynasty was hard to cut into.

Answers to their personal inventory reveal that justice and humanism were their governance ideals. Their palpable human side set them apart. Thus, the Mughals became a brand that was hard to compete with. In fact they commanded an impressive, almost unbelievable brand loyalty, even as late as 1857. It is remarkable that many of the pioneers of India's first war of independence chose Bahadur Shah Zafar II, the last Mughal ruler, to be projected as a replacement for the foreign rulers. Indeed, Babur's progeny had, by then, become the children of Hindustan. They were inseparable from it, like whiteness in milk, colours in flowers, or the inexplicable fragrance of wet mud.

ONE

ZAHIRUDDIN MUHAMMAD BABUR

1483–1530

'When one has pretensions to rule and a desire for conquest, one cannot sit back and just watch if events don't go right once and twice…With whatever artifice your portrait is made, you are still more. They call you "soul". But without artifice you are more than a soul…'

—BABUR'S REFLECTIONS[1]

Babur was a lineal descendant of Chingiz Khan (1162–1227) and Timur (1339–1405). Both of them were unbeatable conquerers in their respective times. His mother, Qutlugh Nigar Khanum (d. 1505), was the daughter of a Mongol chief, Yunus Khan (d. 1487). She was a 14th generation progeny of the line of Chingiz Khan. His father, Umar Sheikh Mirza (d. 1494), traced descent from Timur's son, Miran Shah (1336–1405). Thus Babur was a fifth generation patrilineal descendant of Timur. His dynastic legitimacy was matchless due to this mingling of blood. Paradoxically, it attracted friends and enemies in equal numbers. For him, his bloodline was like a pool of enthusiasm. He drew from it to rebuild his confidence after every smashing failure.

Amongst the major players in the political field of the fifteenth–sixteenth century, Transoxiana and Cisoxiana were the Persianized Mirzas—descendants of Amir Timur, non-Persianized Khans—descendants of Chingiz Khan, Sultans (usually suffix), the blue-

---

[1]Cf. Babur, *Baburnama*, Wheeler M. Thackston translated, edited & annotated, introduction by Salman Rushdie: *The Baburnama: Memoirs of Babur, Prince and Emperor*, The Modern Library, New York, 2002, pp. 67 & 115.

blooded Uzbegs of Turkistan and Otrar. Uzbeg hero Shaibani Khan was dreaded by the Turks. Besides them, the Begs—Turic tribal and military lords, Tajiks—Persianized nobles, Dughlat Amirs—nobles of Kashghar and Uralipa, and the Tarkhan Mongols of Samarqand were the most prominent. Titles like Sayyid, Maulana, Khwaja, Mir, etc. indicated some intellectual/religious/spiritual attainment. Generally, Turco-Mongolians were brave warriors, but civil sophistication was the forte of Persianized elements. In the early 14th century, a lot of Chaghtayid Mongols converted to Islam. However, they did not immediately unlearn their earlier cultural systems. As a contrast, the Timurid residents of Samarkand and Bukhara were custom-built for Persianized Islamization. Timur was a Barlas Turk. His clan was a subdivision of the Chaghtai Turks, who were related to Chingiz Khan's son, Chaghtai. Besides, Timur had married a princess of the Mongol royal family. His title 'Gurgan' declared his status as a son-in-law of blue-blooded Mongols. He respected that designation. This intermixing notwithstanding, the Timurids and Mongols were divided by Persianization. Babur belonged to an urban pocket. His lot referred to the Mongols as 'Moghuls'. He disapproved of their cruel military tactics, barbarianism and political undependability. He was smitten with his paternal Timurid-Turkish ancestry. His title 'Mirza', was a short form of the Timurid designation Amirzadeh (son of a noble).

Umar Shaikh Mirza ruled over Farghana. This fertile alluvial valley was enclosed by mountains on the north, east and south. These became impassable in winters. The fortress of Akhsi was an important urban settlement. Umar Shaikh usually resided here. He aspired to be an urbanite, as sophisticated as his relatives at Herat or Samarqand. In his autobiography, Babur shares his memories of his father. The qualities that Umar Sheikh's descendants inherited from him are numerous enough to be noticed even in a quick review. His liberal nature was well known. He was a disciple of Khawaja Ubaidullah Ahrar (d 1490), a renowned sufi saint of his times. Perhaps the majestic mysticism of the Great Mughals could be traced back to his mystical inclinations. His insistence on justice was another ideal that his royal descendants tried to imbibe. Babur narrates that once, a caravan was trapped in deep snow. Only two of the travellers survived. His father took all the goods and beasts of burden in his custody. However, despite being hard up, he didn't use any of them. Instead, he summoned the rightful heirs from Samarqand and Khurasan, and handed everything to them. The whole exercise took almost two years.

Umar Shaikh was fond of reading. He was familiar with the works of Jalaluddin Rumi (1207–73), Amir Khusroe Dihlavi (1253–1325) and Abul Qasim Firdausi Tusi (940–1020), to name a few. This shows his interest in classic works of sophisticated Persian. One of his dangerous qualities, which his descendents inherited, was his love for intoxicants. He consumed both wine and opium. In fact, he even cajoled Babur to drink wine. Eventually Babur too became a regular drinker. Umar Shaikh was also short tempered. He could often be found involved in brawls. His scars told stories of his ambitions and anger. All in all, he was an unpretentious man, well-rounded in physical and mental attributes. Personally, he kept the pen and the sword in equilibrium. Professionally, his state balanced culture and war.

Babur was born on 14 February 1483. He was Umar Shaikh's eldest son. Yunus Khan, his maternal grandfather, and other Mongol relatives visited Farghana to celebrate his birth. They found his name Zahiruddin Muhammad too complicated, so he was given a pet name—Babur. He had two brothers and five sisters. His sister Khanzada Begum (b. 1478) was his only full sibling.

Umar Shaikh's accidental death on 8 June 1494 took Babur by surprise. He was at Andizhan, and the news reached him the next day. Besides the personal loss, he had to face political predators of all sorts. Power vampires hovered around his kingdom to depose him. His claim to the crown was ignored, as if it didn't exist at all. Luckily, at this point his immediate family stood by him. Three aggressors emerged almost simultaneously. Ahmad Mirza (d. 1494), his paternal uncle, attacked from the southwest. Mahmud Khan, his maternal uncle, approached from the northwest, and a distant Mongol relative, Abu Bakr Dughlat (d. 1514), arrived from the extreme eastern end.

Ahmad Mirza's attack pretty much proved the hypothesis that internal wars between Timur's descendants were self-destructive. In fact, besides being Babur's uncle, he was also his father-in-law. His daughter, Ayesha Sultan Begum, had been married to Babur in 1488. The groom was just five years old, and all that he later remembered of the event was that as per the Turkish custom, he was asked to lift the bride's veil. Qutluq Nigar Khanum had enthusiastically travelled 300 miles to Samarqand for this wedding. Obviously, the marriage was meant to strengthen the exclusivity of Timurid blood and to weaken internal rivalries. However, the plan clearly seemed to have failed, and so did the marriage, eventually. Sometime in early 1500, the marriage was consummated. Babur was young and very shy. His mother had to literally push him into spending time with his bride. He visited her once in 30 or 40 days and gradually they grew apart. Around this phase, he became infatuated with a boy from the camp market. Incidentally, his name was Baburi, matching with his own. But this was just an infatuation, which burnt bright but died fast. He remembered being lost in thoughts of his beloved and then becoming speechless in front of the boy. However, Babur was not a homosexual; his negative comments about those who were are ample proof of that. He seemed aware of the infeasibility of such an attachment. As far as the intense verses that he wrote for Baburi go, they seem to be amplified and super sweetened versions of his relatively less serious emotions. Perhaps they were 'an idealizing strand in his poetry, an almost inaccessible love expressed in homoerotic literary genre.'[2] The other paternal cousins who were married to him were Masuma Begum and Zainab Sultan Begum. It may also be noted that Babur's maternal aunt, Mihir Nigar Khanum, was married to Ahmad Mirza.

---

[2]*Exploring Medieval India Sixteenth to the Eighteenth Centuries* vol-2, Meena Bhargava (edited), Orient BlackSwan, New Delhi, 2010, p. 238.

Babur's well-wishers whisked him off to a *Namaazgaah* (mosque) outside the city, so he could be saved from harm in any eventuality. Fortunately, the attacks were contained and losses were limited to small townships on the western borders. The 12-year-old king rewarded his loyalists. However, encouraged by an important minister, Hasan Yaqub, Babur's younger half-brother Jahangir (b. 1485) refused to recognize his authority. Such internecine strife was often fuelled by warlords who used princes of blood as puppet rulers. For most people, the prospect of personal gains swayed the choice between loyalty and betrayal. Babur was also challenged by two non-Chinggised Mongols, Sultan Ahmad Tambal and Ali Dost Taghai. They had served his father and had initially been loyal to him as well. Their rebelliousness encouraged others to also disobey the young king. In mid–1495, Babur visited his maternal uncle Mahmud Khan at Taskent. He had hoped that this would impress on the local lords to submit to his authority. It didn't.

In the following year, 1496, he got an opportunity to prove his mettle. Sultan Ahmad Mirza had died on his way back to Samarqand. His brother, Sultan Mahmud Mirza, who held Badakshan, succeeded him. He was a tyrant. Babur reports that a certain man's wife was abducted by one of his officers. When the aggrieved fellow complained to Mahmud Mirza, the latter replied that his wife had been with him for many years. He could very well let her be with another man for a few days. Babur also laments that the Mirza kept a lot of catamites to satisfy his homosexual urges. He was always on the lookout for attractive, beardless youths, to be inducted as his catamites. He turned his officers' sons and his sons' officers into sexual slaves. His influence made it fashionable to keep catamites. His sons were also shamefully immoderate debauches. Within a year of taking over Samarqand, Mahmud Mirza died. He was succeeded by his 18-year-old son Baisunghar Mirza. The latter's succession was challenged by two of his brothers. Babur joined those rebels. He believed that Mahmud Mirza's oppression had led to this situation, and philosophized: 'Beware of festering inner wounds, for inner wounds surface in the end. Distress no one in so far as you are able, for one cry of anguish can upset the whole world.'[3]

Anyway, Babur and his allies besieged Samarqand. After seven months of stubborn persistence, the city fell in November 1497. Then it dawned on the victors that they didn't really have much to celebrate. The long siege had devastated the place internally. The areas that had surrendered willingly couldn't be looted. The others had already been denuded by bands of plunderers. The city was in such distress that it needed assistance, seeds and monetary advances. It had nothing to give. The military adventurers who had joined Babur in hopes of making quick gains were disappointed. Impatient, annoyed and shamelessly unapologetic, they began deserting. Their vanishing act was so quick that Babur was left practically alone to consolidate his hollow victory. However, none of this was as bad as what was to happen at Farghana in the following days. The treacherous Sultan Ahmad Tambal dashed to Farghana. Jahangir Mirza also took off with him. With Babur's brother as an ally, Tambal was hooked up for usurpation. After all, Jahangir Mirza was also Umar Shiekh's son, and that took care of the question of Timurid legitimacy. Andijan, Babur's stronghold, was besieged by traitors while he was at Samarqand. His mother, his maternal grandmother Ehsan Daulat, and other relatives were trapped in the fort. Their desperate petitions for help put Babur in a fix. He was sure to lose Samarqand if he left without consolidating his authority there. But he hardly had any other choice. He didn't have the heart to ignore his mother's pleas and stand idle. Thus dictated by emotion, he left Samarqand in March 1498 and lost it as expected.

Perhaps his family's insistence on his return to Farghana stemmed from their political sagacity. They may have anticipated that Samarqand was a giant but nebulous zone, while the ownership of Farghana was far more crystalline. A bird in hand is better than two in the bush. Ehsan Daulat was particularly famous for her courage. Once, her husband, Yunus Khan, was defeated and arrested

---

[3] *Baburnama*, p. 28.

by an adversary, Shaikh Jamal. The latter presented her to one of his favourite generals. When the man approached her in private, she had him stabbed by her female attendants. The dead body was unceremoniously tossed to the street below. When this news reached Shaikh Jamal, he immediately summoned her. She argued that since her husband was alive, she could not accept any illegitimate groom. So she was allowed to join Yunus Khan in the prison. She was an intelligent woman, whose advice was sought even in political and military matters.

Anyway, Babur had no sooner left Samarqand than the disheartening news of the loss of Andijan arrived. Both Samarqand and Farghana were lost. Tambal had assassinated his tutor, Maulana Muhammad Qazi, a Naqshbandi sufi. The latter was the face of Babur's sympathizers at Farghana. Babur had never known such pain and distress. Not just kingdom-less, but also homeless, he took refuge in a small town at the western entrance of Farghana. At 15, Babur had lost his inheritance to his ambitions. Regretful tears flooded his eyes, and they just wouldn't stop. Fortunately, the safe arrival of his mother and grandmother stabilized him. Reverting to positivity, he convinced himself that if one had pretensions to rule and a desire for conquest, one could not just sit back and watch if things did not go right once or twice. Thus he went to Taskent to ask for his maternal uncle Mahmud Khan's help.

Whatever assistance he received from his uncle wasn't enough to recover any of the places. Month after month, he wandered about in anxious disappointment. A Mongol chieftain helped him through the freezing winters. Luckily, the very element of disloyalty which had had him dethroned now came to his rescue. Annoyed with Tambal's arrogance, his commander Ali Dost Taghai defected to Babur's camp. This changed the game. With Taghai's help, Babur occupied a town near Andijan. Emboldened by his return, the locals revolted against Tambal. Disturbances erupted at Akhsi as Babur's Mongol comrades massacred his enemies there. Tambal seemed to be losing control. However, just before he was to besiege Andijan, Babur fell ill. His injuries and illnesses had always bothered him, because they slowed him down. He could hardly ever afford to be lagging. Although he had gotten back on his feet after a previous illness, due to premature strain his ailment relapsed. The second bout was far more severe. He literally lost his speech for four days. Water was dribbled into his month from a piece of wet cotton. The warriors who had joined him became apprehensive and were on the verge of deserting him. But once he was relatively better, he got into action immediately. Despite running a fever, he rode ceaselessly for three days and three nights. The exertion paid off, and many of the enemy platoons were hammered.

His officers opined that they should be allowed to reclaim their personal goods from the Mongols who had looted them earlier. This recovery could have refreshed hostilities with those of the Mongols who had submitted to him. In fact, retrieval of goods from those who had voluntarily submitted was pretty much against the norms. However, Babur was pressurized by his allies to permit this. He agreed in haste, but regretted the decision later. Indeed, identification of goods, horses, etc. and their subsequent restoration to their rightful owners was a very delicate task. It caused confusion and ill will. Mongol bands that had only recently yielded to him became rebellious. His bigger agenda against Tambal suffered. It was a political blunder, but it taught him caution and foresight. He observed: 'In taking realms and administering kingdoms, although some things appear rational on the surface, one has to consider a hundred thousand things behind every act.'[4]

In June 1499, Andijan was finally recovered. Nevertheless, Tambal and Jahangir remained active in the region. They unsettled Babur's rule every now and then. Ultimately, peace was negotiated in February 1500. It was settled that Akhsi and its neighbourhood would be held by Tambal and Jahangir. Babur would keep Andijan and its environs. A futuristic provision of the treaty stated that the two parties would jointly conquer Samarqand. Thereafter, Babur would relocate there.

---

[4]Ibid., p. 77.

Andijan would be given to Jahangir. This settlement hardly pacified Babur. His kingdom had been partitioned. The only thing that he had gained was time; time to wait for another opportunity to stamp out Tambal.

Babur appreciated the bravery of two opponents in a combat he witnessed in 1499. He wrote: 'In this battle two warriors fought outstandingly. For our side, Samad by name and for the other side, a Moghul, Shahsuwar, by name. Shahsuwar gave such a blow that it passed right through Samad's helmet and sank well into his head. Despite his wound Samad struck so hard that his sword broke off a piece of bone, the size of the palm of the hand from Shahsuwar's skull. Shahsuwar had no helmet. They trepanned his head wound and he recovered. There was so one to trepan Samad's head so he died three or four days later.'[5]

Within four months of Babur's pact with Tambal, an opportunity to re-invade Samarqand appeared. Tarkhan Mongols of Samarqand revolted against their nominal ruler, Sultan Ali Mirza. The latter was Babur's cousin. The Mongols invited Babur to take his place. Although his position in Farghana was still insecure, he decided to give Samarqand a second shot. Unfortunately, while he was still on his way, Shaibani Khan, the dreaded Uzbeg superhero, occupied Bukhara. It was rumoured that Samarqand was his next destination. On hearing this, Babur made a detour to Kish. To his dismay, Shaibani Khan actually occupied Samarqand within a week or so. This was just the beginning of Babur's contest with this man.

Shaibani Khan was the leader of a Turko-Mongol-Uzbeg confederacy. After Chingiz Khan and Timur, he was the only one who succeeded in bringing various tribes under an umbrella of common goals. While the Timurids lost kingdoms to in-house divisions, the Uzbegs ensured that the descendants of Timur also lost their heads, on which they could wear crowns. Many Timurid princes were killed by them. In this context, Babur was lucky to have survived despite his repeated encounters with Shaibani Khan. With time, occasional

---

[5]Ibid., 77–79.

Uzbeg raids grew into full grown military challenges. While Timurid and Mongol loyalties yo-yoed with the flow of power, Shaibani Khan embraced ascendancy with his band of steady followers.

Babur was in a fix again. He blamed Sultan Ali Mirza's mother, Zuhra Begi Agha, for the loss of Samarqand. Apparently she had sent a message to Shaibani Khan that if he married her, she would ensure that her son handed over Samarqand to him. This, according to Babur, was a stupid and irrational proposal, perhaps designed and taught to her by some traitor. He felt that in her lust to get a husband, that wretched, feeble-minded woman had brought destruction on her son. Shaibani Khan did marry her but treated her less than a concubine. She was ignored and sidelined. Sultan Ali Mirza and his close associates were assassinated. An influential *sufi*, Khwaja Yahya Ahrari, and his son were banished to Khurasan, but were killed on the way by Uzbegs. They were Babur's supporters. These murders roused popular resentment against the Uzbegs. To avoid taking responsibility for the unlawful killings, Shaibani Khan distanced himself from this episode. He claimed to have no knowledge of the plot. Babur felt that he was lying. Even if he wasn't, as the leader of the Uzbegs, he was accountable for the *sufis'* murders. He wrote that Shaibani's irresponsible excuse was worse than the crime itself. If officers had free reign to engage in such acts of cruelty without the knowledge of their leader or king, what was the use of such leadership or kingship?

Anyway, Babur was jammed in the middle of nowhere, once again. This episode gave him a taste of the generosity of hypocrites, which is typically extended to those who don't need it. The supposedly big-hearted and open-handed chieftains cold shouldered him because he was in need. His well-off cousins were treated better. He recalled ruefully that the headman of Fan had presented his cousin Sultan Masud Mirza with 70 or 80 horses and performed other services of equal value. In contrast, he sent a second-rate horse to Babur, not even bothering to go himself. People renowned for their generosity had turned stingy. A people well-known for their cooperative nature had forgotten how to be helpful. These experiences taught him to be wary of good weather friends and flatterers. He wrote: 'Who has seen, O heart, good of the people of the world? Expect no good of him in whom there is no good.'[6]

The Tarkhans, who had initially shown loyalty towards Babur, ditched him. They felt that facing the Uzbegs was too hazardous. So they sided with Khusrau Shah, the Qipchaq Turk who had ruled over Badakshan since 1494. On the homefront, Ali Dost Taghai changed sides again. He rejoined Tambal. In a repeat of Babur's last sojourn at Samarqand, his family in Andijan became unsafe again.

However, the newness of Shaibani's rule in Samarqand encouraged Babur to continue to try his luck there. He anticipated that the people of Samarqand and Shaibani Khan had not yet become attached to each other. Besides, Samarqand had been the capital of the Timurids, hence Babur's chances of getting popular cooperation were substantial. Thus, banking on local backup and surprise tactics, Babur stormed into Samarqand and occupied it.

Shaibani Khan couldn't have imagined that some 19-year-old Timurid would dare to take such a risk. But Babur did. And it worked—at least for the time being. Babur was indeed welcomed by the locals. Thus his relative popularity and the power of Timurid legitimacy stood proven. When he entered the city at dawn, the people were still asleep. Some shopkeepers who were working early looked out of their shops and recognized him. They called down blessings upon him. A little while later, when the news of his arrival spread, there was a general spirit of jubilation among the locals. Excited by the unexpected victory of a Timurid, they stoned and clubbed the Uzbegs to death. Their bodies floated in the gutters. Shaibani Khan escaped.

Now, Babur's family was to join him at Samarqand. Ayesha Sultan Begum had given birth to his first child—a daughter, Fakhrunnisa. Everything seemed hunky dory, but then Shaibani Khan returned. It was sometime in April–May 1501. Despite Babur's desperate efforts, his forces were out-manoeuvred by the Uzbegs' Tulghama flank assault.

---

[6]Ibid., p. 97.

They encircled his forces and rained arrows on them. They were very well-organized, both in advance and retreat. The Mongols on his side turned with the tide. Babur said that had he won, they would have looted the booty, but now that he was losing, they unhorsed his men and plundered them.

Babur backtracked to Samarqand and a lockdown followed. The Uzbegs laid a siege. A veteran commander like Shaibani Khan would not have his prestige dented by a young Timurid. The siege dragged on. Months passed and resources inside Samarqand diminished. The lockdown caused a serious shortage of food. The poor and the unfortunate ate dogs and donkeys. Horses were fed on shavings and chips of wood, and leaves of Mulberry and Elm. Desertion became increasingly frequent in Babur's camp.

Perhaps the only man who could have bailed him out of this grave situation was Sultan Husain Baiqara, the Timurid ruler of Herat. Babur sent him urgent messages for help. But instead of helping him, Baiqara's comradeship tilted in favour of Shaibani Khan. Apparently, he had missed the big picture of the Uzbeg–Timurid conflict. The price for such neglect was high. The Uzbegs later slaughtered many princes of Baiqara's bloodline. After all, it was their grand plan to liquidate Timur's descendants.

Anyway, with his petitions for help being ignored at every quarter, Babur decided to back off in July 1501. In what seems like a political understanding, his elder sister Khanzada Begum was left behind at Samarqand to be married to Shaibani Khan. In return, the later allowed him safe passage. The *Shaibaninamah* claims that she had fallen in love with the Uzbeg, and the marriage wasn't just a diplomatic bargain. Eventually, she bore him a son called Khurram Shah. Later, Shaibani Khan divorced her, and thereafter she married a prominent noble, Mahdi Khwaja.

Babur's exit meant that Samarqand was lost. He had won and lost Samarqand twice. It was devastating. On the other hand, Tambal was in a very dominant position at Farghana. Babur's commanders were so terrified of him that one Ahmad Beg had to motivate his colleagues to fight Tambal by saying: 'How much of a man is this Tambal for you to be so scared? If your eyes are afraid, shut them and let's go face him.'[7]

In the ensuing flight from Samarqand, Babur was so disoriented that despite his expertise at riding, he fell from his horse. His head was hurt. His brain normalized only in the evening. Throughout the day, he couldn't register anything. Events seemed like dreams and phantoms. Andijan had been occupied by Tambal, and once again Babur had lost both Samarqand and Farghana. He took shelter in a small village called Dakhkat. The freezing winters of 1501–1502 were spent here. His attempts at seeking help from his maternal uncle, Mahmud Khan, failed. To get rid of his needy nephew, the Khan formally assigned the town of Auratipura to him. This was held by Mohammad Husain Mirza Dughlat, who was married to one of Babur's Mongol aunts. Obviously, Dughlat refused to part with his dominion. Babur was quite helpless unless the Khan actually backed up his claim with military support. Unfortunately no such patronage was extended. In a state of utter disillusionment, Babur composed the following lines: 'With whatever artifice your portrait is made you still are more. They call you "soul" but without artifice you are more than a soul.' In this phase he had an insightful verse of Saadi inscribed near a tomb: 'I heard that the fortunate Jamshid inscribed on a stone at a fountainhead: At this spring many like us who boasted, passed away in the twinkling of an eye. With valour and might we seized the world and yet we did not take it with us to the grave.'[8]

In those days, Babur usually walked barefoot. His soles hardened—so much so that mountainous rocks and stones made no difference to him. During his wanderings, he met a woman who was 111 years old. One of her relatives had served in Timur's army. She recalled anecdotes narrated by him. Ninety-six of her children, grand-children, great grandchildren and great-great grandchildren lived in Dakhkat. If the dead ones were also counted, the number

---

[7]Ibid., p. 109.
[8]Ibid., p. 114.

would go up to 200.

As he wandered aimlessly, randomness characterized his days. He wrote: 'No one remembers anyone in tribulation. No one gladdens anyone in exile. In this exile my heart has not been gladdened. No one can be comforted at all in exile.' And 'Other than my own soul I never found a faithful friend. Other than my own heart I never found a confidant.'[9]

In June 1502, Babur visited his uncle at Tashkent again. He tried to convince the Khan that they must unite to snub the Uzbegs before they became too formidable. He argued that a fire should be put out while it is still a spark. If left unchecked, it would become an all consuming inferno. Urging his uncle to take quick action, he said that one should shoot an arrow so quickly that the enemy doesn't even get an opportunity to string his bow. But the Khan was not convinced and remained non-committal. In fact, he became cold and distant. Visiting his affectionate grandmother was the only happiness Babur could find. In her house, he felt like himself.

Luckily his other Chaghtai uncle, Ahmad Khan, was more perceptive. He arrived from North China to mobilize the Mongols against the Uzbegs. After a long time, Babur saw a ray of hope. A tripartite alliance was formed between him and his uncles. Shaibani Khan was their ultimate target, but Tambal had to be butted on priority. In the middle of all this military planning, the family get-togethers were an emotional relief. Everyone gathered at Shah Begum's house and sat around talking about old times until midnight. Babur met Ahmad Khan for the first time. He noted that in comparison to his other urbanized maternal relatives, this uncle's dress and behaviour were far more conventionally Mongol. Ahmad Khan never let go of his sword. It was his weapon of choice. He kept it either by his side or in his hand at all times. He said that the six-flanged mace, the flail, the hatchet and the battleaxe work only in one place when they strike, but when a sword hits the mark, it works from head to toe.

Now Babur and his uncles headed for the recovery of Farghana.

---

[9]Ibid., p. 117.

In one of the battles with Tambal, Babur was caught off guard. An arrow pierced straight through his thigh. Taking advantage of this injury, Tambal landed such a blow on his head that it went numb. Luckily, he was wearing an under-helmet cap on his head. Although not a single thread of the cap was cut, his head was badly wounded. Ironically, this sword had been presented to Tambal by Babur himself. It was a big, broad one, made by Babur's friend Noyan. These injuries were a painful setback. Babur could walk only with the help of a staff. A Mongol named Atika Bakhshi, an expert surgeon, treated him. Babur seemed quite impressed by this doctor. The fellow could heal even those whose brains had spilled out. He could easily treat any sort of wound with his herb bag. For some wounds, he prescribed salve-like medicines, for others the medicines were to be swallowed. An animal's foot was rubbed on Babur's thigh and no dressing was applied. Besides that, some herbal medicines were prescribed. The doctor told him he had once had a patient whose leg bone had been shattered. He had hollowed out the flesh, taken out all the bone splinters, made a paste, and put it in place of the bone. When the paste solidified it became just like the bone. Babur was fascinated by the surgical and medicinal accomplishments of this doctor.

While Babur was off the grid due to his injuries, his uncles drew up a new plan. They proposed that Farghana would go to Ahmad Khan and later, when they conquer Samarqand, it would be given to Babur. Of course, Babur was smart enough to understand that this had nothing to do with his betterment. It was a mistake to bring his uncles to his ancestral dominions. Instead of helping him recover Farghana, they wanted the place for themselves. Who would have known better than Babur that conquering Samarqand was easier said than done? It was an ambitious dream, but not easily doable. But he was in no position to question or contradict his uncles, so he played along. Andijan was besieged by the Khans.

With Mongol pressure building upon him, Tambal played two cards. First, he used underhand diplomacy to break Babur's alliance with his uncles. He believed that without Babur by their side, the

Mongols would not be able to get a foothold in this area. Second, he sent an invitation to Shaibani Khan to come over. He hoped that even if the Uzbeg commander took over the place, Tambal would be amply rewarded. Interestingly, both the plans worked. As soon as rumours of Shaibani Khan's arrival spread, the Mongols backed off from Andijan. In fact, they were literally chased out. So much for their dream of conquering Farghana and Samarqand! In the meantime, the fort of Akhsi was handed over to Babur by Tambal's brother. At this juncture, Jahangir Mirza finally decided to ally with his elder brother. This put Tambal in a tight spot. With his legitimizing blood prince gone, he became desperate. Akhsi was attacked and Babur was again driven out. In fact, granting him easy access to the fort had all along been a part of Tambal's plan of separating him from his uncles.

The winter of 1502–1503 was a nightmare. Babur wandered like a vagabond: hiding from enemies and fighting the weather. There were days when he had to do without food and nights when he slept in the open. He realized that no fear was greater than the fear of death. At times he felt that he just couldn't go on anymore. He philosophized: '. . . whether one lived to a hundred or a thousand, in the end, one had to die. Be it a hundred years or one day, in the end one must depart from this noxious place. I readied myself for death.'

Sometime in early 1503, Babur rejoined his uncles. In June 1503 they actually fought Shaibani Khan jointly, but were defeated. His uncles were captured. Mahmud Khan and his five sons were murdered by the Uzbegs in 1512. Ahmad Khan had died earlier. Babur escaped. He suffered painful hardships yet again. An additional fear was that adventurers in his camp could disunite him and Jahangir Mirza, and use the prince as a string puppet to legitimize their own power. His well-wisher Baqi Beg warned him that two sovereigns in one province and two generals in one army always cause strife and tribulation. Ten poor men can sleep on one rug, but two kings cannot fit in one clime. If a man of God eats half a loaf of bread, he gives the other half to the poor. A king may take possession of an entire clime, but he will still hunger for another. Thus his loyalists opined that Jahangir Mirza should not be allowed to move around freely, lest such leniency later became a cause of regret for Babur. The latter, however was inclined to take an easygoing and trusting view. He didn't like to punish the people he loved just because they had indulged in some breach of etiquette. Although Jahangir Mirza had betrayed him on earlier occasions for territory and liege men, Babur was grateful that he had now joined him, all uncertainties notwithstanding. Jahangir Mirza had followed him through tough journeys and had given him no reason to doubt his intentions. Unfortunately, Babur was mistaken. Jahangir Mirza did leave him again, and went away with venturesome commanders.

This betrayal still did not teach Babur to distrust his brothers, but it did teach him to trust the legacy of his bloodline. He realized that the dynastic legitimacy that he and his brothers carried in their persons was in itself priceless. His royalty did not depend on possessing Farghana or Samarqand. He was born royal. Shaibani Khan had known this all along. That is precisely why the ruthless draining of Timurid–Mongol blue blood was always a part of his plan. Indeed, Babur was lucky to have survived the Uzbegs. He resolved that he had to live to fight another day. Farghana or no Farghana, he had to build a kingdom. Kingship flowed in his blood. Thus, instead of being a celebrated refugee at the court in Herat, he decided to go to Kabul. The erstwhile ruler of this province, Ulugh Beg Kabuli, his paternal uncle, had died in 1502. The new ruler, Muqim Arghun, was so intimidated by Babur's arrival that he surrendered voluntarily and moved to Qandhar.

This was a fresh beginning. The runaway became a ruler. From 1504 to 1526, Kabul anchored the fluidity of Babur's life. Despite its shifting tribal politics, there was something calm about Kabul. It settled in his heart just as much as he settled there. He studied, read, wrote, thought and philosophized. Gatherings of friends and experts of fine arts were regularly organized. A vibrant island of Persianized Timurid urbanity emerged in the sea of Afghan turbulence. On the personal front, he fathered 18 children and made time to supervise their upbringing. His son Kamran was with him till 12 years of age, and Babur took keen interest in his education. He himself wrote a treatise on Muslim law to help his son understand it. Babur fondly called him 'Shaikh Muhammad' to acknowledge the boy's interest in theological studies.

At Kabul, Babur didn't have to dodge death as often as he did during his Farghana days. But challenges had a way of finding him wherever he went. The submission of local tribes had to be periodically reinforced by military raids. His brothers Jahangir Mirza and Nasir Mirza were assigned Ghazni and Lamghanat respectively. His Mongol relatives were also given advantageous postings. By 1505, Nasir Mirza had become somewhat independent. In 1507, ambition dragged him into a direct conflict with the Uzbegs. Thoroughly defeated, he returned to Kabul in tatters. Babur immediately forgave his follies. Jahangir Mirza remained loyal to him from 1506 onwards.

Babur's commitment towards his relatives was promoted by his own emotional vulnerability and a tendency to self-censure if he was harsh with anyone. Kinship actually did mean something to the Timurids, at least till Babur's and his sons' times. To encourage himself to forgive and let go, Babur often quoted the proverb: 'Entrust to fate him who does you evil, for fate is an avenging servant for you.'[10] Perhaps the one man whom Babur found unforgiveable was Shaibani Khan. When Husain Mirza of Herat began mobilizing the Timurids to form a confederation against the latter, Babur was more than enthusiastic to join in. He wrote: 'We felt it was necessary to go to Khurasan for several reasons. One was that when a great Padishah like Sultan Husayn Mirza, who sat on Timur Beg's throne, sent out a summon to all parts, to his sons and Begs and was mounting a campaign against a foe like Shaibani Khan, if others were going on foot we would go on our head and if others were going armed with clubs we would go armed with rocks.'[11]

---

[10]Ibid., 188
[11]Ibid., 192.

Although the inviter, Husain Mirza, died in May 1506, Babur continued his march towards Herat. In October 1506, he met the Mirza's sons. He estimated that his sophisticated cousins were outstanding in social graces, but were strangers to the realities of military command and the rough and tumble of battle. No wonder they failed to notice the Uzbegs' potential to destroy them. Uzbeg torridity was evaporating Timurid blood, but they did not seem to care. As long as wine flowed in their cups, they were happy. Looking through the lens of his experience, Babur prophesized their doom. He was right. Within eight months of his departure from Herat, the city was captured by Shaibani Khan. That was sometime in May 1507. Some of his relatives were beheaded straight away, while others were tortured and then killed.

Politically the visit was a failure, but personally Babur gained much. He made fascinating memories and met Masuma Sultan Begum, his future wife. Here he was initiated into the drinking club, something that he had resisted for so long. Later, he pledged to give it up when he turned 40. When he turned 39, he drank too much, since his self-imposed deadline of promised abstinence was very close. However, Babur never forced anyone who did not drink to try it. Recollections of the visit highlighted Babur's relative simplicity. For the meeting with his cousin Badiuzzaman, it was pre-decided that Babur would kneel as soon as he entered the camp. Badiuzzaman would quickly rise and come forward to receive him. Babur did his part promptly, but Badiuzzaman's movements were slow. Someone had to tug on Babur's belt to signal him to slow down. Perhaps his prestige could have been compromised if he went too close to Badiuzzaman before being welcomed. But Babur didn't seem to care. In fact, he didn't always insist on being treated as high and mighty. Later, roasted goose was served at a party. Babur didn't know how to carve or disjoint it. So he decided not to eat it. When Badiuzzaman questioned his disinclination, he told the truth. He was grateful when his cousin carved and disjointed it for him. He appreciated that Badiuzzaman was without equal in social sophistication.

However, Babur knew that as far as far as military enthusiasm was considered, he and his cousins were not on the same page. He felt that they weren't really serious about fighting the Uzbegs. Thus, going back to Kabul seemed to be the best option. Despite his restlessness to go back home, his journey to Kabul began only in late December. Snow had fallen. Some of his men lost their limbs to the cold. His party was hit by a blizzard, but Babur refused to take shelter in a cave unless it accommodated all his men. He remembered a Persian proverb: 'Death with friends is a feast',[12] and was ready to die with his men. Luckily, they found a cave that did accommodate everyone. However, when he reached Kabul, his face was unrecognizable due to frostbite. His friend Ahmad Yusuf didn't recognize him. Despite Babur's shouting, 'Hey Dost! Hey Dost!' (Hi Friend!), Yusuf struck at him with a sword but, luckily, missed.[13]

Anyway, the end of his worries was still far. There had been a coup at Kabul. Wais Mirza, son of his uncle Mahmud Mirza, had been raised to the throne of Kabul. A popular rumour that Babur had been arrested by his cousins at Herat had facilitated this revolution. Babur's maternal relatives and Mirza Husain Dughlat were the main conspirators. He had reached just in time to contain the conspiracy. He spared the conspirators' lives, something that would become increasingly difficult for his descendants to do. The involvement of his maternal grandmother and aunt in this conspiracy was an emotional setback. Babur pondered that just because his mother had passed away (June 1505), it didn't mean that his maternal relatives would treat him as if he wasn't Yunus Khan's grandson. Anyway he forgave them. And he did it with great humility and affection.

After the destruction of Heart, Babur was the only Timurid royalty powerful enough to face the Uzbegs. The latters' threat was such that sheer survival seemed like an ambitious plan. A situation of a direct face off with Shaibani Khan was averted in 1507 for which Babur thanked his experienced advisor Qasim Beg Quchin. The latter

---

[12]Ibid., p. 234.
[13]Ibid., p. 239.

had convinced Babur by saying that whatever the youth see in the mirror the old can see in baked brick. At this time, his safe return to Kabul was marked with the adaptation of a grand title: Baadshah.

Another man who parallel Babur's ascendency was Shah Ismail Safavi, the Safavid ruler of Iran. It was he who killed Shaibani Khan in December 1510. He took the Khan's skull to be carved and covered with gold. It was turned into a cup. These developments rekindled Babur's Samarqand dream. He was directly helped by Shah Ismail in occupying Samarqand and indirectly in losing it yet again. It was on 8th October 1511 that a victorious Babur entered Samarqand for the third time. The local's acceptance was spontaneous. However, rumours of his conversion to Shi'ism alienated the orthodox Sunni elite of the city. They were already annoyed with Shah Ismail's treatment of influential Sunnis of Samarqand in 1510 and were not ready to accept his protégé as their ruler. This time Babur could have obtained and retained Samarqand on his own. He had sought the Shah's assistance by way of abundant precaution. Interestingly that was what derailed his mission. As local support dipped, his vulnerability increased. Ultimately he was defeated by Ubaidullah Khan Uzbeg in 1512. This finally closed the Samarqand chapter. By 1514 he was back to business at Kabul.

The *Baburnama* (Babur's autobiography) doesn't account for the years between 1508 and 1519. In January 1519, we find that he was engaged in subjugating some Pashtun tribes. This campaign mentioned *tufang*s (matchlock weapons) for the first time. This action is popularly known as the Bajaur Campaign. It was Babur's first step towards Hindustan. The Bajauris had never seen firearms. Due to their ignorance of the power of such weapons, they didn't fear it and even made fun of it with obscene gestures. To seal some kind of a political alliance Babur married the daughter of a Yusufzai chieftain. She was known as Bibi Mubarika Afghani Aghacha. After Bajaur, he occupied Bhira in February 1519. With reference to the earlier Timurid occupation of this place it was declared to be Babur's paternal inheritance. Thus plundering the locals was prohibited and soldiers who defied this order were either executed or their noses were slit to deter others. In March 1519, a kind of a notice was sent to the Lodi Afghan ruler of north India. It stated that these Hindustani territories belonged to Babur's Turkish ancestors and therefore they were his. Of course the Afghans did not take these demands seriously. Events of the time between 1520 and late 1525 are also missing from the *Baburnama*. On 17 November 1525, Babur left Kabul with the intention of subjugating the Lodis of Hindustan. Ibrahim Lodi was their influential ruler. His capital was at Agra. His governor in the northwest, Daultan Khan Lodi surrendered before Babur and was reduced to the status of a zamindar. Alam Khan Lodi, another prominent noble had fallen out with Ibrahim Lodi. He came over to Babur's camp.

On 26th February 1526, Hamid Khan, the governor of Hissar Firuza was defeated by Humayun; Babur's eldest son. The Afghans were defeated in another preliminary combat on 2nd April 1526. The final confrontation happened at Panipat; a small town near Delhi. The historical battle that changed the face of Hindustani politics and society is named after this town: The battle of Panipat, 20th April 1526. The usually accepted approximation asserts that Babur had just 12,000 men to combat Ibrahim's one lakh. He adopted the Ottoman-Turkish battle formation. This was the flank assault. In it the officers and ordinary soldiers charged at the same time undertaking the same kind of risks. They shot arrows even as they galloped. In retreat too they were well organized and never went pell-mell. These tactics had always impressed Babur. The first line of his army had carts tied with leather ropes. In between the carts stood soldiers on foot holding shields. Behind then were matchlock men. The cavalry was to march through the gaps in between. They were to charge in an enveloping manoeuvre known as *Tulghamah* (Rapid wheel). In Central Asia, soldiers used passwords to avoid injuring men of their own party. Two words were used as sign and countersign. During action the soldiers exchanged the passwords; one saying the sign and the other the countersign. In this way they distinguished between friends and enemies. Words like Durdana, Lulu, Tuqpay and Tashkent are examples of such passwords. Babur's forces were shielded by the town of Panipat in the right and artificial ditches on the left. His forces were subdivided into neat and structured flanks. Ibrahim's plan was to literally crush the small army that he was facing. Babur's tactics would have worked only if the Afghan forces moved towards his battle formation. He couldn't have charged first. Finally when the Afghans charged with the intention of storming over and past the Turks, they were surprised by the latter's unique battle line up. Their speed was broken. The Afghan front-liners slowed down, but the lines behind them were unaware of the barriers ahead so they kept moving speedily.

Now, Babur's forces moved to encircle and compress the Afghan forces towards their own centre. In a matter of just four hours, some fifteen or sixteen thousand Afghans were killed. A near contemporary; Abdul Qadir Badauni informs that so many soldiers were killed here that the battle field of Panipat became haunted. Strange sounds emanated from there. People were scared to go by it at night. Ibrahim Lodi died fighting. His head was presented to Babur by Tahir, an axe-man. Babur guessed that perhaps Ibrahim Lodi was miserly, inexperienced, unenergetic and irresolute. In fact Ibrahim was not so bad; it was only that Babur was better. Occupation of Hindustan, per se was never a part of Babur's stratagems for most of his career. However once it was set in motion, it moved so fast the even a veteran daredevil like him found it hard to brace up for the consolidation of his celebrated conquest.

Babur distributed generous rewards to his allies. But Panipat was only the tip of the iceberg. After the initial flush of funds subsided, challenges arose. Afghans were regrouping against him. The non-Muslim rajas had finally perceived the presence of a go-getting empire builder in their vicinity. They were alarmed and anxious to check him. The locals were obviously uncomfortable with the rise of a new brand of rulers. During Babur's initial days at Agra, his soldiers felt strange vibes of antagonism and hatred. The locals ran away and shops were shut. No one knew when this otherness would subside. Many of his commanders wished to return to Kabul. He desperately wanted them to stay but there was no way that he could stop them. He had believed that his comrades would follow him even if he walked into water or fire. Now he knew that they wouldn't. When Khwaja Kalan, his friend and a senior commander, was leaving Hindustan, he wrote to Babur: 'If I cross the Indus in safety, may my face turn black if I ever desire to see Hindustan again.' Babur was quite hurt by the man's disdain for his new home. He replied: 'Give a hundred thanks O Babur that the Generous Pardoner of all has given you Sind and Hind and a vast kingdom. If you cannot endure the heat and say: "I would see the face of cold," there is Ghazni.'[14] In an attempt to understand the Hindustanis he read the *Tabaqat-i Nasiri* of Minhaj al Siraj Juzjani. This book narrates the history of the Sultanate period. And of course, he observed everything around him with great keenness: the political setup; that Hindustan was not being ruled by a single house, the population, quick settlement of villages, availability of labour, water table, methods of irrigation, florae and faunae, religious and cultural practices, etc. He remarked that the Hindustanis had a great system of numbering. It was noted that the animals and birds considered sacred by the locals were not to be injured or killed. At a later date he wrote for those who left Hindustan: 'O you who have gone from this country of India feeling pain and distress, you thought of Kabul and its wonderful climate and hotly left India. There you have apparently found pleasure and joy, and many good things, yet we have not died, thank God, although we have suffered much pain and untold grief you have no more physical distress, but then neither do we.' Indeed Babur believed that affairs are mortgaged to their time[15] and that all is well that ends well.[16]

The post-Panipat scenario was not a simple win-win situation. But there was not other way that Babur would allow the undoing

---

[14]Ibid., p. 358.
[15]Ibid., p. 381.
[16]Ibid., p. 374.

of his victory. His combat with Rana Sanga of Chittor was an acid test of sorts. It is speculated whether the Rana had earlier promised support to Babur and then backed off. In any case he was now heading a confederation of rulers to oust the Timurid. A big number of Babur's loyalists had already left. His Mongol allies had been unable to forge any local alliances at Panipat due to lingual and other barriers. However now they were better placed to betray him. The broad pattern of his strategy and tactics had already been exposed in 1526. Besides, the Rajput rulers had very deep roots in the political field of Hindustan. Many influential Muslims were also on their side. Thus the retention of Panipat's victory itself meant more wars. In the mean time his canon master Ali Quli went into a strange kind of depression. He was encountering some error in the casting of a mortar. The fellow was so upset that he was ready to throw himself into molten lead and Babur had to go out of his way to drag him out of this low phase.

On 25 February 1527, Babur took a pledge to give up wine. It was a personal decision. A kind of thanksgiving for all that he had achieved. But within two days of his promise, the idea of abstaining from alcoholic drinks caught the fancy of the elite. It became a fad. In about a week or so 300 people pledged abstinence. Gauging the mood of the moment Babur decided to use the idea of religious idealism to enthuse his soldiers. He reminded his warriors that only God is immortal. Human life is, in any case, short and unpredictable. It should be used wisely to serve God. Thus religious emotionalism was used as a war strategy—a military plan. Personally Babur didn't have much to do with communalism per se. Finally abstinence became the symbol of Mughal solidarity against their enemies. The plan worked. Gold and silver goblets were melted and sold. The money thus obtained was given in charity. Salt was added to barrels of aged and expensive wine. It was turned into vinegar. However it may be noted that armies were never ever composed on religious lines by any of the contestants. Every big player knew that religious sentiments were dragged into political games for giving a temporary psychological high to the simple common soldiers. Coalitions had to do more with common economic and political interests rather than common faith. Anyhow, the much anticipated battle of Khanua fought on 17th March 1527 was won by Babur. He added the title *Ghazi* (holy warrior) to his seal. However, he found it really difficult to curb the urge to drink and wrote that by renouncing wine he is confounded. He is confused and bewildered. People become penitent and repent. But he, poor thing, was penitent for having repented.

By December 1528, most parts of the north Indian plains and Punjab had been consolidated. However none of it was easy. The demands and difficulties that lay beyond Panipat took a toll on Babur's health. He fell ill every now and then: August 1527, October 1527, September 1528, November 1528, March 1529 and so on. About his fever in October 1527 he wrote: 'By day fever rages in my body. Sleep flies from my eyes when it is night. These two are like my grief and patience, the more the one increase the less the other becomes.' It lasted for 25–26 days. On an earlier occasion he was drenched in sweat every time his fever receded. He was bled to drain the infection but that also didn't help. The doctor had given him Narcissus and Julep and some purgatives. During this illness he had to give up drinking temporarily. He pacified himself by watching others drink. A couplet which he wrote in December 1528 kind of captured his worries: 'Finally neither friends nor companions will be faithful. Neither summer nor winter. Companions will not remain. A hundred pities that precious life passes away. O alas! that this celebrated time is futile.' In May 1529, he said: 'I despair of governing and kingship. I shall retire to this garden (Bagh-i Zarfishan at Agra) and ask only for Tahir the ewer bearer as a companion. I shall grant the kingship to Humayun.'

In 1530, Babur had organized an excursion to Dholpur. This was to help the ladies of the harem in managing their grief over the death of two infant princes, Alwar and Farukh. While the royalties were there, Humayun left his post at Badakshan, leaving it in charge of a young Hindal; Babur's youngest son. Although Babur wasn't particularly pleased with this initiative, he allowed Humayun to proceed to Delhi. Before the posting in the north-west frontier could be restrategized Humayun fell ill. The royal jaunt was curtailed and his distraught mother, Maham, reached her son's beside. In these circumstances her conversation with Babur is recorded as follows: 'Do not be troubled about my son. You are a king; what griefs have you? You have other sons. I am distress because I have only this one.' And Babur replied, 'Maham! Although I have other sons, I love none as I love your Humayun. I crave that this cherished child may have his heart's desire and live long, and I desire the kingdom for him and not for the others, because he has not his equal in distinction.'[17] Therefore, Babur was doubly tortured by the sight of his careworn beloved and their comatose son.

Disillusioned and disappointed with the ineffectiveness of medication, they turned to frantic prayers. It was contemplated that the Koh-i-Noor diamond should be given as *sadqa* (alms giving) for Humayun's life but that, Babur thought was too little. The *sadqa* had to be something bigger, better, unmatchable but well-matched with his son; it had to be him. Accordingly he took supplicatory rounds of Humayun's bed, begging God for his son's life in exchange of his own. Perhaps his prayers were accepted and the malady switched from Humayun to him. Babur enfeebled as Humayun recovered. Despite his hectic military career Babur had always found time for his family, whether it was escorting his mother for a visit to her relatives or taking his wives and children for a picnic. His illness wrapped the whole harem in gloom. His daughters Gulrang and Gulchihra were married in great haste since his concerns regarding them were typically like those of any ordinary parent. However one of his wishes that remained unfulfilled was meeting his youngest son Hindal. At his dying father's behest, Humayun promised that he would never quarrel with his brothers nor entertain any evil intentions towards them.

---

[17]Rumer Godden, *Gulbadan Portrait of a Rose Princess at the Mughal Court*, The Viking Press, New York, 1981, pp. 65–66.

Babur finally died on 21 December 1530. Initially he was buried at Aram Bagh in Agra. He was entitled *Firdaus-Makaani* (resident of the best paradise). Humayum and Maham made elaborate arrangements for prayers in his favour. Charitable meals were distributed in his name. Revenues of two provinces were dedicated for these activities. Sometime, between 1533–1544 his remains were carried to Kabul and interred in a simple grave. His grandsons Jahangir and Shahjahan visited his grave in 1607 and 1640 respectively. His legacy continued to inspire his progeny.

Besides his incredible resilience, another vital aspect of Babur's personality was his recognizable humanity. Emotionally vulnerable, he cried while eating a Kabuli melon which someone had brought for him to Hindustan. Sometime he displayed childish naughtiness. For example, he offered colocynth; a very bitter purgative fruit to his Central Asian friend, and told the fellow that it is sweet Hindustani watermelon. The unsuspecting man took a big bite with great relish and an amused Babur recalled that the bitterness did not leave his friend's mouth till the evening. He recorded his meeting with Hulhul Anika; perhaps the only female drunkard Babur ever met. After the drinking party she probably tried to seduce him, but he avoided her by 'acting' drunk. He had many fun memories of his drinking parties. At one time, his friend Abdullah was so drunk that he threw himself in cold water in a fully clothed state. Thereafter he felt so cold that he pledged to never touch alcohol ever again. Once, his friend Dost Muhammad was too drunk when hostile Afghans intruded his party. This man couldn't even ride on his horse for the flight. So another drunk friend suggested that they should cut off Dost Muhammad's head and take it with them so that it is not defiled by the Afghans. Babur somehow never lost his senses to drinks. He ensured that Dost Muhammad was somehow lugged on his horse and taken to safety. He narrated funny rivalries of poets. One day Ali Sher Beg and Kamaluddin Ali Bannai (author of *Shaibaninama* and *Futuhat-i Khani*) were at a chess party. Ali Sher stretched his leg and it touched Bannai's back. To tease the latter, Ali Sher commented that it is a sad state of affairs that in Herat, one could not even stretch out a leg without poking a poet in the ass. This implied that even the rustics claimed to be poets here and Bannai was one of them. To this Bannai retorted that he agreed, because if Ali Sher pulled his leg back in, he would poke another poet.

Anyway, Ali Sher was quite a brand leader. The designs that he wore become popular as 'Ali Sheri'. Babur amusingly records that the blue handkerchief which Ali Sher tied over his head due to earache had become a branded fashion item for the local ladies. It was popular as the Ali Sheri comforter. Babur named one of his page boys Rhinoceros Maqsud, because he was thrown off his horse by the horn of a Rhinoceros. Speaking of light takes on serious poems, Babur records that Shaykim Beg Suhayli had written the following lines: 'One night of grief the whirlpool of my cries swept the celestial spheres away. The dragon of my torrential tears carried off the inhabited quarter of the world.' He jokes that when Maulana Abdul Rahim Jami heard these lines he quipped: 'Mirza are you out to compose poetry or to frighten people?'[18] Personally, Babur avoided playing hurtful jokes on others. Specially, since he began writing the *Mubin*. However in 1525 he spontaneously composed some vulgar lines to tease one Mulla Ali Jan who was usually the butt of jokes. After a couple of days Babur fell ill. He had fever and cold and his sputum was bloody. He was worried like crazy; especially due to the internal bleeding. He felt that this was divine retribution for his vulgar verse. He wrote: 'I realized where the admonition was from and what I had done to deserve this suffering.' He actually wrote a verse to warn his faltering tongue: 'What am I to do with you O Tongue? On your account my inwards are bloody. No matter how gracefully you compose humorous poetry, part of it is obscene and part is false. If you wish not to burn for this crime, turn your reins from this field.' He somehow felt lucky to have received divine admonition before he could break more hearts with rudeness and collect demerits. Someone had said: 'What is one to do with the

---

[18]*Baburnama*, p. 207.

loveliness of every coquette? There where you are, what is one to do with others?' And the teaser that Babur regretted adding to this was: 'What is one to do with a dope like you? What is one to do with every female ass with a hole as big as a cow's'.[19]

His ability to forgive was exemplary. In fact, in the *Baburnama* he advises not once but twice to let fate be the avenger rather than taking upon oneself to avenge betrayals. He believed that affairs are mortgaged to their designated time and one has to be patient. In the Wais Mirza conspiracy of 1506–07 Muhammad Husain Mirza Dughlat had tried to dethrone Babar. But the Baadshah gave asylum to his orphaned eight-year-old son from 1508 to 1512. This boy, Mirza Haider Dughlat in his book *Tarikh-i Rashidi,* says that Babur welcomed him with open arms. The Baadshah embraced him lovingly and assured that he would treat him as his own child. He should neither feel insecure nor grieve for the loss of his family. The child felt that Babur's words drove away the bitterness of orphanage and the poison of banishment from his mind.

Babur's maternal grandmother Shah Begum and his maternal aunt Meher Nigar Khanum had been co-conspirators in the Wais Mirza episode. Their betrayal had hurt him emotionally. Mirza Haider's account specifies how Babur tried to save these women from embarrassment despite himself feeling hurt. He said to his grand-mother that a child has no right to be angry with his mother if her affection shifts to another sibling. A mother's authority cannot be challenged by a child. He laid his head on her lap and said that he wanted to sleep for a while. Only Babur could have displayed this mixture of strength and vulnerability. He granted forgiveness and asylum to many enemies and rivals. He even spared the life of Buwa, Ibrahim Lodi's mother who tried to get him poisoned. One of Ibrahim's cooks in Babur's employ and three were also involved in this plot. The cook put a piece of thin bread at the bottom of Babur's plate and then sprinkled some poison over it. On top of this he laid a dish of meat. The poison could not have been added

---

[19]Ibid., pp. 306–312.

to the cooking pots because the cooks were made to taste from the pots. The deadly toxin had been especially bought from Etawah. It made Babur sick the moment he tasted a bit of the meat. He ran to the wash basin but vomited on the way. The vomit was fed to a dog. The animal's stomach swelled and he lay motionless for a day. Poisoning was confirmed. Babur was enraged. Although Buwa's helpers were sentenced to death, she was only arrested and later banished. Until this episode, Babur had maintained Ibrahim's mother and son quite honourably. The lady had been granted an expensive estate.

Babur was very affectionate towards his family. He was exceptionally respectful towards his elderly relatives and made it a point to visit them at least once a week. No one, not even his favourite wife Maham could stop him from doing so. Although he may not have loved all his wives equally, he treated them with respect. As a father, he comes across as any other ordinary man who loves his children more than himself. He took personal interest in the settlement of his son-in-law Muhammad Zaman Mirza, husband of his daughter Masuma Sultan Begum. The marriages of his daughters; Gulrang, Gulchihra and Gulbadan were a matter of concern for him. He took great interest in grooming his children. He was keen on nurturing them into well-rounded individuals. Despite the uncertain circumstances of his life, he loved reading and writing. He noted his memories. These became his mesmerizing autobiography, the *Tuzuk-i Baburi/Baburnamah*. The script, *Khatt-i Baburi*, was his innovation. In this all the letters were written separately and were not joined as they usually are. He wrote a copy of the Quran in this script and sent it to Mecca. He also wrote a religious text called *Mubayyin* and a versified rendering of the *Risala-i Walidiyya* of the Central Asian Sufi, Khwaja Ahrar. In poetical compositions the only poet considered at par with him was Mir Ali Sher Navai of Herat.[20] Babur was also a competent critic of literary works. He comments that Abdullah's *Layli Majnun* is famous, but not as good as it is reputed

---

[20]Cf. *Two Studies in Early Mughal History*, Yusuf Husain, Indian Institute of Advanced Study, Shimla, 1976, p. 108.

to be. His *Timurnama* is an imitation of the *Sikandarnama* and his *Haft Manzar* is an imitation of *Haft Paiker*. Mirza Haider Dughlat recalled that Babur personally supervised his education like he did for his own children. He used both encouragement and severity to make him study. Every bit of progress was noticed and rewarded. He thought books were appropriate gifts to be sent to his sons. He was generally observant. He noticed the arrangement of leaves, colours of flowers and camp fires glowing at a distance. He noted things like methods of irrigation, population, markets, work force, clothes, dancing style, singing style, foods, belief systems, people being introverts or extroverts etc. He records that once a snake as big as a man's forearm and a fathom long was killed. From inside that snake came a smaller snake that must have just been swallowed. It was completely whole. The smaller snake was only a bit shorter than the big one. Then from inside the smaller one came a big rat. It too was whole, and none of it had been digested. When he described diseases, he usually also mentioned the treatment which was being administrated.

Babur was a people's person. He opined that ten friends were better than nine. Nevertheless, he mentions the type of people who are not his type. He didn't entertain predictors of the future, especially the 'gloom and doom' kind. Although he did seems to believe in charms. He disapproved of temperamental and tantrum throwing men. He disliked the miserly and the niggardly kinds. He wrote that nothing could be more indicative of stupidity and craziness than degrading oneself by swallowing the flattery of deceitful and ambitious men. Advising caution against reckless talk and action, he cited the proverbs: 'He who reaches hastily for the sword will bite the back of his hand in regret,' and 'A mere word can stir up strife that will bring down an ancient line.'[21] Timing was always a matter of importance to him. He emphasized that unnecessary delays lead to regrets.

Though he had fought many wars for worldly possessions, life's

---

[21]Ibid., pp. 104 & 251.

eventual temporariness always haunted him. Even at the peak of his success he remembered that nothing will go with him. In this context he felt that a good name is too precious to be exchanged with anything of this fleeting world. He wrote: 'In the end only qualities survive a person in this world. Anyone who has a modicum of intelligence will take steps so that he will not be ill-spoken of afterwards. Why should someone who has a trace of awareness not take pains that his actions be approved? The wise have said that a good memory is a second life.'[22] He employed his reflexive piety and mystical liberality to adhere to some moral code. Intra-Muslim/Shia-Sunni/Muslim-non-Muslim contests, in a religious context, didn't seem to make much sense to him. Perhaps that is why he saw no harm in donning the Shia symbolic pointed cap at Samarqand in 1511. That, of course, cost him Samarqand. In the few years that he spent in Hindustan he didn't discriminate on religious lines. He declared that the residents of Hindustan were under his protection, because they were his subjects. Their religion didn't matter. In politics the Muslim Afghans/Uzbegs etc. were as much his enemies as were the Hindu Rajputs. He was clearly in favour of rationalism and evolution. In this context his comment on the Chingizid Code (*Tora-i Chingizi*) and Chingizid law (*Yasa-i Chingizi*) are inspiring: '... However, Genghis Khan's code is not a binding text according to which a person must act absolutely. Rather, it is necessary to act in accordance with a good rule when someone leaves one behind; if an ancestor has set a bad precedent, however it should be replaced by a good one.'[23]

Thus Babur was inexplicably dynamic. He had brushed with death so many times that he loved life. He wrote 'Ease and relief seem all the more pleasurable after hardship and distress' and that he who reaches the point of death appreciates life.[24] However there remained a mysterious void in his heart which perhaps his experiences had dug. He wrote: 'Is there any cruelty or misery the Spheres can inflict,

---

[22]Ibid. pp. 219–220.
[23]Ibid., p. 224.
[24]Ibid., pp. 111 & 374.

Have I not suffered? Is there any pain or torment my wounded heart has not suffered? My heart is steeped in blood, like a rosebud. Even if there were a hundred thousand springs, what possibility would there be of it opening?'[25]

Anyway, despite believing in the infallibility of fate he strived to achieve what he wanted. Despite his ability to guard many political secrets he easily displayed emotions of joy and sadness. Despite getting mounds of skulls made to deter enemies, he could cry for days over the death of a friend. Despite being a powerful king he remained a vulnerable father. Despite all the uncertainities he certainly enjoyed life. Despite loving his past, he loved his present. He loved Hindustan with all his heart.

At the time of his death, Babur was only 48 and had ruled for 36 years. Each of those years had been packed with activity and adventure. Challenges were unending. But he seemed to have a pact with himself to fight back, always and every time. He finished the most difficult part of establishing the Mughal Empire. He initiated it.

❧❦❧

---

[25]Ibid., p. 233.

TWO

NASIRUDDIN MUHAMMAD HUMAYUN

1508–1556

Although one's image be shown in the mirror,
It remains always apart from one's self,
It is wonderful to see one's self in another form,
This marvel will be the work of God.

—HUMAYUN IN A LETTER TO SHER KHAN[26]

Humayun was born on the 6th of March 1508. He was Babur's eldest son. His mother, Maham Begum, belonged to the family of Sultan Husain of Herat and perhaps was the Baadshah's favourite wife. Babur mentions two of the chronograms composed for his birth: *Sultan Humayun Khan* and *Shah-i Firoz Qadr*. Both proclaimed the prince's luckiness. On the 3rd or 4th day of his birth he was named Humayun. On the 6th day, Babur hosted a grand feast. Offerings to the prince made an unprecedented heap of silver coins. Besides Humayun, all the other children born to Maham died in their infancy. Amongst Babur's surviving sons were Mirza Kamran, Mirza Askari and Mirza Hindal. Kamran and Askari were full brothers. Their mother, Gulrukh Begum belonged to the Beg Chick tribe of the Mongols. Their full sister, Gulizar Begum, was married to Yadgar Nasir Mirza. Hindal was born to Dildar Begum. He and his full sister Gulbadan Begum were adopted and brought up by Humayun's mother. Humayun's childhood was spent at Kabul. He respected Babur not just as his father, but also as a king. In 1519,

---

[26]Cf. *Humayun Namah*, Gulbadan Begum, Annette S. Beveridge (translation & notes), Sang-e-Meel Publications, Lahore, p. 145.

Babur's return from Bajaur was a hush-hush affair. The princes were apprised about it when he was already at the city's gate. Mounting their horses would have taken too long so their pages quickly carried them to pay homage to the monarch. Like his mother, Humayun also trusted omens and he never outgrew his belief in the prophetic significance of events. He was appointed as the viceroy of Badakshan when he was 12 years old. Babur and Maham went there to settle him. When Babur started for Hindustan on 17 November 1525 he summoned Humayun to join him. Babur's fondness of this prince becomes apparent from his detailed reminiscences of Humayun; his reaction at watching a rhinocerous hunt, the parties he attended, the death of his story teller, his first shave, etc.

In the Hindustan campaigns, Humayun featured as Babur's right hand man. On 25th February 1526, he was deputed to bear down on Hamid Khan, the governor of Hissar Firoza. Veteran commanders like Khwaja Kalan and Hindu Beg were sent to assist the young prince. Babur had laid out the battle strategy, but Humayun improvised the tactics on field. He sent about a hundred and fifty soldiers to scout around the enemies' camp. His main army turned-up when the Afghans were engaged with the scout. Taken by surprise they were defeated. The news of his son's first big victory reached Babur on 2nd March 1526. Humayun was awarded a royal robe, a horse from the royal stable, a crore of cash and the district of Hissar Firoza and its dependencies. Three days later, the captured men and elephants were presented to Babur. Execution of the prisoners with ammunition gave the Mughals an opportunity to unnerve the Afghans. Rahmat Piada was dispatched to Kabul to give the good news to the royal family. At this time, another first for Humayun was shaving: 'Having put the razor and scissor to his face'; as Babur puts it. Twenty-eight years later while reading his father's memoires Humayun annotated these lines with his own comments that since his late Majesty (Babur) has mentioned his shaving among these events, he follows him in mentioning it. At that date, he was 18 years old. Now he is in his 46th year.[27]

---

[27]*Baburnama*, p. 449.

At Panipat Babur had sent a few thousand soldiers for a spy sneak attack on the Afghans. When an important commander was injured on this mission, Humayun was sent to replace him. On the day of the main battle; 20th April 1526, he commanded the right wing of his father's army. Later on Babur's orders he sped post haste to appropriate the treasures at Agra. Perhaps the Mughal victory had not sunk in yet because the Afghan guards at Agra's citadel resisted his entry. Thus camps were pitched outside and a vigil was maintained to ensure nothing was smuggled in or out of the fort. Amongst the fallen allies of Ibrahim Lodi was Raja Bikramjit of Gwalior. His family, then residing in Agra's fort, tried to escape but was detained by Humayun's soldiers. The latter immediately took them under his protection. The grateful royalties presented him many gems and jewels. Amongst them was the famous diamond Koh-i-Noor. Babur was aware that it originally belonged to Alauddin Khalji and its worth had been valued at the whole world's expenditure for half a day. When Humayun presented it to him he returned it to his son straight away. Besides the largest portion of Agra's treasure, Humayun was also given a room full of riches which had not been inventoried. Later, in an award ceremony he was presented a girth sword and a horse with a golden saddle. Sambhal was added to his land assignments and a force was sent to settle Afghan turbulence there. While loud celebrations marked Humayun's victories, Kamran quietly held his father's original base at Kabul and Qandhar. Babur was as confident of him as he was of Humayun. If he trusted Humayun with the treasure of Agra he also trusted Kamran with the custody of Ibrahim Lodi's son. However he supervised both of them.

In the post-Panipat scenario, Humayun offered to go to the east to deal with Afghans like Nasir Khan Nohani, Ma'ruf Farmuli, etc. He departed on 21st August 1526. The Afghan army at Jajmau was so overawed by the prince's advance party that they submitted without a fight. He subjugated Dalmau as well. Afghan commander Fath Khan Sarwani was sent to Babur. On this occasion, Babur banned the use of a title which was popularly employed by the Afghans to honour their dignitaries: *Azam Humayun*. He explained: 'Because of my own Humayun, it was considered inappropriate to invest anyone with such a title.'[28]

Even before his victory over the eastern Afghans could sink in, Humayun was informed about the confederation of Rajputs and others under Rana Sanga. Babur's letter dated 31st October 1526 updated him about the challenging developments. He reached Agra on the 6th of January 1527. Around this time Babur had released Nahar Khan, son of Hasan Khan Mewati. He had hoped to wean the latter off the Rajput alliance by doing so. To his dismay, Hasan Khan joined Rana Sanga even before his son reached him. Paradoxically, the more battles that the Mughals won, the more battles awaited them. They swung between feasts and fights. Humayun attended many parties in the days preceding the battle of Khanua. Back then, he used to be a reluctant drinker.

Like Panipat, at Khanua too Humayun headed the right wing of the Mughal army. Babur was quite proud of his contribution and narrated much about the bravery of his 'dear eldest son'. After this victory, Humayun was awarded the treasury of Alwar. Thereafter, he left for Badakshan. Most of his troops were Badakshis and they had been promised recess after matters were settled with Rana Sanga. Around 3rd April 1527, Babur travelled up to Firozpur to see him off. Strangely Humayun made a detour to Delhi and appropriated its treasures for himself. Babar was shocked and very furious. He had never expected such misappropriation from his trusted son. Humayun received extremely harsh letters of reproach from his father.[29] Perhaps this strange usurpation of funds was born of Humayun's dissatisfaction with Badakshan's resources or the fact that Babur was being unreasonably generous with his commanders. In fact, he took up the matter of his province's impoverishment with his father rather soonish. Anyway, opening of treasuries was his go it alone show and it reflected his general reputation of being trustworthy. No one else

---

[28]Ibid., p. 350.
[29]Ibid. p. 399.

could have pulled off such audacity.

Sometime around mid 1527 he was back at Badakshan. His absence had emboldened the Uzbegs. In their father's absence, both Humayun and Kamran found it difficult to safeguard their dominions. Runners travelled between Agra and Kabul, Qandhar and Badakhsan with absolute regularity. A matter that summoned Babur's immediate attention was that both Humayun and Kamran were looking at Kabul with covetous eyes. By mid 1528 Humayun could hardly cover up his desire for possessing it. Kamran had been its viceroy for quite a while. He felt that if any of the princes had a right over Kabul it was him. In September 1528 Babur summoned Askari to Agra and gave his province, Multan, to Kamran. This was to compensate for the exceptionally slender income from Kabul. Around this time Humayun wrote to Babur that he was lonely at Badakshan and wanted to relocate to Kabul. His grumble about Kamran was also being reported to their father. In response, Babur wrote him a long letter on 26 November 1528. Broadly speaking, Babur congratulated Humayun over the birth of his son, advised him to improve his writing skills and use less of jargon and clarified that he doesn't appreciate the idea of his sons competing over the possession of Kabul. The letter follows:

To Humayun. Thinking of you with much longing, I greet you. My words are these: On Monday the tenth of Rabi'I [November 23], Beggina and Buyan Shaykh came. From your letters and reports we have become acquainted with the situation on both sides of the Hindu Kush. I give thanks for your son, a son to you and a beloved one to me. May God ever grant me and you such joy. Amen, O Lord of the Universe. You have named him 'al-Aman'. May God bless him. However, although you yourself may write it thus, you have not considered the fact that frequently the common people will say either 'Alaman' or 'Ilaman'. Moreover, names with 'al-' are rare. Nonetheless, may God bless and keep both him and his name. For my sake and yours, may He keep al-Aman in fortune and happiness for many years, for many decades. God has ordered our affairs through His great grace and generosity. Such an event has not happened in how many decades?

Item: On Tuesday the eleventh rumours were heard to the effect that the people of Balkh had summoned Qurban and let him in.

Item: Kamran and the Kabul begs were ordered to go join you, and you all will proceed to Hissar or Samarqand or whichever direction is in our best interests. Through God's grace you will defeat your enemies, take their territory, and make your friends happy by overthrowing the foe. God willing, this is your time to risk your life and wield your sword. Do not fail to make the most of an opportunity that presents itself. Indolence and luxury do not suit kingship.

Conquest tolerates not inaction; the world is his who hastens most. When one is master one may rest from everything except being king.

If, by God's grace and favour, Samarqand is also subdued, you stay there yourself and, God willing, I will make Hissar royal demesne. If Kamran thinks Balkh is small, write me. God willing, I will make up the deficiency to him out of those other territories.

Item: You know that this rule has always been observed: six parts to you and five to Kamran. Always observe this rule yourself and do not break it.

Item: Conduct yourself well with your younger brother. Elder brothers need to have restraint. It is my hope that you will get along well with him, for he has grown up to be a religiously observant and fine young man. Let him also display no deficiency in homage and respect for you.

Item: I have a few complaints of you. For two or three years now none of your men has come. The man I sent returned exactly a year later. Is this proper?

Item: In your letters you keep talking about being alone. Solitude is a flaw in kingship, as has been said, 'If you are fettered, resign yourself; but if you are a lone rider, your reins are free.' There is no bondage like the bondage of kingship. In kingship it is improper to seek solitude.

Item: As I asked, you have written your letters, but you didn't read them over, for if you had a mind to read them, you would have found that you could not. After reading them you certainly would have changed them. Although your writing can be read with difficulty, it is excessively obscure. Who had ever heard of prose designed to be an enigma? Your spelling is not bad, although it is not entirely correct either. You wrote iltifat with the wrong t; you wrote qulinj with a y. Your handwriting can be made out somehow or other, but with all these obscure words of yours the meaning is not entirely clear. Probably your laziness in writing letters is due to the fact that you try to make it took fancy. From now on, write with uncomplicated, clear and plain words. This will cause less difficulty both for you and for your reader.

Item: You are going on a great mission. Consult the experienced begs for strategy and tactics and do what they say. If you want to make me happy, stop sitting by yourself and avoiding people. Don't leave the decision to your brother and your begs, but invite them in twice a day, consult with them on whatever has come up, and make your decisions with the agreement of these supporters of yours.

Item: Khwaja Kalan learned to be free and easy with me through constant contact. So should you mingle with others as I did with him. If, through God's grace, the situation over there should demand less attention and you do not need Kamran, station trustworthy men in Balkh and let him come to me.

Item: There were such conquests and victories while we were in Kabul that I consider Kabul my lucky piece and have made it royal demesne. Let none of you covet it.

Item: Conduct yourself well. Make friends with Sultan Ways. Bring him in and act upon his opinion, for he is an experienced man. Keep the army disciplined and in training. Buyan Shaykh has had verbal instruction from me that he will communicate to you. With longing, peace. Written on Wednesday the thirteenth of Rabi'I [November 26].[30]

Thus it was clarified that Kabul would always be Babur's territory. If his sons wished to expand their dominions they would have to personally exert for it. In fact Humayun actually planned to invade Samarqand. Babur himself dissuaded him from doing so. Who could have known better than him that how dangerous the Samarqand dream could be. By early 1529 Babur had made it quite clear to his sons that he didn't appreciate deadly familial rivalries and out-of-place demands. However he did indulge them by sending precious gifts. He sent 10,000 *Shahrukhi* gold coins as a congratulatory gift on the birth of Humayun's son and on Kamran's wedding. A tunic and a belt for each of his elder sons, a jewel-studded girth dagger, a jewel-studded inkpot, a mother of pearl inlay box, etc. His poems in the Baburi script were also presented to them. Humayun was advised to suppress thieves and bandits if he didn't have any other pressing engagement. Kamran was preoccupied with handling Persian insurgency at Qandhar. In August 1529, he went to Lahore to meet Babur and returned to Qandhar sometime after 4 March 1530. He pampered his father a lot in what was to be their last meeting.

On 29 December 1530, at 23, Humayun inherited his father's

---

[30]Ibid., pp. 422–23.

vast but unconsolidated empire. His dominions were a tapestry of diversity; geographical, cultural, lingual, etc. So was the army; a mixture of various races and tribes. The nobility was unsure of its loyalty but sure about giving precedence to short-sighted self-interest over anything else. Factions within the nobility were contending for the crowning of Muhammad Zaman Mirza in place of Humayun. The Mirza was Babur's son-in-law and the scion of the celebrated bloodline of Sultan Husain Baiqara. Muhammad Sultan Mirza of the same bloodline was another rival. The Afghans had proclaimed Mahmud Lodi, Ibrahim Lodi's brother, as their king. Bahadur Shah, the ruler of Gujarat was dangerously ambitious. And of course there was Sher Khan; obscure as yet, but destined to outshine all his contemporaries including Humayun. The latter was eventually deposed and exiled by him. Humayun knew that in such a volatile situation the most bankable people were his blood relations. Thus he sought Kamran's cooperation and also asked him to 'remove the veil of secrecy from the face of his desires.'[31] He assigned Kabul and Qandhar to him, but took away Multan. This clarifies that Humayun had inherited Babur's undivided empire. In his coins, Kamran designated himself as Baadshah and Humayun as Sultan-i Azam, his overlord.

Humayun's first brush with Bahadur Shah was in March 1531. The latter had occupied Malwa. However, before matters could come to a head, Humayun had to rush to Chunar to stop the advancing Afghans. The fort of Chunar was critically located in the route connecting Agra–Delhi to Bihar–Bengal. In March 1529, Babur had subjugated its governor, Taj Khan Sarang Khani. The latter was to hand it over to a Mughal officer—Junaid Barlas. However, before the exchange could actually happen, both Babur and Taj Khan died. Now it was held by Sher Khan, a reasonably powerful Afghan leader. This man had earlier worked for Babur for almost an year and a half and was well aware of the Mughal way of functioning. The Mughals besieged the fort, but distractions around Awadh and Punjab did not allow

---

[31]Cf. *The Mughal Nobility Two Political Biographies*, Iqtidar Alam Khan, Permanent Black in association with Ashoka University, Raniket, 2016, p. 8.

Humayun to press on. On the Punjab front, Kamran had occupied Lahore without his prior permission. Kamran's petition requesting his brother's endorsement arrived later. Of course, Humayun endorsed because the trouble of handling the north-western tribes—Biluchis, Gakkars, Afghans and Hazaras—would now become entirely Kamran's responsibility. This arrangement suited him as well. On the other hand, Kamran was happy at the prospect of improved finances. He regularly sent gifts and words of praise to Humayun. In reward for one such laudatory poem, Humayun gave him the prestigious *jagir* of Hissar Firoza. It was a win-win situation for the brothers.

By October 1532 most of the Afghan commanders had been eliminated. Mahmud Lodi had fled to Bihar. Sher Khan didn't intervene to save any of the big wigs of his fraternity. Perhaps, he wanted to be the face of Afghan oneness. He was a master planner. In fact, he strategized so silently that the Mughals almost failed to notice him. No wonder his rude reply to Humayun's demand of the Chunar fort scandalized the Baadshah. The Mughals laid siege to the fort. Incidentally, both Humayun and Sher Khan were pulled out of the encounter by their respective adversaries; Bahadur Shah of Gujarat and Nusrat Shah of Bengal. In a hasty treaty, Sher Khan pledged loyalty to Humayun and sent his son Abdur Rashid Qutb Khan to serve him. In return he was allowed to keep the fort.

By March 1533 tension was diffused on the Gujarat front. In a corridor of peace between 1533 and 1534, Humayun commissioned Khwandmir to write an account of his reign. The book thus compiled is known as the *Qanun-i Humayuni*.[32] It records Humayun's efforts towards organizing the administration of his domains. The author situates Humayun's authority within the idea of the king being the shadow of god on earth. However, he also refers to him as the Sun that justly distributes light to everyone. Akbar's idea of the Baadshah being a ray of divine light could well be an offshoot of Humayun's theory of kingship. Huamyun encouraged artisans and traders. Taxes

---

[32]*Qanun-i Humayuni*, Khwandmir, Baini Parshad (translation), Bibliotheca Indica Series, The Royal Asiatic Society of Bengal, Calcutta, 1940.

and duties were duly regulated to save all sections from economic exploitation. As a prince he had once sought guidance from omens by asking the names of the first three persons he met. The names were *Murad* (desire), *Daulat* (wealth) and *Sa'aadat* (accomplishment). As a monarch he marked socio-political classes by these names. His brothers and powerful nobles were designated as the *Ahl-i Daulat* (people of wealth), saints and scholars were called the *Ahl-i Sa'aadat* (accomplished people) and artists and other talented persons were in the *Ahl-i Murad* (desirable people) category. Days of the week were allotted in advance to different types of engagements. Saturdays and Thursdays were reserved for meeting learned scholars. Sundays and Tuesdays were for meeting ministers and looking into political and economic affairs. Mondays and Wednesdays were days of pleasure and parties. Fridays were reserved for pious works. Drums were beaten when the Baadshah sat on his throne and guns were fired when he left. When the court was in session, distributors of prizes and executors of punishments used to be in a state of readiness to realize royal orders. Justice wasn't delayed at all. Seekers of justice could beat the *Tabl-i Adl* (The drum of justice) outside the palace. The number of beats signified the seriousness of their complaint. Small dispute–1 beat, non-receipt of wages–2 beats, theft or kidnapping–3 beats, murder/death–4 beats. The administration was divided into four units called the *Aatish* (fire); *Hawai* (air), *Aabi* (water) and *Khaki* (earth). The unit supervisors looked after affairs directly or vaguely linked with these elements. For example, arms and ammunition came under *Aatish*, wardrobe and stables came under *Hawai*, wine cellars and canals came under *Aabi* and agriculture and building came under *Khaki*. The colour of the Baadshah's clothes was in accordance with the dominating planet of the day. Saturday–Saturn– Black, Sunday–Sun–Yellow, Monday–Moon–White, Tuesday–Mars– Red, Wednesday–Mercury–Blue/Ash, Thursday–Jupiter–Brown/gram colour and Friday–Venus–Green. The embellishments on his crown formed the digits, 77. The alphabetical value of 77 made the words Izz (honour). Thus his crown was called the *Taj-i Izzat* (The crown of honour). His turban was usually of a single colour. As a mark of differentiation, the courtiers wore multicoloured turbans. He was fond of designing his clothes. The *Ulbaaqcha* was designed by him. It was a front open, long waistcoat. One of his inventions was a huge house boat called the *Chaar Taaq* (Four quarters). It was built in four sections which could be brought together. It was a magnificent floating palace. It had gardens. Flowers like jasmine and tulips blossomed there. Markets on the *Chaar-Taaq* catered to all kinds of requirements from fancy clothes and exotic dishes to weapons and ammunitions. Humayun is known to have travelled from Delhi to Agra on this floating palace over the river Yamuna. He also designed a folding bridge which was carried with the army. It was assembled as and when required. A three-storied moving palace of wood was yet another one of his innovations. A golden dome topped this moving wonder. Curtains of seven different hues were used to give it a colourful look. Luxurious tents were made of the finest cloth. The *Bisaat-i Nishat* (Carpet of Pleasure) was perhaps his most fun invention. It was a round carpet divided into circles corresponding to the orbits of the various planets, with the sun in the centre. Figures in various kinds of action were painted on the area outside the circles. Humayun sat in the centre and others sat in the represented planets in accordance with their stature. The players had to throw a dice and then copy the position of the action on which the dice had fallen. For example they had to stand or recline or twist or even sleep as per the picture on which their dice fell. Perhaps Humayun hoped to build an informal ease with his nobles by such games. He promoted the use glass goblets instead of metal ones so that one could see if a fly or something else fell into their drink. He practiced the *Tula-Daan*, an ancient Indian practice in which a person was weighted against precious items and then the items were given to charity. He incorporated the observation of *Nauroz* (Persian New Year) in the calendar of court celebrations. Between February and March 1533, he mapped out the city of Din Panah. However this phase of developments ended with the rebellion of Muhammad

Zaman Mirza and Muhammad Sultan Mirza. They were defeated and imprisoned by Yadgar Nasir Mirza but managed to escape to Gujarat and sought asylum with the local ruler. Bahadur Shah had previously agreed that he would not shelter Humayun's enemies, but he did welcome the rebellious Mirzas. This widened the breach between him and the Mughals. Thus Humayun left for Gujarat on 8th November 1534. This gave Sher Khan a free hand to strengthen himself in Bihar. Interestingly, despite his victory in the battle of Surajgarh in 1534, Sher Khan did not proclaim himself to be a sovereign. Not yet. Indeed, his political quietism was quite dangerous.

Humayun's success in the initial series of combats with Bahadur Shah was impressive. He enthused over the combat enough to have personally scaled the walls of the fort of Champanair. This was sometime in mid July 1536. For Bahadur Shah it was a run of bad luck. He fled from place to place destroying whatever he couldn't carry. His famous cannons called Laila-Majnun were also smashed. Moreover, his artillery in-charge, Rumi Khan and another important officer Alam Khan defected to Humayun. The Mughals who were in the possession of the fort of Champanair were unable to locate the treasure therein. Humayun was advised to get Alam Khan tortured for the disclosure of the fort's riches, but he devised a more diplomatic plan. A banquet was thrown in the officer's honour. Questions regarding the treasure's location were posed to him when he was drunk. The latter happily informed that it lay right underneath the large bath over which they were sitting. Men were immediately summoned to empty the tank with buckets. However, Alam Khan promptly showed a secret plug hole by which the tank could be drained in an instant. The treasure was retrieved and generously distributed. Every soldier's shield was filled in proportion to his rank. Besides this, a well full of gold and silver ingots was also discovered.[33]

A section of the nobility opined that Bahadur Shah should be reinstated in Gujarat as a Mughal vassal. Perhaps they were bribed

---

[33] *Tazkirat-ul Vaqiyat*, Jauhar Aftabchi, Major Charles Stewart (translation), *Tezkereh Al Vakiat*, Idarah-i Adabiyat-i Delli, Delhi, 1972, pp. 5–6.

by the Gujarat ruler. But Humayun differed. He appointed Askari as the viceroy. However, soon after Humayun's departure the situation slipped from Askari's control. He approached Tardi Beg; the Mughal governor of Champanair for assistance. Unfortunately the latter suspected him of treachery and informed Humayun accordingly. A confused Humayun believed the rumours and thus Askari was denied assistance. The latter could not have hung on without assistance from the centre. Disappointed, he abandoned his post and moved towards Agra in a huff. It was feared that he would usurp the throne at Agra. Thus, Humayun also abandoned all projects and rushed towards the capital. Soon after, Bahadur Shah reoccupied Ahmadabad. Though the misunderstandings between the brothers were sorted on their way to Agra, the mistrust had cost them a lot of time, energy and money. They lost Gujarat.

While Humayun was busy with the Gujarat campaign, a lot had occurred on other fronts. In June 1535, Sam Mirza; younger brother of Shah Tahmasp the ruler of Persia, had laid siege to Qandhar. He was defeated by Kamran. Then in April 1537 the place was besieged by Shah Tahmasp. Even a veteran like Khwaja Kalan couldn't defend it. Ultimately, it was recovered by Kamran. Thereafter he stayed at Qandhar for a year to douse Persian ambitions. After their escape from Gujarat the Mirzas were again up to rabblerousing. They were checked by Kamran and Hindal. Thus Humayun and his brothers were workings like a team, trying to get a grip. Despite all the losses Humayun wasn't complaining. Askari was rewarded for his services and Hindal's wedding was celebrated with royal grandeur. On the other hand, Sher Khan continued to hex the empire with his conquests. In 1535–36, he had extracted tribute from the ruler of Bengal and in June 1537, he invaded that state. His son had quit Mughal services. Finally he became too towering, to be ignored. Humayun resolved to tackle him. However before starting for his Bihar-Bengal campaign, he sought the advice of Khwaja Nura; a famous sufi of Lahore. The sufi predicted his defeat and advised him against the endeavour.[34] Nevertheless, he went. He asked Kamran to stay in Lahore until his return and directed him to speed to Agra-Delhi in case of any emergency.

Humayun started for Bengal in 1537. He besieged the fort of Chunar in 1538. A drama was played to break through the fort's defence. Rumy Khan's loyal slave, Khilafat, was flogged. The latter then acted as if he had defected to the Afghans. On seeing his wounds the Afghans were convinced that indeed the man had a reason to betray the Mughals. They trusted him. He was taken inside the fort and his wounds were dressed. He went around the place, marked the best spots for an offensive attack and then escaped back to his master. His inputs indeed made a difference. The fort fell. Arms of 300 Afghan artillerymen were amputated on Rumy Khan's orders. Humayun was furious to hear of such cruelty. Anyway, Rumy Khan was soon poisoned by jealous Mughal nobles. This was sometime in June 1538. Precious months were lost in occupying just one fort. Besides, Sher Khan had already shifted the treasures from there to Rohtas. This delayed the opening of a second front against the Afghans in Bihar-Bengal. Thus Bengal fell to Afghan pressure. Now Humayun demanded its treasures and the fort of Rohtas from Sher Khan. The latter replied that Bengal had cost him 5–6 years of hard work and the lives of many loyalists. He wouldn't give it to anyone. Around this time he formally assumed the title of *Sher Shah Al-Sultan*. Originally, his name was Farid Khan but he is popularly referred to as Sher Shah. Meanwhile the defeated king of Bengal, Syed Mahmud, sought asylum in the Mughal camp. Humayun's generous promise to reinstate him drew the Baadshah deeper into the local politics of an unfamiliar region. In the following months Syed Mahmud and his sons died but Humayun continued to march towards Bengal. When he reached its capital, Gaur, in late 1538, the place was brought under his control within four day. This seemed like a big achievement, but actually it wasn't. Sher Shah wanted exactly this to happen. He had already emptied Bengal of its riches.

---

[34] *The Mughal Nobility*, p. 16.

Humayun had nothing much to gain. Now the Mughals were literally locked in there. Returning back to Agra wasn't going to be easy in any way. What Humayun thought to be a victory was really the beginning of a war. The Mughal army was exhausted. A stopover in Bengal was essential, but Humayun tarried too long. His months of hibernation in the harem were a bit too much. Grumblings of the nobility began. Hindal and Yadgar Nasir Mirza had left for Agra midway down the route to Bengal. Now the prince was eyed as a potential puppet ruler by the anti-Humayun faction.

Instead of challenging Humayun in Bengal, Sher Shah occupied almost everything from Bihar to Jaunpur to Awadh. He knew that Humayun would anyway leave Bengal when Agra would be threatened. Mir Atika who had visited Bengal during this time had noted an anti-Humayun wave in the Mughal camp. Babur was informal at social gatherings but no one could dare challenge his authority. Humayun didn't command that kind of authority. In a meeting preceding his departure to Agra, he proposed to appoint Zahid Beg as the governor of Bengal. He said that the latter had urged him many times to grant him a promotion. Thus he was being appointed as a governor. Surprisingly, pat came the officer's audacious reply: 'What? Could you find no other place to kill me other than in Bengal?' Having said this Zahid Beg left the meeting in a huff and Humayun openly pledged to kill him. He said: 'I must put this scoundrel to death.'[35] Influential ladies of the harem interceded for him, but Humayun refused to budge from his stand. Ultimately Zahid Beg, Khusroe Beg Kokaltash and Mirza Nuruddin—a son-in-law of Babur, fled to Agra and sought Hindal's protection. They incited him to declare his independence, which he did. Interestingly many of the local lords actually recognized him as the ruler of Agra-Delhi.[36] In desperation Humayun's supporters invited Kamran for help. He was the only one who could knock some sense into Hindal's head. Indeed his arrival restored order. Hindal back-tracked from his rebelliousness.

---

[35] *Tazkirat-ul Vaqiyat*, p. 13.
[36] *The Mughal Nobility*, p. 16.

After all, Kamran's presence in Lahore paid off.

After a harassing journey, Humayun reached Chausa in March 1539. Sher Shah was waiting there to liquidate his prestige and power. His brothers at Agra didn't come to help him. He was disappointed and his army was demoralized. It is a mystery whether they didn't come or they couldn't come. The nobles who had instigated Hindal's rebellion perhaps wanted Humayun dead and thus they refused to cooperate with his brothers. Or maybe Kamran too had lost confidence in Humayun's capabilities and didn't want to waste resources on a lost cause. Unsure of his exhausted armies' energy, Humayun opened negotiations with Sher Shah. Shaikh Khalil, a saint from the line of the celebrated sufi, Shaikh Fariduddin Ganj-e Shakar and perhaps another sufi by the name of Maulana Muhiuddin Muhammad; a disciple of Shaikh Bahlul, were requested to mediate. A treaty was concluded according to which Sher Shah was to get Bengal and Chunar. In return he had to recognize Humayun's supremacy and give him a safe passage to Agra. However, before the Mughal army could move, the Afghans launched a surprise attack. The night before the attack, Humayun was warned by Shaikh Khalil, but he wouldn't believe that such a breach of treaty was possible. Of course it was. Humayun miscalculated. The Mughals were stupefied by the suddenness of the strike. They began deserting the battle field. In fact many of the nobles left the field without even receiving a single wound. Humayun was badly injured. His life was saved by a water carrier; Nizamuddin. The grateful Baadshah promised to seat him on his throne for a day and make him as famous as his famous namesake sufi Shaikh Nizamuddin Auliya.[37] Humayun's daughter Aqiqa and some other women of his harem were lost in the ensuing confusion. Those who survived were honourably sent to Agra by Sher Shah. After this loss, Humayun swore to never ever take members of his harem on military expeditions. He finally reached Agra in July 1539. The landlords en route half-heartedly offered him some gifts but the only one which he accepted was an embroidered saddle for Kamran.

---

[37] *Tazkirat-ul Vaqiyat*, p. 18.

Humayun was shaken, both physically and mentally. On Kamran's intercession, he forgave Hindal immediately. In fact he was ready to swear on the Quran to convince Dildar Begum that he had pardoned her son. A political congress of the brothers was in progress when Nizamuddin the water carrier arrived. He wanted the Baadshah to fulfil his promise. Humayun was wildly enthusiastic about keeping his word, much to the annoyance of the royalties and the nobility. Kamran wrote disgustedly: 'Gifts and favours of some other kind ought to be the servant's reward. What propriety is there in setting him on the throne? At a time when Sher Khan is near, what kind of affair is this to engage, your Majesty?'[38] The hostile nobles cited this humility to malign him as a whimsical freak. However Humayun did what he had to. Only he had the power to pay the price of such commitments. Nizamuddin was enthroned.

While Humayun was recovering from his injuries Kamran offered to lead the Mughals against Sher Shah. He was not allowed. Humayun argued that this was his war. The Afghans had humiliated him and only he would avenge it. Maybe he was protective about Kamran and thought that his brother would underestimate Sher Shah. Or maybe he was insecure that if Kamran actually won, his prestige as the Baadshah would diminish further. Given that Kamran didn't come to his rescue at Chausa, he might have doubted his brother's intentions. However, Kamran's vexations turned to alarm when he fell ill at Agra in February 1540. Semi-paralytic, he could hardly move or speak. He suspected that Humayun had got him poisoned, so that he could occupy Kabul and Qandhar, if he lost Agra-Delhi. From this point onwards the brothers' relationship slipped continuously. No one was interested in helping them patch up, like Babur would have. After Humayun recovered, he requested Kamran to join him in combating the Afghans but the latter refused. He didn't want a share in Humayun's possible failures and misfortunes. Reluctantly he contributed a 3,000-strong contingent to accompany Humayun

---

[38] *Gulbadan Portrait of a Rose Princess at the Mughal Court*, Rumer Godden, The Viking Press, New York, 1981, p. 80.

and another 1,000 soldiers to be stationed at Agra.[39] That was all.

At Benaras, Sher Shah had assumed the title of *Sultan-ul Adil*. His confidence inspired many commanders to join him. The fateful battle of Kannauj in which he and Humayun faced each other was fought on 17 March 1540. Hindal commanded the right wing, Askari the left and Humayun was at the centre. Babur's sons lost. This was just the beginning of their trials. As a ripple effect of this defeat, the Persians and the Uzbegs were emboldened in the north-west and sedition brewed at Lahore. Kamran too was tripped by the roll-out of his brother's accident-prone plans.

After the smashing defeat at Kannauj, it wasn't safe for Humayun to be seen at Agra. He secretly headed towards the house of Syed Rafiuddin; a saintly non-political man. Hindal dashed to collect their family treasures and valuables from the citadel. After a quick breakfast of melons and bread, Humayun rode off in the direction of Lahore. Still considering the locals to be his subjects, he disallowed their plunder or harassment. The head of a soldier who had defied this order, was hung on a spear to scare the others into obedience. Humayun reached Lahore in July 1540. Here, he was almost alone in proposing that another attack should be launched against Sher Shah. The others felt that invasion of Kashmir was militarily a more viable idea. To buy time while the Mughals made up their mind, Kamran opened negotiations with Sher Shah. The latter also played along but kept preparing for the invasion of Punjab. Kamran suggested that he should be allowed to go to Kabul to settle the dislocated nobles' families. He would join the Kashmir campaign after that. Humayun suspected that he won't. Nobles urged Humayun to order Kamran's assassination. He snubbed them and said: 'No, never for the vanities of this perishable world will I imbrue my hands in the blood of a brother, but will forever remember the dying words of our respected parent (Babur) who said to me, "O Humayun beware, beware do not quarrel with your brothers nor ever form any evil intentions

---

[39] *The Mughal Nobility*, pp. 15–24.

towards them." These words are engraved on my heart forever.'[40]
Interestingly Kamran too echoed the same type of sentiments. While
Humayun was at Lahore the coins struck there had only his elder
brother's name. This indicates that Kamran acknowledged Humayun
as their father's primary heir.

Around October 1540, Sher Shah was close to Lahore. Now,
Karman decided to march to Kabul without any further delay.
Humayun's plans for Kashmir fizzled out and after Kamran, he too
exited from Punjab. The suggestion to usurp Kabul and eliminate
Kamran cropped up again. It was again vetoed. Humayun said: 'I
refused this request when at Lahore and will certainly not agree to
it.' Thereafter, Kamran left for Kabul and Humayun for Sindh. Now
Kamran was Babur's only child with any dominions of his own. He
tried to strengthen his position by marriages and political alliances.

Humayun's efforts for a political alignment with Shah Husain
Arghun, the ruler of Sindh failed. However he was luckier on the
personal front. In 1541, he was at Pat when Dildar Begum invited
him for a feast. There he saw Hamida Banu Begum, daughter of
Mir Baba Dost. The latter was Hindal's preceptor and was distantly
related to the royal family. At 33, Humayun fell in love at first sight
with a much younger Hamida. He requested Dildar Begum to get
her married to him. Hindal was quite upset by this proposal. Initially,
he argued: 'I regard this girl in the same light as a sister or daughter.
His Majesty is the king, suppose he does not make adequate provision
so that there is some vexation later?' He also added: 'I thought you
came here to do me honour; not to look out for a young bride.
If you commit this (ridiculous) action, I will leave you.' Humayun
was livid that his brother had made such cheeky comments. Dildar
Begum intervened. She told Hindal off and promised Humayun that
his proposal shall be actualized. The next day, on Humayun's request
she sent for Hamida. The latter refused to come and replied: 'If the
intention is that I should attend on his majesty, I have had that
honour on that day. For what else should I come?' Then Humayun

---

[40] *Tazkirat-ul Vaqiyat*,p. 26.

sent Subhan Quli to request Hindal to convince her. Obviously the prince refused. He said that nothing that he says would make any difference to her. Anyway when Subhan Quli personally requested her, she said: 'For the kings to see (a woman) once is lawful, the next time she becomes a stranger seeing whom is unlawful. I will not come.' When Humayun heard this reply he said: 'If she is a stranger a (*na-mahram*) we will (marry her to) make her accessible (*mahram*).' Finally Dildar counselled Hamida. She said to Hamida that she would anyway marry someone, then why not a king. Hamida argued: 'Yes, but let me be given to someone whose collar my hand can reach, rather than that I be given to a man whose skirt, as I know well, my hand will not reach.' Finally after 40 days of relentless persuasion she agreed. Humayun himself fixed the date and hour of the wedding in accordance with auspiciousness. It was on a Monday, midday. Mir Abul Baqa performed the marriage and was paid 2 lakh (tankas) as the fees. After 3 days he left with his bride for Bhakkar and an annoyed Hindal proceeded to Qandhar.[41]

Desertions from Humayun's camps were alarming. At times he sat up the whole night to keep an eye on his officers. He reached Rohri in Sindh on 26 January 1541. For seven months he kept trying to take Bhakhar from here. His attempts failed. Then he moved to Thatta and on 7 November 1541, besieged the fort of Sehwan. This attempt also conked out. In 1541–42 under threat from Mirza Shah Husain in Sindh, Humayun and his entourage were to cross a river in vessels made of cattle hide. The Baadshah and some officers were yet to cross and a single boat remained. Hotspur Tardi Beg, one of his officers, insisted on preceding him. This agitated the superintendent who felt that Tardi was flouting the protocol. In the following showdown Tardi hit him with his horsewhip and in the heat of the moment the superintendent also drew out his sword. Humayun was informed and instead of being angry with Tardi for trying to cross before him, he decided to guard his noble's honour.

[41]Shireen Moosvi, *Episodes in the Life of Akbar Contemporary Records and Reminiscences*, National Book Trust, New Delhi, 1994, pp. 1–3.

The superintendent's hands were tied with a handkerchief, symbolizing handcuffs and he was presented before the noble. Embarrassed by the Baadshah's magnanimity and ashamed of his conduct, Tardi quickly untied the fellow, apologized for his conduct and gave him presents to seal the reconciliation. Later, when the group was being pursued by Askari, Humayun's request to Tardi for a horse was turned down. Therefore, he had to seat Hamida on his own horse during that chase but he never held a grudge. Anyway, he started for Bhakkar on 23 February 1542, but went to Rohri again. He had left Yadgar Nasir there in January 1541 and wanted his assistance in refreshing his endeavours. But Yadgar Nasir had been bought off by Shah Husain Arghun. The example of his treachery encouraged others also to defect. Once, Humayun kept awake the whole night to stop his senior nobles, Munim Beg and Tardi Beg from running way. However in the morning when they went out for a wash the nobles rushed towards their horses to escape. Humayun had to literally run after them to stop them. Nothing fruitful could be achieved at Rohri. Then in April 1542 he started for Marwar on the invitation of Raja Maldeo. But the Raja got cold feet due to Sher Shah and backed off. The disappointed adherents of Humayun advised him to usurp the Raja's lands. He dismissed the idea saying: 'If you could make me king of the whole world, I could not attempt so foul an action or be guilty of such ingratitude.'[42] Thus in August 1542 he turned towards Phalodi and then via Jodhpur and Jaisalmer reached Amarkot on 22 August 1542. Many of his loyalists perished in the desert due to lack of water. Hamida's pregnancy in the midst of a travel laden with dangers definitely added to her burdens. In this state when it was sometimes difficult to find something as basic as water, she had a craving for pomegranates. The possibility of finding one in the middle of a desert was almost nonexistent. Humayun was saddened by his inability to fulfill such a mundane wish of his beloved wife. Fortunately, the Mughal party chanced upon a merchant who had a single piece of the required fruit. It was immediately procured.

---

[42] *Tazkirat-ul Vaqiyat*, p. 37.

Humayun's happiness over this fluke could easily equal his dejection over losing his kingdom. His child-like enthusiasm reflected his spirit of living in the moment. In the last lap of the journey towards Amarkot, a heavily pregnant Hamida rode a horse borrowed from an officer called Roshan Beg. However, due to the indisposition of the horse that he was riding, the officer demanded the one that he had lent. Humayun immediately alighted from his own and seated Hamida on that horse. Roshan's animal was gracefully returned and the Baadshah started walking on foot. After a tiresome walk he mounted a camel, not the ride preferred by royalties. Eventually, another officer Khalid Beg offered his horse to Humayun.[43] The fact that an officer could demand his animal back from Hamida is a reflection on Humayun's approachability. Rana Prasad, the ruler of Amarkot welcomed him. He wanted Humayun's assistance in getting even with Shah Husain Arghun. The latter had killed his father. In the middle of all this chaos, Hamida gave birth to a boy. This was on 15 October 1542. Jauhar Aftabchi the author of *Tazkirat-ul Vaqiyat* who was present on the occasion noted: 'The moon of the fourteenth is called *Badr*. Thus did prince Muhammad Akbar, the conqueror, the full moon of the world and faith, illuminating both the worlds, came into the world and was named Jalaluddin which is the same as Badruddin (full moon of the faith) and there is no light in any night like that of the light of the night of the full moon. Thus the virtue of that night is that it illuminates both the worlds.' To celebrate his son's birth Humayun distributed musk amongst the nobles. That was all that he could afford. He said that he wanted to thank God for giving him this son and that he hoped that one day his son's fame would fill the world just as the fragrance of the musk had filled the room.[44] He was happy beyond measure. Indeed, Humayun lived it up no matter how testing the times were. He saw his son after 35 days of the child's birth. Meanwhile, Shah Husain tried to instigate the Rana of Amarkot against him. The Shah sent the Rana an honourary dress

---

[43]Ibid.,pp. 42–43.
[44]Ibid., p. 45. Also see *Episodes from the life of Akbar*.

and a bejewelled dagger. Humayun was informed and according to his fancy, the gifts were returned. A dog was sent to Shah Husain; wearing his gifts. Around April 1543 the alliance between the Rana and Humayun snapped. At that time the latter was stationed at a place called Jun. Around July 1543, Humayun's progression towards Qandhar alarmed Kamran and Askari. The latter was governing the place. Humayun's advance trackers informed him that he might be arrested by Askari. The threat was so urgent that Humayun fled to Persia. Due to the dangers involved in this journey Akbar was left behind in the care of trusted servants. Thereafter, Askari took him in his personal custody. He kept his baby nephew not just safe, but loved and pampered.

Kamran rightly anticipated that the Persians, who had made four attempts on Qandhar in the last ten years, would certainly seek Humayun's assistance in capturing it. He was right. Thus he sponsored attempts to sabotage the pact between Shah Tahmasp and Humayun. When Humayun reached Persia in January 1544, Shah Tahmasp had to take the call on handling his kingly guest who at the moment, wasn't exactly a king. The immediate hospitality that the Shah extended to Humayun was exceptionally grand and his whole entourage was happy kicking their heels. However the feasibility of a political and military alliance with him was still being debated amongst the Irani bigwigs. Three noblemen: Raushan Beg Kukeh, who was Humayun's foster brother; Khawaja Ghazi Diwan and Sultan Mohammad envenomed the Shah's mind against Humayun. The trio claimed that they could conquer Qandhar for the Shah with half of what the monarch would invest in resurrecting Humayun to do that. Secondly, if the latter deserved any help then his brothers would have surely helped him and that there must have been a reason for their indifference towards him. Besides these suggestions, another matter which disoriented the Shah was an old intelligence report that during a divination, Humayun had written the Shah's name on arrows of an inferior quality and his own on superior ones. This had hurt the Shah's ego and he now asked Humayun for a clarification. The Baadshah accepted his slip-up and said that since his empire was much larger than the domains of the Persian monarch he had considered the Shah inferior to himself, however only God's will prevails. Rubbing in the irony that now he was forced to take refuge in the very place he considered lowly, the Shah retorted with sarcasm that indeed due to his foolish vanity, 'villagers' drove him out of his 'vast empire'.[45]

Eventually the Shah's siblings managed to bring him round to support Humayun. His brother made a case on moral and ethical grounds and his sister, Shahzaadi Sultanam, on political ones. She pleaded that as it is the Persian Empire has no dearth of antagonists, the Turks, the Uzbeks and others are perpetually on the lookout to devour it, they could very well do without adding the Mughals to this long list of foes. Thus, harming Humayun would be a political blunder. If her brother did not intend helping him then he must clarify this immediately and ensure the fugitives' safe exit from Persia. The Shah was sagacious enough to value this counsel and he rightly understood that for the maintenance of a favourable balance of power in the region it was critical to help Humayun. The first step now was to snub the in-house opponents. The Shah felt that the three instigators mentioned earlier were diverting him from the path of dignity by their unworthy counsels. They had to be put down; literally. Feet tied with rope, face first; they were to be lowered into a deep well called the *Diwan* of Suleiman. Their painfully slow death would be an example to deter other challengers of this diplomatic coalition. Incidentally the ropes which were brought to drop them at the bottom of the pit fell short and so they were hauled up to be descended again the next morning. Making use of precious luck, Raushan Beg managed to send a petition to Humayun. He confessed his offence, implored forgiveness and begged the Baadshah to intercede for him to be pardoned by the Shah. In response Humayun dispatched a supplication to Shah Tahmasp with a request to forgive the trio as an act of pious alms giving so that his late father, Shah Ismail's soul

---

[45]Ibid.,pp. 69–70.

may rest in peace. Despite his adamantine resolve in such matters the Shah pardoned them.[46] In admiration of Humayun's benignant gesture he remarked that to forgive people who wish you death is not something that the weak can do. It needs exemplary forbearance and clemency, therefore his trust in this man's capabilities cannot be misplaced. Indeed he was right.

Meanwhile Kamran was left with no option but to wait for Humayun's return to deal with him. The suspense was killing. Besides, Kabul and Qandhar were overcrowded with unemployed and dissatisfied nobility. The nobles who had been displaced from Hindustan had nowhere else to go. Some of them had come with Kamran voluntarily. The latter didn't have enough lands to satisfy their expectations or ambitions. They were a volatile lot and had to be monitored. It was likely that they would join Humayun if he returned.

Low down whispers about Humayun's return began sometime in October 1544. As a precaution, Akbar was shifted to Kabul; in Kamran's custody. Finally, in March 1545 Humayun actually appeared and besieged Qandhar. Sometime in mid 1545; while the siege was still on, Bairam Khan came to Kabul as Humayun's envoy. He brought classified letters from Humayun. No one was privy to his meeting with Kamran. He stayed at Kabul for six weeks. He was allowed to meet nobles and also Hindal. His visit gave an impression that the brothers might unite. Droves of deserters from Kabul joined Humayun. Kamran sent their aunt Khanzada Begum to intercede for Askari's safety in case he was captured by Humayun. Finally in September 1545, Qandhar fell. Badakshan, which Kamran had held since 1544 also slipped away. Mirza Sulaiman, Yadgar Nasir and Hindal joined Humayun. On 16 November 1545, Kamran surrendered Kabul without any resistance; but he managed to escape arrest. Destiny was rewriting Humayun's stars. No one could believe that this was actually happening.

Kamran sought asylum in the Hazara region for the most

---

[46]Ibid., p. 72

of 1545–50. A niece of the Hazara chief Khizr Khan had been married to him. After a failed attempt at capturing Zamin Dawar, he progressed towards Sindh. The fickle-mindedness and treachery of the nobility which had helped Kamran in 1540 helped Humayun in 1545. In Sindh, Kamran married a daughter of Shah Husain Arghun. Meanwhile Humayun fell ill at Badakshan. Nobles considered deserting him; again. He was almost comatose. Askari was put under arrest by his loyalists. Hamida took upon herself to nurse him because no one else could be trusted in such delicate times. This was in late 1546. Taking advantage of this situation, Kamran appeared around Kabul. He took away Akbar from the citadel. Hisamuddin Ali, the governor of Zamin Dawar was castrated, tortured and killed. Some of Humayun's officers were imprisoned, blinded or eliminated. Some joined Kamran either out of fear or free will. As in 1540 and 1545, 1546 also recorded a shift in loyalties. As soon as he got better, Humayun besieged Kabul. To deter him from using canons Kamran threatened to seat his son Akbar on the fort's ramparts, in the direct line of firing. Humayun immediately banned the use of ammunition but the blockade of supply lines continued. Anyway he had been reluctant to use violent tactics against the fort since many family members were residing there with Kamran. Since kinship still meant something to the Timurids, Kamran was literally accused of blasphemy for threatening his 5-year-old nephew. The ladies of the family were flabbergasted. The fort fell in 1547 after four months of the siege. Kamran escaped and Hindal was dispatched to pursue him. He saw Kamran fleeing, being carried on a man's back. Taking pity on his brother's condition, he gave him a horse and let him escape. Kamran emerged again, around late 1547 and captured Badakshan. Pir Muhammad Khan, the ruler of Balkh helped him. Again, the nobles were tempted to desert Humayun. Kamran had to be subdued to stop them. Humayun's peace propositions were rejected by his brother. He had written to Kamran: 'Oh my unkind brother, what are you doing! Every murder that is committed on either side, you will be answerable for, on the day of judgement, come and make peace so that mankind may be no longer oppressed by our contest.' To this Kamran replied: 'He shall obtain the bride of the kingdom who embraces her across the edge of the sharp sword.'[47] Anyway, in June 1548 Humayun finally succeeded in defeating him. This time Kamran came to meet him. He was well treated. It was decided that they would jointly invade Balkh and Kamran would get that territory. Humayun went ahead with the plan, however when he was already halfway into the enemies' area, his intelligence gatherers reported that Kamran had backed out. Humayun had to revert immediately to save Kabul from his brother. He was seriously injured in an ambush. His clothes were so blood soaked that he had to change into a sheep skin coat and a silk trouser presented by an old woman. Some of the clothes which he had earlier discarded were presented back to him by their second owners. He had no choice but to wear them. Once, he became so restless and sleepless that he placed his head on the lap of a noble and the latter sang a lullaby to put him to sleep. Failure of the Balkh campaign shattered him. Besides on his fears about Kamran's intention of usurping Kabul in his absence were coming true. Indeed Kamran occupied it in June 1550. In August–September 1550, Humayun started from Badakshan to retrieve it once again. This time he proposed to Kamran that Akbar could be married to his daughter. The royal couple would jointly rule Kabul. Then the brothers could be united against the Afghans in Hindustan. Kamran was tempted, but those who had betrayed Humayun to join him, persuaded him to reject the offer. They said that they would rather have their heads hung at the gates of Kabul than to surrender it. Eventuality they were defeated and the gates of Kabul were actually adorned by their severed heads. Askari was captured and by mid 1551 he was exiled. Kamran's son-in-law, Aq Sultan, also joined Humayun. Due to the ever diminishing support, Kamran fled to Sindh. He reappeared round March 1551. On 20 November 1551 he launched a surprise attack on Humayun's establishment at Ju'i Shahi. Hindal was killed in this encounter. When the blitz was over and Humayun

---

[47]Ibid., p. 91.

enquired about Hindal, nobody dared to break the shocking news. When he finally saw the dead body, he was inconsolable. The whole of Babur's clan sunk in sorrow. Kamran included. It was heard on the grapevine that the prince was cursed to death by a deer that he had hunted that very morning. He was shot with the same type of arrow that he had used to shoot the deer.

Kamran had unwittingly crossed a line. He was being hunted by a very desperate Humayun. Most of his supporters vanished. Around March 1552 he fled to Hindustan and headed for the court of Jalal Khan-Islam Shah Sur, son of Sher Shah; Humayun's nemesis. The Afghan king was not interested in getting dragged into what he thought was a squabble between Babur's sons. Perhaps he missed the big picture. The announcement of Kamran's arrival to his court was: 'Your majesty be pleased to cast a glance hither for Kamran the *muqaddamzada* (son of a headman) of Kabul invokes blessing.'[48] Surely Babur would have rolled over in his grave. Once some courtiers nastily referred to Kamran as *moro* (Peacock). This was to mock him. When he asked for the meaning of this word, they lied that it meant a great dignitary. Kamran sensed their cunningness and said that in this case, Islam Shah is a greater *moro* and perhaps Sher Shah was the greatest one. After this, Islam Shah forbade his courtiers from cracking such jokes. For almost a year Kamran was held hostage by the Afghans. Finally he escaped in a woman's disguise. Desolate and desperate, he now sought shelter with Sultan Adam; a Ghakkar chief. The latter handed him over to Humayun, but took a promise that the prince would not be killed. Humayun was as good as his words, so Kamran lived. In fact he outlived Humayun. Humayun's loyalists pressurized him to get his brother bumped off. They believed that a mixture of kinship and kingship makes a deadly concoction. In 1550, in an oath taking ceremony, the nobles had pledged to be loyal to Humayun and had also made him promise that he will pay heed to their advice. Under their pressure it was decreed that Kamran would be blinded. Humayun's discomfiture was so obvious

---

[48] *The Mughal Nobility*, p. 46.

that Jauhar Aftabchi had to ask him for a reconfirmation of the order. Kamran withstood the pain of a rod being run through his eyes with exceptional courage. He objected only when someone put lime and salt on his raw wounds. This was sometime before October 1553. He threatened Humayun that he would commit suicide if he was taken to Kabul in such a miserable state. Humayun honoured his wishes and sent him to Mecca. He visited his brother before the departure. Kamran's wife, Mah Chuchak Begum, princess of Sindh accompanied him against her father's wishes. Chalma Beg also went along. With their help, Kamran performed the Haj pilgrimage thrice. He died on 5 October 1557.[49] His children remained in Humayun's custody. Their uncle treated them well.

Tribes of Afghanistan and the rulers of Persia, Balkh and Sindh were also involved in the strife between Babur's sons. The larger question of Shia or Sunni dominance in this tract was important for local politics. For example, the Shia Persians supported Humayun, since he was a more liberal Sunni in comparison to Kamran. They were extremely good to him up till Kamran's blinding. After the latter exited the political scene, their attitude became hostile towards Humayun as well. Humayun's defeats taught him that centralization and an insistence on loyalty were key components of governance. Before 1540 he was already trying to rearrange the nobility. He made separate departments which would report directly to him. Routine administration was delinked from military functions. He wanted to use his officers' expertise to strengthen his administration. His brothers hadn't been treacherous in the beginning. They had fissures of differing opinions, which were widened by the selfish and short-sighted nobles. It was obvious that Sher Shah's organizational skills were much more sophisticated in comparison with his own. On his return Humayun was ready to implement changes in the composition and handling of the nobility. By 1553, the political compulsions forced the nobility to remain under central command. Visionaries who were ready to be a part of a big and steady empire were retained. Officers prone

---

[49]Ibid., pp. 48–50.

to yo-yoing loyalties were dropped.

On 12 November 1554, Humayun left Kabul. He reached the Indus by 31 December 1554. Sher Shah had built the fort of Rohtas in anticipation of Mughals' return. However when the test actually came, Tatar Khan the Afghan governor of Rohtas was so overwhelmed that he literally surrendered the fort and fled. On 24th February 1555 Humayun reached Lahore and then by May, he was in Sirhind. 22nd June 1555 was the fateful day when Sikander Sur, Kala Pahar and other Afghan big wigs faced him. They were defeated. On 20th July 1555 the victorious Mughals entered the fort of Salimgarh at Delhi. Humayun had returned to Hindustan. It was a miracle.

Years of hardships hadn't changed Humayun's prioritization of justice for the common man. While appointing Jauhar Aftabchi as the *Tehsildar* of Haibatpur, he told him the story of a dishonest Mughal who snatched a blanket from a poor man on the first day of his appointment as a Collector. When the poor fellow protested against this exploitation the new appointee replied that didn't the scoundrel know that the government had appointed him to 'collect'? Jauhar understood the sarcasm and he records that on receiving this hint he said: 'I am aware of my own unfitness for public employment, but trust that through your Majesty's favour and having had the honour for so many years of pouring water on the royal hands, I shall not discredit the appointment to which I have been nominated. Humayun responded thus: 'good produces good and evil causes evil'. Jauhar later reported to Humayun that in his *pargana* people's wives and children were enslaved by money lenders because of the debts they were trapped in. He further informed that he had recovered hoarded grains concealed in deep dry wells and the same were sold in the market. The money thus generated was used to repay usurers and free people who were in their captivity. This pleased Humayun and he promoted Jauhar to a higher rank.[50] Thus Humayun was trying to restructure governance but an accidental fall from the stairs of his library proved fatal. This was in January 1556. After the fall,

---

[50] *Tazkirat-ul Vaqiyat*, pp. 112–113.

his ear bled and he slipped into a coma. An urgent message was sent to the crown prince Akbar. The Baadshah died after two days. He was 51 and had ruled for 25 years in all. Like his father, he too was out of time; before the empire could be consolidated. For the Mughals his incredible story became an ideal of perseverance. Humayun never gave up. His attitude towards life could be summed up in the positive 'So what!' He trusted easily, was deceived easily, forgave easily, thanked easily and allowed himself to hope despite anguish, love despite hostilities and above all, he welcomed happiness with open arms however, whenever and wherever it dropped by.

THREE

JALALUDDIN MUHAMMAD AKBAR

1556–1605

*There exists a bond between the Creator and the created which
cannot be brought within the space of language... To be a pir
(mystic guide) should mean to have power of recognizing sorrow
and providing its relief, not letting the beard grow, wearing out
the robe and raising a tumult through worldly talk.*

—REFLECTIONS OF AKBAR[51]

I t was rare for the power vampires of medieval times to accept a
minor as their sovereign. Akbar was indeed lucky. He was just
14 at the time of his coronation in February 1556. Internally
and formally he remained unchallenged. His *ataliq* (tutor/guardian)
Bairam Khan was unanimously accepted as the *Wakil–us Sultanate*
(Prime Minister). Bairam Khan immediately abolished the office of
the *wazir* (sole in-charge of the revenue department, independent of
the *wakil*) which had been instituted by Humayun. Now the *wakil*
controlled the finances as well. The nobility's mysterious unanimity in
accepting him as the *wakil* was rooted in their fears. After Humayun's
expulsion from Hindustan in 1540 they had suffered unspeakable
losses and anxieties. Thus, dealing with the forces that had uprooted
Babur's sons from Hindustan was a clear priority. Unity of command
was essential and Bairam Khan was an excellent commander.

Bairam Khan was an old loyalist of Humayun. He was present in
his Gujarat and Bengal campaigns. After the Mughals were defeated

---

[51]Cf. *Episodes in the Life of Akbar Contemporary Records and Reminiscences*, Shireen Moosvi,
National Book Trust, New Delhi, 1994, p. 126–127.

at Kannauj in 1540, he had fled to Gujarat. He joined Humayun again in April 1543. He helped Humayun in seeking asylum at Persia. Thus Bairam Khan combined efficiency and ambition. He was useful but could also be dangerous. Humayun knew that. No wonder when he started for the re-conquest of Hindustan in 1553 he asked Bairam Khan to relinquish the governorship of Qandhar and accompany him. Perhaps it was feared that in his absence Bairam Khan would usurp Qandhar. Not only did Humayun take Bairam Khan to Hindustan, he ordered the latter's trusted men to stay back in Afghanistan.

Munim Khan, a trusted noble, was left in charge of Kabul and Qandhar and the royal harem in Humayun's absence. He had been Akbar's tutor and was a great favourite of Humayun. One day Akbar wanted to miss his lessons and requested Munim Khan to grant him leave. The latter obliged the prince. Someone reported this to Humayun. When Akbar visited him he told the prince to refrain from asking such favours in future. Interestingly he added that Munim Khan had not complained about him. This was done to ensure that Akbar held no grudges against the noble. Anyway, since Akbar was going to Hindustan, Bairam Khan was appointed as his tutor and Munim Khan was attached with Mirza Hakim; Humayun's younger son.

Humayun's death was quite a thunder for the Mughals. They were shaken inside out. Bairam Khan kept Kamran's son, Mirza Abul Qasim, under his personal surveillance. A blood prince could always be used as a puppet by adventures. Thus reaffirming Akbar's *baadshaahat* (kingship) and Bairam Khan's *wikalat* as the nobilities' best bet for sustaining their own legitimacy. Shah Abul Ma'ali, a noble who didn't attend the festivities of Akbar's coronation was arrested. His absence was interpreted as a protest against Bairam Khan's *wikalat*. Even the plea that he was mourning Humayun's death was rejected. Bairam Khan ensured that all those who could challenge him were kept at a safe distance from Akbar. He built a group of personal loyalists. However there remained a neutral and non-committal group as well. These super-diplomats were waiting and watching the movement of power's fulcrum. Akbar was lost in the chaos around him. Bairam Khan was the man of the moment. Everyone looked up to him for deliverance from the Afghans. But he was looking beyond the Afghan challenge, much further into the continuation of his dominance, Afghans or no Afghans. In fact his obsession with his future became so strong that he lost touch with the here and now.

Bairam Khan ignored Munim Khan's request to help him save Kabul from Mirza Sulaiman, the ruler of Badakshan. This was the first manifestation of his arrogance and indifference towards Humayun's people and possessions. Kabul was invaded in May 1556. Haram Begum; the Mirza's wife had visited Kabul in 1551, after Hindal's death. She wanted to meet his sisters and offer condolences. However she had also fought with her husband and wished to get away from him. Meeting the Mughal princesses gave her a pretext to leave Badakshan. Later she patched up with her husband and informed him about Kabul's weak defence arrangements. Emboldened by Humayun's death the Mirza attacked Kabul. Munim Khan was sure that help would come from Hindustan. He was wrong. Bairam Khan wanted the royal family and veteran royalists to be stranded at Kabul or perhaps even be killed in the war with the Badakshis. Their arrival in Hindustan would have jeopardized his wherewithal with Akbar. Rumours about Bairam Khan's high handedness had been trickling into Kabul for quite some time but they hadn't been taken seriously. Now they were. Anyway Munim Khan wisely impressed upon Sulaiman Mirza's envoys that help from Hindustan was on its way. His poker face attitude was quite an act. It worked. The Badakshis feared that if armies from Hindustan actually arrived they would be sandwiched between two Mughal forces. Thus a treaty was quickly signed and Sulaiman Mirza retreated.[52]

A party led by Muhammad Quli arrived to escort the royal harem to Hindustan. However in view of Bairam Khan's recent betrayal

---

[52] *The Mughal Nobility*, pp. 38–43.

Munim Khan decided to escort the royalties himself. Muhammad Quli was asked to take over the governorship of Kabul in his absence. He was reluctant but Hamida Banu persuaded him to agree. However he laid a condition that his wife's house in which Munim Khan was residing should be vacated for his residence. When Munim Khan didn't vacate it speedily, Hamida summoned Bayazid Bayat; Munim Khan's representative at Kabul, and scolded him saying that it wasn't easy for her to persuade Muhammad Quli to take charge of Kabul and why was the handing over of his house not being expedited. [53] Thus, she was influential indeed.

While the royal harem was preparing for their relocation to Hindustan, the Mughals there were preparing for war with deadly opponents. Mubarriz Khan Sur-Adil Shah held Chunar. However it was Hemu, his Brahmin/Vaish (Hindu caste names) associate whom the Mughals really dreaded. They confronted him on 7th October 1556 at Tughlaqabad, a few miles from the Qutub Minar. Enthusiasm in the Mughal camp was pathetically drizzly. No wonder they lost to Hemu's crisp assault. The latter occupied Delhi and took the title of Bikramjeet / Vikramaditya; the name of a legendary ruler of ancient India. His checkered record of victories kind of justified that. Tardi Beg who was in command on that fateful day had been keen on a quick clash. Perhaps his eagerness was motivated by personal ambitions. He wanted to prove his worth in the battlefield before Bairam Khan's arrival. The phobic *Wakil* feared precisely that. Accordingly Bairam Khan had sent personal supporters on the field to ensure that Tardi Beg doesn't succeed in his absence. He delayed the backup forces also. Abul Fazl reports that on the day they lost the battle, divisiveness overflowed from the Mughal camp. The cowards were hesitant to fight out of fear and the brave hesitated out of caution. So despite the compromises that the Mughal nobility had made to defeat their enemies, they were defeated. This outcome disturbed the balance of power not just in the Mughal-Afghan and Mughal-Uzbeg context but also in the Mughal-Mughal context. It was impressed that Bairam

---

[53]Ibid., p. 45.

Khan was indeed critical to the survival of the empire. He decided to punish Tardi Beg for his over enthusiasm, the fact that he used to address Tardi Beg as *toqaan* (elder brother) notwithstanding.[54] He conveniently forgot that the latter had handed over the custody of Mirza Kamran's son Mirza Abul Qasim to him. The veteran noble was killed on superfluous charges of treason. Leaving the field to save one's life in the face of imminent defeat/death and then reporting to the central command for further directions wasn't exactly treason by medieval standards, but that is exactly how it was interpreted. On the witness of Pir Muhammad Khan Shirwani and Ali Quli Khan, Tardi Beg was executed on 22nd October 1556. It is unclear whether Akbar was pressurized to sanction the latter's assassination or was the permission taken *post-facto* or was it not taken at all. One afternoon, Bairam Khan brought the noble to his tent and had him slain there. The nobility received a severe jolt. Money and power were used to suppress any serious or open condemnation of the act. For example, Maham Anaga, Akbar's chief wet nurse, an influential person in the harem was bribed. Tardi's loyalists were imprisoned. Special care was taken to prevent the leakage of this news at Kabul. The assassination was made officially public only after a month of the Mughals' victory in the second battle of Panipat (5th November 1556) and Akbar's second coronation. In this battle, an arrow pierced Hemu's eye and went through his skull. His severed head was sent to Kabul. However the news of Tardi Beg's assassination was still withheld. It was only in January 1557 that Baraim Khan conveyed it to Munim Khan through a letter. Three months had already passed and the news sounded more like an injunction than information. The latter cancelled his plan of personally escorting the royal harem. Going to Hindustan would have endangered his life. So, Shamsuddin Muhammad Atka was deputed for this work. Within six months of the execution, Bairam Khan had practically isolated Akbar and was looking forward to be the *de facto* ruler.

[54]*Muntakhab-ut Tawarikh*, Abdul Qadir Badaoni Ibn-I Muluk Shah, Vol. II, G. S. A. Ranking (translation), Saeed International, New Delhi, 1990, p. 7.

To contain Bairam Khan's audacity, Hamida Banu decided to marry Akbar to his rival, Mirza Abdullah Mughal's daughter. Munim Khan was her maternal grandfather. This was to restore a balance of power amongst the nobles. Around March-April 1557 the royal harem reached Lahore. Akbar was there. He was married in accordance with his mother's wishes; Bairam Khan's opposition notwithstanding. Ceremonies and celebrations of the wedding stated that the *Wakil's* advice was of no consequence for the royal family. Hamida Banu was young but she had been Humayun's partner in his political trials and that experience stood her in good stead. She was determined to halt Bairam's blitzkrieg. Generally speaking, the royal ladies received power and wealth through a channel of male relations: father/husband/son etc. Therefore Hamida's worries over Akbar's subservience to Bairam Khan were understandable for reasons beyond maternal affection. Maham Anaga also distanced herself from Bairam Khan after Hamida's arrival from Kabul.

Meanwhile towards the end of 1557 Haram Begum had another showdown with her husband. Again she came to Kabul and requested Munim Khan to make arrangements for her journey to Hindustan. He extended her great hospitality but on Sulaiman Mirza's request, dissuaded her from going there. This time she felt genuinely indebted to the welcoming Mughals and promised she would ensure that her husband and son wouldn't attack Kabul. Ultimately she went back to Badakshan. Thus Munim Khan somehow managed the show at Kabul without any help from the richer part of the empire.[55]

In Hindustan it was becoming clearer that though Bairam Khan had been useful in tough times, it was definitely not his ticket to dominate the royal family. The Afghans had been disseminated and now his arrogance out-weighted his abilities. The general opinion was in favour of curtailing his powers. An attempt was made on his life at Mankot in the middle of 1557. Untamed elephants of the royal stable ran into his camp. He was sure that this was not an accident. To clear his name from the list of suspects of a murder

---

[55] *The Mughal Nobility*, pp. 50–51.

conspiracy, Shamsuddin Muhammad Atka brought all his sons to Bairam Khan's camp. He swore on the Quran that the episode was indeed an accident. Bairam Khan was hardly convinced. Alarmed and angry, he re-strategized his moves. He married Babur's granddaughter Salima Sultan Begum. Maham Anaga helped in fixing this match. More nobles were admitted into the dominating clique. By April 1558 there was a group of nobles who passed proposals prior to their presentation before Akbar. Gradually Bairam Khan's exclusivity was reduced. Most members of the Khan's club were sycophants and opportunists, so the moment he slipped clumsily on the path of ascendency, they applied the reverse gear and drove straight into Akbar's camp. Akbar, in any case, was a politician of genius and could not have been overshadowed for too long. Eventually with the support of the harem he began asserting his rightful position.

In March 1560 Akbar went to Delhi on the pretext of visiting his ailing mother. Bairam Khan was unaware of his movements. Kamran's son was also removed from Agra. From Delhi Akbar issued a *farman* (royal order) of the *Wakil's* dismissal. The nobles were ordered to report to him directly, at Delhi. This triggered off massive desertions from Bairam Khan's camp. By July 1560 his position slipped beyond retrieval. He fled towards Punjab and rebelled when his attempts at patching up with Akbar failed. On August 23rd 1560 he was defeated by Syed Muhammad Atka. He supposedly chose to proceed to Mecca. In fact, such 'choices' practically implied banishment. However he was assassinated on the way in 1561. Now, Akbar married Salima Sultan Begum; his widowed cousin. She exercised great influence over the royal household. Bairam Khan's son, Muhammad Rahim Mirza was adopted by him. The latter grew up to be an important noble of the royal court. He became popular as Abdur Rahim Khan-i Khanan.[56]

In September 1560 Akbar invited Munim Khan, his old tutor and the governor of Kabul to be the new *Wakil-us Sultanate*. He addressed him as Khan Baba, exactly the way he used to address Bairam Khan. Shamsuddin Muhammad Atka was disappointed at

---

[56]Ibid., pp. 46–60.

being by passed for this priced post. He was pacified with rich land grants. Akbar indeed had numerous issues to resolve. Bairam Khan's supporters were still angry at the way fate had betrayed them. One of them, Bahadur Khan, had killed a soldier who had audaciously put his comrade Wali Beg's severed head on public display. Maham Anaga's lobby wanted unlimited rewards for helping Akbar tackle Bairam Khan. The senior Chaghtai nobles had anyway always felt entitled to privileges. Whatever little that Humayun had done to constitute a dependable nobility had been undone by Bairam Khan. However it is difficult to guess whether the empire could have survived without the latter's initial leadership. Akbar knew that the divisive and fickle nobility had cost his father and grandfather quite a lot. He resolved to battle the genii.

In the new setup, Maham Anaga fortified her position by befriending the new *Wakil*. She had two sons: Adham Khan and Muhammad Baqi Khan. In December 1560 she was an active participant in debates related to the release of high profile prisoners. Once, Akbar's request for just rupees 17 was turned down by the imperial treasurer. His plea was that the treasury was empty. Maham Anaga sent the required amount to him out of her own purse.[57] The revenue department had literally collapsed. Obviously the centre's share of the revenue was being usurped by the governors. Defiance was in the air. According to Abdul Qadir Badauni, the following *hadis* (sayings of the Prophet) had indeed come true: 'A time will come on men when none will become favourites but the profligates, and none be thought witty but the obscene, and none be considered weak but the just, when they shall account the alms a heavy imposition, and the bond of relationship a reproach, and the service of God shall be a weariness unto them, and then government shall be by the counsel of women, and the rule of the boys and the management of eunuchs.'[58] Finally, after April 1561, Akbar began recovering his dominions. Now he had to fight the very people who

---

[57]Ibid., p. 60.
[58]*Muntakhab-ut Tawarikh*, p. 64.

had helped him fight Bairam Khan. The ladies and eunuchs of the harem were diplomatically sidelined. As a soft and subtle warning to all the ambitious ladies, Akbar ordered the illustration of Ziauddin Nakshabi's *Tutinama*. This fourteenth-century text is a collection of stories which advice women against moral transgressions. It cautions them about the dangerous consequences of immodest desires.[59] To cut his new *Wakil* to size, he retrieved the prestigious *jagir* (territorial revenue assignments) of Hissar Firoza from him. The modest tract of Alwar was granted instead. Maham Anaga's overconfident son Adham Khan had not furnished the correct accounts related with the Mughal victory against Baz Bahadur of Malwa. He had slyly retained some ladies of the harem, dancing and nautch girls and elephants etc. for his own use. Akbar paid a surprise visit to his camp and demanded the centre's share. The same was done with other governors. Finally when he returned from his authoritarian mission, Akbar was loaded with treasures. It was quite clear that he would not allow misappropriation of the empire's earnings. In August 1561, he summoned Shamsuddin Muhammad Atka to Agra. In November 1561, Atka was given the charge of civil and military administration. Thus he used Atka to curtail the powers of Munim Khan and Maham Anaga. Many nobles were shunted from their postings. Audits and transfers continued and so did the growth of mutual jealousies in the nobility. Akbar didn't intervene to sort out differences between the nobles. Perhaps he wanted the most ambitious ones to destroy each other. All this boiled down to Atka's murder on 15th May 1562. He was killed by Adham Khan. The latter's mother, Maham Anaga's authority had been challenged by Atka. Adham Khan's rage was triggered off when during a visit to the central offices everyone stood up enthusiastically to welcome him but Atka reluctantly rose just half way. Spilling his sustained anger he killed the poor man. Others like Munim Khan and Shihabuddin Ahmad Khan who was a relative of Maham Anaga were jealous of Atka and encouraged Adham Khan to cut him to pieces. The murderer then appeared in

---

[59]Ibid., p. 186.

Akbar's personal apartment with the naked sword still in his hand. Enraged by this audacity, Akbar had him killed immediately. He was thrown off a building twice. Badauni described the incident as follows: 'Then with his sword in his hand he (Adham Khan) swaggered in and took his stand at the door of the royal inner apartments. Then the Emperor also seized a sword and coming out, asked him, "Why did you commit such an act?" He answered, "A disloyal fellow has met with his deserts." Then they bound him hand and foot, and cast him down from the topmost terrace of the palace, and since he was still breathing, the Emperor commanded them to throw him down a second time.'[60]

Akbar ensured that Adham Khan was buried before Atka. Thus the murderer was buried before the murdered. Such a quick dispensation of justice pacified Atka's clansmen. Everyone noticed that Maham Anaga's personal influence over Akbar couldn't save her son. She also died on the fortieth day of her son's death. Thus it was clear that Akbar had zero-tolerance for overstepping in any field. He couldn't be taken for granted.

In July 1562 Munim Khan recovered his full powers as the *Wakil*. However his request for the *jagir* of Lahore was politely turned down. Sometime between August 1563 and March 1564 Khwaja Muzaffar Ali Turbati was appointed as the *Wakil*. He was designated as: *Wakil-i kul Sahib-i ikhtiyaar wa Wazir-i-batadbir-wafir-iqtidaar* and *Diwan-i wizarat-i kul* (A *Wakil* possessing wide authority and an efficient and powerful *Wazir*, in-charge of all financial matters).[61] Although Munim Khan was designated as the *Khan-i-Khanaan* (Khan of Khans) and *Sipaah-Salaar* (commander in-chief) yet he had to report to Turbati on financial matters. Interestingly Turbati had earlier served him at Hissar Firoza and used to report to him. This humbled Munim Khan. Akbar could promote or demote anyone. He boldly rejected the recommendation of the Shah of Persia to give a high sounding title to Sultan Mahmud Bhakkari. In 1561 he roamed the streets

---

[60]Ibid., pp. 49–50.
[61]*The Mughal Nobility*, p. 72.

of Agra in disguise to get a real picture of his subjects' concerns. In 1562 he abolished the custom of enslaving prisoners of war. In 1563 the pilgrimage tax was abolished. In 1564–65 he appointed Sheikh Abdun Nabi as the *Sadr* (Central minister in charge of revenue-free grants). In 1564 *Jazia* (a tax levied on able-bodied non-Muslims in lieu of military service) was abolished. In 1565 he gave revenue free land grants to temples. Many *Nishans* (orders of members of the royal family) to this effect were issued. Hamida's nishan regarding the protection of the cows of Mathura is a classic example:

> Be it known to the karori and diligent officer of the Pargana of Mahavan (in Mathura the hub of Radha-Krishna worship) in the sarkar of the darul khalifa of Agra, that according to the farman of the Exalted and the Just (Emperor-Akbar), the cows belonging to the indisputable prayer-offerer (well wisher) Bithaleshwar, *Zunnardar* (wearer of the sacred thread—Brahmin) may graze wherever they are, and not a single individual of the Khalisa and jagirdar should molest them or prevent them (from grazing). They must allow his cows to graze and that the aforesaid person (Bithaleshwar) should feel perfectly at ease.[62]

This practice was continued by even his supposedly super orthodox great-grandson Aurangzeb. Raja Todar Mal was appointed to manage the empire's Ministry of Finance. Initially the Muslim nobility raised objections to this appointment but Akbar brushed them aside.

Akbar had become so assertive that he had an influential officer, Shah Abul Ma'ali, arrested for overtaking him on horse or perhaps for saluting him while seated.[63] Reactions to his assertions manifested in the rebellions of five powerful nobles between 1562–67: Mirza Sharfuddin–1562, Shah Abul Ma'ali–1564, Abdullah Khan–1564, Ali Quli Khan–1565–67, Asaf Khan's desertion–1565–66 and revolt of the Mirzas–1566. Most of the Irani-Shia Muslims, non-Muslims

---

[62] *Edicts From The Mughal Harem*, S. A. I. Tirmizi, Idarah-I Adabiyat-Delli, Delhi, 1979, p. 4.
[63] *Muntakhab-ut Tawarikh*, p. 33.

and the Indian Muslims, were loyal to Akbar during these uprisings. Thus their position improved between 1562–67. Hereafter Akbar dissolved clan-based centres of power. Land grants of members of a single clan were scattered over distant regions. The size of the grants was reduced. Executive and financial responsibilities were bifurcated.

In 1566, Akbar's half-brother, Mirza Hakim, besieged Lahore. Earlier on Kamran had taken Lahore without Humayun's prior permission and the latter had graciously granted the province to his brother. Unlike his father, Akbar started towards Lahore to thwart his brother's assertion. When he reached Punjab in January 1567, Mirza Hakim withdrew to Kabul. Taking advantage of the hostilities between the brothers, Akbar's opponents declared their allegiance to his brother. On his return from Punjab Akbar subdued the rebels. He was adamant about punishing disloyal nobles. In fact he had turned down even Khwaja Abdul Shaheed's (grandson of Khwaja Ahrar; to whom his forefathers were dedicated) request to release Mirza Sharfuddin. When the latter's intercession was not well received by the Baadshah, the Sufi is said to have cursed him saying that since Akbar has lost justice and mercy, may he also lose *Aman* (peace/security), *Amaan* (mercy/grace) and *Imaan* (faith/religion).[64] Anyway Akbar was sure that he would not mix reverence for anyone with his political/professional decisions.

In the 1570s the huge provinces of Gujarat and Bengal were added to the Mughal Empire. Akbar travelled a lot to understand the modalities of management. He kept the spying machinery well oiled. Genesis of an efficient administration was his priority. It is reported that in 1577 when he was hunting around the area of Palam (near Delhi) he decided to spend the night in the local village headman's house. The next morning he made it known that he would stay in some other peasants' houses as well. Their names were recorded and they were duly compensated later. Reorganization of the army was an important issue. In 1574–75 he ordered that the officers would be given *ulufa-i naqad* (cash payment) instead of *jagirs*. He

[64]Ibid., p. 187.

designated all the core areas of his dominions as *Khalisa* (literally-pure, used for territories administered directly by the central government). The *Mansab* (grade/rank) of officers was fixed. Lands were brought under *Zabt* (measurement). A standard unit of measurement was used to know the correct size of plots. Akbar had himself invented a measuring rod made of reeds of bamboo for this purpose. In the colloquial language it was called *baans*. Quality of land and the value of product were also taken into account by the assessors. Revenue was fixed in accordance with the current produce and its value in the market. The estimated revenue was called *Jama* and the actual collection was called *Haasil*. One hundred and eighty two *amils* (revenue collectors) were appointed to facilitate the process of assessment and collection of taxes. The *amils* were also called *karoris* since the area that each one of them held fetched approximately a crore of tankas. Clerks were appointed to keep elaborate records. The village bigwigs like the *muqaddam* (headman), *patwari* (record keeper) etc. were used as intermediaries. The zamindars (hereditary proprietors of land) that cooperated with the government were encouraged and the contumacious ones were destroyed. A Court Hall of the Finance Department (*diwan khana-i kachehri*) was established to look into the cases of financial crimes. Raja Todar Mal was the overall in-charge of this organization. People dreaded the correctness of his calculations and the severity of his punishments. In fact Akbar was so impressed by the neat balance sheet of Gujarat presented by this Raja that he immediately gifted him a precious sword. Now the central government had a better control over the nobles and the farmers were saved from exploitation as far as possible.

In the military set-up Akbar revived the system of *daah-o-chehra/ daagh-o-mahaal* (branding of horses and maintenance of the descriptive rolls of soldiers). This was to ensure that the *mansabdaars* (office holders) actually maintained the exact number of troops that they were being paid to maintain. Dishonest *taabin-bashis* (commanders of troops) made money by presenting ad-hoc soldiery at the time of muster. They collected household servants or poor farmers or whoever they could lay their hands on and passed them off as soldiers. The fake army was disbanded as soon as the official auditing was over. It had become such a profitable trade that anyone; weavers, cotton-cleaners, carpenters, green grocers, etc. aspired to become military commanders. Akbar wanted to check such frauds. His method was incredibly simple. He had the soldiers weighed. If they were found to be grossly underweight and weak it was understood that they were not a part of the regular soldiery. Then they were interrogated and coaxed to tell who had recruited them and when. However the Baadshah was kind towards the exploited men. He took some of them in his direct service. The corrupt officials were punished. The soldiers were categorized as the *Du-aspa* (one soldier and two horses), *Yak-aspa* (one soldier and one horse) and *Nim-aspa* (two soldiers and one horse).[65] Besides the core of the empire in the Agra-Delhi region, this practice was implemented in Gujarat in 1578 and Malwa in 1579. The commanders had to ensure that their cavalry was duly branded by the officers appointed for this work. The troops were to be presented for muster at least once a year. Akbar began assigning ranks to his officers. Their salaries and the number of troops that they were to maintain were to be proportionate to each other. He wanted to give an opportunity to all and any talented persons to serve him. Ideally people were recruited at a lower rank and were gradually promoted if they were found to be efficient. By 1579 refinement of the revenue and military system lead to the evolution of the *Zaat* and *Sawar* numerical ranks in the *Mansabdaari* system. The former indicated an officer's personal salary and rank and the latter indicated the number of troops that he maintained and his professional status. Besides these recruits were the *ahdi*s (imperial troopers/gentlemen troopers). They were standalone soldiers of exceptional bravery and talent. They reported to the Baadshah directly and were often employed as personal security guards of the royal family. They were very highly paid and were mustered every four months. Another category was the *daakhilis*. They were paid by the imperial treasury

---

[65]Ibid., p. 194.

but were assigned to the officers. The infantry was also reorganized into two bands called the *banduqchis* (artillery men) and *shamsherbaaz* (sword bearers). Akbar had been to the sea-coast only once in 1572, nevertheless he had commissioned the building to two big vessels in 1594 and 1596. He had shifted base to Lahore in 1585. After Mirza Hakim's death, he occupied Kabul to safeguard the gateway of his possessions in Hindustan. He annexed Kashmir (1586), Sindh (1589) and Qandhar (1592) to exploit Hindustan's geography to draw a scientific boundary of his empire. The Hindukush range was set as a firm line of demarcation. Man Singh's relentless efforts led to the annexation of most of Bengal. Orissa was occupied in 1592. Akbar left Lahore in 1598. Berar and Khandesh were annexed in 1596 and 1600 respectively. Ahmadnagar was subjugated between 1598 and 1600. If he didn't have to return to Agra due to the political unrest of 1601 perhaps, more states in the Deccan region would have been added to the Mughal Empire.

Akbar was smart at maintaining diplomatic relations with his royal neighbours beyond Hindustan. He wasn't interested in seeking wars in areas that he couldn't effectively consolidate. However. sealing the borders of his empire was important to him. He selected wars that led to effective expansion. Rebellions of the Turani-Chaghatai nobles prompted him to re-knit the fabric of his own nobility. Reforms in this direction had been underway since a long time. The Kachwaha Rajputs of Ajmer had joined Akbar in 1561 and this saw the beginning of his liberal policies towards the Rajputs. Chittor fell in 1567 and within three years of that many kings of Rajputana joined the Mughals. Mewar was an exception; it resisted for a very long time. The position of the Rajputs witnessed rapid and remarkable rise in the following decade. Akbar's marriages with the daughters and nieces of the Rajput royalties influenced him personally. For example, Abul Fazl reports that both at home and on travels, Akbar drank water of the Ganges (the river and its water is considered sacred by the Hindus). It was brought for him in sealed jars. Food could be cooked in rain water or water from the Yamuna or Chenab but a bit of Ganga water was definitely mixed with it. *Abdaar Khana* was a department in charge of looking into the water supply for the royal household.[66]

Besides the influence of his liberal parents and teachers, the Chishti *Khanqah*s (hospices) introduced Akbar to an impartial way of thinking. In addition to his regard for Khwaja Muinuddin Chishti of Ajmer (d. 1236), he was particularly indebted to Shaikh Salim Chishti of Sikri (d. 1572). The first of his sons to have survived infancy was born at the Shaikh's *khanqah* at Sikri. Akbar was close to Shaikh Muhammad Ghaos and his son Shaikh Muhammad Ziyauddin. The *sufis* introduced him to the ideas of *Fana* (an inexplicable state of existence in non-existence) and *Wahdat ul wujud* (unity of existence) etc. In 1573 he regarded Khwaja Muinuddin Chishti as his spiritual preceptor and swore to himself to kill anyone who said the saint was *gumrah* (misguided-lost). After 1575 he tried to learn the *Chilla-i Ma 'kus* (concentrating on God while suspended head down in a well for forty days and nights) from Shaikh Chaya Laddha.[67] Shaikh Mubarak and his sons Faizi and Abul Fazl (the author of *Akbarnama-Ain-i Akbari*) assisted the Emperor in the ultimate fine-tuning of his secular inclinations. The idea of justifying taxes as wages of sovereignty against a backdrop similar to the European Theory of Social Contract was a socio-political stance framed by them. Akbar's theory of kingship rested on the belief that when God did not withhold His bounty from anyone then how could the king who was *Zill-i Ilahi* (shadow of God) discriminate? The Sun shines for everybody and that is how the king's bounty should be; undiscriminating.[68] In an effort to understand Hinduism and popularize its understanding in the Persian-speaking world, Akbar established a *Maktab Khanal* translation bureau in 1573. He ordered the translation of many

---

[66]Abraham Eraly, *The Mughal World Life in India's Last Golden Age*, Penguin Books India, New Delhi, 2007, p. 67.

[67]Iqtidar Alam Khan, *India's polity in the age of Akbar*, Permanent Black, and Ashoka University, Ranikhet, 2016, pp. 161–162.

[68]*Akbar And His Age*, Iqtidar Alam Khan (edited), Northern Book Centre, New Delhi, 1999, introduction by Irfan Habib, pp. xi-xvi.

Sanskrit works. Some examples are the *Singhasan Battisi* (*Nama-i Khirad Afza*), *Atharva Veda* (*Atharban*), *Mahabharata* (*Razm-nama*), *Ramayana*, *Harivansha Purana* (*Haribans*), *Lilavati* (Bhasrakacharya's work on Arithmetic dated 1150), *Tajikanilkanthi* (*Tajik*; a work on astronomy), *Rajtarangini* (Kalhana's famous History of Kashmir)and *Panchtantra* (animal tales with lessons on wisdom). The *Iyar-i Danish* was inspired by the *Panchatantra* and Faizi's *Nal Daman* was a retelling of an indigenous tale in Persian. Abul Fazl opined that Indian culture was not studied by the Muslims because there had been no freedom of enquiry under the burden of inherited tradition. 'The path of asking how and why had been closed.' During Akbar's reign, reason was glorified and the doors of questioning and inquiry were reopened.[69] The concluding part of the *Ain-i Akbari* has a chapter on India's religions, thoughts and customs. It is remarkable that it rests on the idea of India as a unit of culture of which Muslims were as much a part as were Hindus, Jains and Buddhists. Irfan Habib emphasizes that this is the first explicit and consistent treatment of Indian culture as a composite one. Thus Akbar established an all patronizing government, run by a multiracial and multireligious nobility. The latter was intellectually unified by spiritualism and commonality of secular interests. The Rajputs became the sword arm of the empire and the right hand of the Emperor. Even a supposedly orthodox man, Abdul Qadir Badauni happily served under the command of Man Singh. When a friend of Badauni pointed out to him that it was improper for a staunch Muslim to serve under the command of a non-Muslim, he replied that Man Singh indeed befitted his position. As long as a commander was loyal to the throne it didn't matter whether he was a Khan or Mirza or Shaikh or Singh. Purity of intentions was the only thing that mattered. Man Singh also treated Badauni with due respect.[70] Akbar had indeed re-written the medieval laws of man-management.

Akbar's personality and governance had been refined by years of

---

[69]Ibid., pp. 12–17.
[70]*Muntakhab-ut Tawarikh*, pp. 233, 239, 241–42.

experimentations and experiences. In the initial phase of his reign the Muslim orthodoxy exercised reasonable influence over him. Mir Murtaza Sharif Shirazi, a Shia, was buried near Amir Khusroe, the famous disciple of Shaikh Nizamuddin Auliya in Delhi. In 1567 on the advice of his orthodox Sadr and Qazi, Akbar ordered the exhumation of his body. They had argued that Amir Khusroe was a native of Hindustan and a Sunni and Shirazi was a native of Iraq and a Shia. Therefore if their graves were close by Amir Khusroe would be very 'annoyed' in his company. Even conservative Sunnis like Abdul Qadir Badauni were shocked by the exhumation of Shirazi's remains. He observed that Akbar had done an act of great injustice towards both the saints. He meant that Amir Khusroe was far more secular than he was being made out to be.[71] In another instance Mirza Muqim of Isfahan and Mir Yaqub of Kashmir were punished because of their sectarian beliefs. The 1568 *Fatehnama* (declaration of victory) of Chittor was framed in the language of Muslim orthodoxy. In 1572 Akbar sent a *farman* to Abdus Samad the *Muhtasib* (officer in-charge of public morals) of Bilgram to eradicate heresy. In the following year the Mahadavi sect of Muslims in Gujarat was suppressed. In fact the Mahadavi saint, Miyan Mustafa Bandagi was arrested. *Jazia* was imposed again in 1575. During 1568–1579 Akbar visited Ajmer with frenzied reverence. Finally the *Ibadat Khana* (Prayer House) discussions set him on the path of re-thinking religion.

The *Ibadat Khana* was established in 1575. It was a place for debates and discourses on religious issues. In the earliest phase the discussions were limited to the Muslims only. The intra-Muslims arguments were themselves so heated that separate places had to be assigned to various sections to maintain order. Initially Akbar was quite interested in knowing the number of legally wedded wives that he could have. He was told that the Quran and the Prophet's tradition didn't allow more than four wives at one time. However some permissive interpreters raised the number to nine and even to eighteen. Akbar was keen that his marriages, which were definitely

---

many more than four, should somehow be legalized in the Islamic framework. To his great annoyance no one could do it. Once he began searching for reasons in religion it became hard for him to be bound by any institutionalized system of belief. He set up lenient Muslims to argue with the orthodox ones. Senior scholars like Makhdum ul Mulk Maulana and Abdullah Sultanpuri were interjected by new experts like Abul Fazl and Haji Ibrahim. Initially even Badauni argued with persons more conservative than himself. Abul Fazl was given the title of *Allami* (highly learned scholar) and he became Akbar's voice against bigotry. Abul Fazl's father Shaikh Mubarak had always been a liberal. He was hounded for that. It was due to the intercession of Shaikh Salim Chishti and Mirza Aziz Koka that he had got an entry into the royal court. Both, Abul Fazl and Badauni, the two major historians of Akbar's reign, had started their careers as *mansabdar*s of the rank of twenty. However while Abul Fazl's status rose due to his closeness to the Baadshah, Badauni's position in the court headed south.

Akbar's supposed alienation from Muslim orthodoxy stemmed from the irreconcilable differences between the various schools of Islamic jurisprudence. The scholars of various schools used their tongues like swords and they didn't hesitate in calling each other fools and heretics. Their refutation of each other led the Emperor to doubt all of them. Badauni says that when Akbar came to know of the worthlessness of the theologians of his own time, he inferred the unknown from the known and rejected their predecessors as well. He felt that the scholars were as proud as the Pharaoh (ruler of Egypt renowned for his relentless pride) and their egos needed trimming.

In this regard Shireen Moosvi cites the *Muntakhab ut Tawarikh* as follows:

> .... till one night the vein of the neck of the Ulama of the age swelled up, and there were loud voices and tumult. His majesty got very angry at this behavior and said to me (Badauni), "in future report any of these people whom you find talking nonsense and I shall expel him from the assembly. " I said in low tones

to Asaf Khan, "If I carried out this order, most of the Ulama (learned scholars) would have to be expelled. " His Majesty asked what I had said. I conveyed to His majesty what I had actually said. He was highly pleased, and mentioned my remark to those sitting near him. He used to summon Makhdumu'l Mulk Maulana Abdullah Sultanpuri to that assembly, in order to annoy him, and would set up to argue against him Hajji Ibrahim and Shaikh Abu'l Fazl, then a new arrival, but now a prime leader of the New Religion and Faith, or rather the Infallible Guide and Representative with full powers with several other new comers.[72]

Badauni's *Muntakhab-ut Tawarikh* describes the developments as follows:

The Samanas (Buddhist ascetics) and Brahmans brought forward proofs, based on reason and traditional testimony, for the truth of their own......His majesty firmly believed in the truth of the Christian religion, and wishing to spread the doctrines of Jesus ordered Prince Murad to take a few lessons in Christianity under good auspices, and charged Abu-l-Fazl to change the Gospel......Every day he (Akbar) used to put on clothes of that particular colour which accords with that of the regent-planet of the day. He began also, at midnight and early dawn to mutter the spells, which Hindus taught him, for the purpose of subduing the sun to his wishes. He prohibited the slaughter of cows and the eating of their flesh, because the Hindus devoutly worshipped them, and esteemed their dung as pure......This reason was also assigned, that physicians have represented that the flesh of cows to be productive of sundry kind of illnesses, and to be difficult of digestion. Fire worshippers also came from Nousari in Gujarat, proclaimed the religion of Zardusht as the true one and declared reverence to fire to be superior to every other kind of worship. They also attracted the emperor's regard, and taught him the peculiar terms, the ordinances, the rites and

---

[72]*Episodes in the life of Akbar*, pp. 63–4.

the ceremonies of the Kaiaanians (an old Persian dynasty). At last he ordered that the sacred fire should be made over to the charge of Abu-l-Fazl, and that after the manner of the kings of Persia, in whose temples blazed perpetual fires, he should take care it was never extinguished night or day, for that it is one of the signs of God, and one light from his lights......From early youth, in compliment to his wives, the daughters of the Rajahs of Hind, he had within the female apartments continued to offer the hom, which is a ceremony derived from sun-worship......On the festival of the eighth day after the Sun entering the Virgo in this year he came forth to the public-audience chamber with his forehead marked like a Hindu, and he had jewelled strings tied on his wrists by Brahmins, by way of a blessing. The chief and the nobles adopted the same practice in imitation of him, and presented on that day pearls and precious stones suitable to their respective wealth and station. It became the current custom also to wear the rak'hi on the wrist, which means an amulet formed out of twisted linen rags. Every precept which was enjoined by the doctors of other religions he treated as manifest and decisive, in contradiction to this religion of ours (Islam).......[73]

Akbar took such interest in understanding Hindu beliefs that priests sat on *charpai*s (cots), which were suspended outside his personal bed-chamber. Their discourse went on till late in the night. Hinduism's popularity amongst his subjects made him particularly soft towards it. Akbar said that a true mystic guide recognizes the sorrows and anxieties of his followers. He helps them fight stress and find peace. A stereotyped appearance was hardly the signature of a master of spirituality. *Sulh-i kul* (Universal Peace/Absolute Peace/Peace with all) was essential to bring harmony in Hindustan.

Akbar's idea of using the words 'Allah Akbar' on his seal was opposed by many. Even a relatively liberal man like Haji Ibrahim expressed an apprehension that the words could have two meanings:

---

[73] *Muntakhab-ut Tawarikh*, pp. 264–69.

God is Great or Akbar is God. Even a whiff of something that compromised Islamic monotheism was obviously unacceptable to the Muslims. They suggested that Akbar should rather use *Lazikrullahi Akbaru* (to remember God is great). However he wasn't convinced. He argued that only fools would imagine any ambiguity in the meaning of the first set of words.[74] The Muslim *ulema* (scholars) were alarmed. Shaikh Badruddin left the *Ibadat Khana* in despair. Mulla Sheri sarcastically wrote that in the rise of Akbar he saw the wealth of Qarun, (Korah; the leader of rebellion against Moses) the rituals of Firaun (The Pharaoh; king of Egypt in the time of Moses. The Muslims consider him to be the very personification of wickedness) and the buildings of Shaddaad (The people of Aad; fourth generation of the line of Noah who lived a luxurious life in southern Arabia. They were known for their physical strength and specially height. They had constructed a paradise-like city which was destroyed by famines and strong winds as a divine punishment for their arrogance and atheism).[75] Badauni wrote that gradually the *Ibadat Khana* became the *Iyadat Khana* (House of sickness).[76] Akbar leapt towards secularization when he opened the doors of the *Ibadat Khana* to multireligious debates. Now experts of various faiths were invited to present their views. The Emperor tried to discover the parallel lines of argument and the common denominator in different religions. He realized soon enough that rituals hindered the formulation of common modalities of life for people. They divided them. So formality/ritualism received a royal dressing–down by *Sulh-i kul*. The biggest take away from these discussions was the idea that a *Sultan-i Adil* (Just King) was above the *Mujtahid* (authorities on Islamic laws who are competent to make an independent judgment/ interpretation). Perhaps the idea drew some inspiration from the Pope of Christianity and the Khalifa of Islam. It gave Akbar an advantage over the Muslim orthodoxy. He used this vision to pave

---

[74]Ibid., p. 213.
[75]Ibid., 204.
[76]Ibid.

the way for exceptionally liberal policies. In 1579 the idea of the supremacy of the Baadshah's discretion in all religious matters was codified in a legal document duly attested by witnesses. It was called the *Mahzar*. It declared that Akbar was the *Sultan-i Islam* and his rulings would be binding on everyone provided that his orders were not contrary to the explicit injunctions of the Quran. Through the *Mahzar*, Akbar tried to unify spiritual and secular headship, within the broad framework of Islamic beliefs. It backfired. The *Mahzar* was a flop.[77] The nobles who resented his revenue and military reforms found a reason to rebel. They were ruthlessly suppressed. He took a U-turn from patronizing sections which opposed the idea of *Sulh-i kul*. Shaikh Abdun Nabi and Makhdum-ul Mulk, who were the face of orthodoxy, were banished. He sought legitimacy for his power from his subjects-from his goodwill for all of them. Akbar was not going to turn away from secularism, *Mahzar* or no *Mahzar*.

From the 1580s, Akbar asserted himself as a spiritual leader of people of all religions. He and his small group of disciples professed *Sulh-i kul*. Monotheism and pantheism lingered in the background of their spirituality. Akbar never founded any new religion. The supposed founding of a new religion called *Din-i Ilahi* is not mentioned in any official record. *Jazia* was re-abolished. He revived the celebration of the Nauroz (Iranian New Year) and held on firmly to the *Jharokha Darshan* and *Tula Daan*. He liberated his personal slaves. Their number ran into thousands. They were then designated as *Chelas* (disciples). By 1582 he invited suggestions from his close associates to promote his subjects' welfare. He decreed that judges should give due weightage to circumstantial evidence. Witnesses should be grilled for contradictions in their narrative and physical signs of discomfiture. He abhorred torture. The dealing with criminals was to be staggered into reprimands followed by threats and then imprisonments. Mutilation was to be used in only very serious cases. The officers were always advised to give capital punishments with caution. However, by 1582 he altogether prohibited the use of this punishment by officers. This

---

[77]Ibid., pp. 274–282.

practice was followed by his successors. By and large the idea was to reclaim criminals by good counsel. Raja Birbal had suggested that honest persons should be posted at the gates of the palace to address the petitions of victims in a fast and fair way. Raja Todal Mal suggested that all the nobles of the court should be directed to give alms every week. Prince Salim Sultan suggested that lowest marriageable age for both boys and girls should be fixed at 12 years. Akbar also felt that child marriages displeased God. He encouraged monogamy as a general practice, however, in case if a female couldn't reproduce due to some reason the man could remarry. He approved of widow re-marraiges of women in reproductive years. He disapproved of sati of females whose marriage hadn't been comsumated.[78] His disapproval of gendered social practices can be noted in his discouragement of widow immolation and the questioning of a lesser share for females in an Islamic division of property. He had himself rescued a widow from immolation (1583). He had allocated an area for the residence of prostitutes in the capital. It was called Shaitanpura. Officers were appointed to regulate the affairs of this locality. Special permission had to be sought to take any dancing girl outside this area. The address where the girl was being taken was noted by the officials for ensuring her safe return. He personally interviewed well-known prostitutes to check out whether any of his ministers had tried to exploit them. The punishment for such cases were fines and even imprisonment.[79] His empathy with the wife of a *dak-chauki* messenger is remarkable. Prince Murad had requested for the transfer of Bahadur; a *dak-chauki* messenger to his station. However Akbar replied that presently messenger's wife was not keen on that posting for her husband so the man cannot be transferred. However he hoped that eventually he may be able to persuade her.[80] Akbar's maternal uncle Khwaja Muazzam had killed his wife in a fit of rage. As a punishment Akbar had him beaten with kicks and sticks and imprisoned him.

---

[78]Ibid., p. 367.

[79]Ibid., pp. 311–312.

[80]*India's Polity in the Age of Akbar*, p. 165.

The following episodes indicate that he was generally against the objectification of women. A beautiful dancing girl called Aaraam Jaan was married to a noble, Khan Zaman. She was well known for her incredible charms and etiquettes. Khan Zaman's friend, Shaahim Beg, fell in love with her. Interestingly enough Khan Zaman had a strange infatuation for Shaahim Beg. The latter was exceedingly handsome. Thus to please him the Khan sent Aaraam Jaan to him. After sometime a friend of Shaahim Beg, Abdur Rahman fell for her. When he asked Shaahim Beg for the girl, the latter obliged. Thus the girl was now transferred to Abdur Rahman. Someone reported this matter to Akbar. He was furious. He blamed Khan Zaman for the shameful transfer of a girl whom he had married, her being a dancing girl notwithstanding. When Khan Zaman heard of the Emperor's wrath he asked Shaahim Beg to go into hiding till the time Akbar's anger subsided. Unfortunately the Beg went to Abdur Rahman's fief. Aaraam Jaan also resided there. In a drunken stupor he demanded the lady back from his host. The latter refused on the plea that he had already married her. However Shaahim Beg wasn't convinced. He called his goons and got his host beaten and tied up. He literally carried Aaraam Jaan away. Now Abdur Rahman's brother, Muayyid Beg stepped into the scene. He attacked Shaahim Beg's lodging. In fact the latter was with Aaraam Jaan when the commotion began. He was killed in the ensuing combat. Abdur Rahman was rescued, but now Khan Zaman was hunting for him to avenge his beloved Shaahim Beg's death. Rahman managed to somehow reach Akbar's court and asked for protection, which he was granted immediately. Khan Zaman didn't dare to take any further action in this matter.[81] In another case a Shaikh of Gwalior fell in love with a singing girl of Agra. He belonged to a respectable family of religious elite. His family sought Akbar's help for thwarting his affections. To douse the Shaikh's desires, Akbar married off the girl to his courtier Muqbil Khan. However despite the marriage the Shaikh and the girl eloped. When Akbar heard of this he understood that the girl was perhaps

---

[81]*Muntakhab-ut Tawarikh*, pp. 15–18.

as much in love with the Shaikh as he was with her. Therefore he ordered that they should be persuaded to present themselves at the royal court. Perhaps he wanted to get them legally married. However the Shaikh's family forbade this proposal. When the doors of the Baadshah's intervention were closed by his own kinsmen, the disappointed man committed suicide. The case of his burial reached the royal court. His relatives wanted a martyr's burial for him. They argued that the man had died for love which is a pure emotion. On the other hand Shaikh Abd un Nabi, the orthodox Sadr of Akbar's court opined that he definitely didn't deserve it because he was an adulterer, besides, suicide was anyway an unforgivable sin. In this case two things are noteworthy. Firstly that Akbar wanted to marry the couple once he realized that the girl was also in love with the Shaikh. Secondly the issue of a lover's burial was a matter worth discussion in the royal circuit. From a very early age Akbar copied Babur and Humayun in his reverence for the elderly ladies of his family. When he was six years old he once suffered from toothache. His step mother Hajji Begum offered to apply some medication on his teeth and gums. Hamida Banu feared that Akbar might be poisoned so she persuaded him to leave while Hajji Begum had gone to fetch the medicine. He refused to go. The Begum understood Hamida Banu's fears and applied the medicine to her own teeth before applying it on Akbar's.[82] As a grown up Akbar respected and pampered Hajji Begum. The latitude that Akbar gave to the non-Muslim women of his harem is commendable.

Akbar imposed restrictions on slave trade in 1594. The head of his own palace security was a man of the Chandal caste (supposed untouchables). He was honoured with the title of Khidmat Rai.

In 1598 he visited Guru Arjan, the Sikh Guru. The official recording of the visit recognized the Guru's great love for God and stated that to be the reason for the Baadshah's respect for the Guru.

In his youth Akbar was fond of hunting. The *Qamargaha* (great battle/lieu de chase) hunting arrangements were made for him. In

---

[82]Cf. *Episodes in the Life of Akbar*, pp. 12–13.

this, in a circumference of about forty leagues, animals were driven inside a circle. The circle was contracted each day. After the Baadshah, the nobles and then the ordinary soldiers hunted. Usually some person of religious merit intervened to stop the sport. However it may be remembered that often, large scale military exercises were also disguised as imperial hunts. Akbar always seemed to have a feeling of guilt while hunting. Eventually an episode in 1578 made him totally averse to it. On 4th May 1578, so many animals were gathered for the royal hunt that the two ends of the *Qamargaha* had come together. Just before Akbar was to begin the sport he fell into a strange trance. No one could explain what had happened to him. Loyalists feared that he wouldn't survive. But he did and the first thing that he ordered was that the hunt was to be called off. In fact, orders were dispatched in all parts of the empire directing people to refrain from killing animals and birds. He gave a lot of gold in charity and cut his hair. Many courtiers also cut their hair to express solidarity. The rumours about the Baadshah's sudden and unexplained illness spread out and caused a couple of rebellions as well. After 1580 he clearly encouraged vegetarianism. By 1595 he had fixed days on which he ate purely vegetarian food. He said that one's stomach should not be the grave of animals. The vegetarian food was called *Sufiyana* (mystical/chaste).[83] A portion of the food cooked for him was first served to the needy. He was so grateful for the food that he got to eat that he sometimes prostrated in thankfulness.

Akbar dressed rather simply. Although many clothes were stitched on his orders most were given away as presents or charity. He took personal interest in patterns and colours of clothes. He promoted the manufacture of silks and brocades. Silken carpets were produced with such finesse that they surpassed even the Persian carpets. He was responsible for the establishment of the Mughal School of Painting. He employed painters, gilders, limners, binders, etc. for his massive painting projects. He laid the foundation of a new fort at Agra in 1565. Fazi described it as the gateway of heaven. Massive building

---

[83]*Muntakhab-ut Tawarikh*, p. 331.

projects were launched at Sikri in 1571. Known as Fathpur Sikri the complex stands as one of the finest examples of architecture. Architectural designs of the various regions of Hindustan were brought together in this project. The Buland Darwaza was constructed to mark his victory over Gujarat. The marble latticework around Shaikh Salim Chishti's mausoleum was one of the most delicate of its kind. His own tomb at Sikandra was a perfect reflection of the Baadshah's personality: simple and strong.

Akbar initiated the Ilahi Era in 1584.[84] In 1586 he commissioned the writing of a detailed and systematic history of his life and reign. This turned out to Abul Fazl's magnum opus: *Akbarnama*. It is well proven that Akbar had a tendency to experiment and search for rational answers. For example, a male deer was mated with a Barbari goat as an experiment ordered by him and a non-productive hybrid deer was born out of the cross-breeding. Experimentation based on the idea of *Zabaan-i Qudrat* (natural tongue/dialect) was more piquant. Some newly born infants were isolated in a palace called the *Gung Mahal* (palace of the dumb) and were raised in a speechless environment. Their caretakers were not allowed to utter a single word in their presence. On their own, the children did not develop any mode of verbal communication, proving the notion that hearing is a key factor in speaking (1579–1580).[85] Badauni reported that questions of Sufism, scientific discussions, enquiries into philosophy and law were the order of the day. There was an insistence on *aql* (reason) over *taqlid* (reflex/ imitation/dogmatism). Ritualism was discouraged and rationalization was encouraged. Akbar argued that if blind following of traditions was all that commendable then prophets would have only followed their predecessors instead of preaching anything reformative. Akbar's reply to his son Murad's query regarding officials who practiced *jismaniat* (physical exercises) for rituals of worship clearly indicated his preference for spiritualism over ritualism. He said that people mostly worship God for the

---

[84]Ibid., p. 310.
[85]Ibid., p. 296.

fulfillment of their wishes. The right way is to worship God for His love and not for any material gains. He professed that obtaining merits for life after death should not be the only objective of good deeds. In fact one should be good because it is good to be good.[86]

Akbar had a wide variety of hobbies. He loved to listen to prose and poetry being read to him. He watched cock-fighting, elephant-fighting, buffalo-fighting, stag-fighting, boxing contests, contest between gladiators, etc. He liked flying tumbler-pigeons and watching birds. He played polo. He enjoyed songs, concerts, dances conjuror's tricks and jesters' funny talks. His patronization of Tansen, the great classical singer is well known. Miyan Baiju also known as Baiju Banwara had also sung for the Baadshah.

Sometimes Akbar even played pranks on his courtiers. A pocket-sized Quran and a notebook of sermons belonging to a scholar Hafiz Muhammad Amin were stolen. Somehow they were recovered by the police and the items were presented to Akbar. The notebook bore the owner's name so Akbar summoned him. He wanted to hand over the lost items himself and see the pleasure on the man's face. Accordingly he told Muhammad Amin that he had a gift for him and presented the man his lost possessions. Muhammad Amin's expression was priceless. The Baadshah also promised him to ensure the recovery of his other belongings.

From 1580 onwards Akbar increasingly moved towards a state of equilibrium in both personal and professional matters. In his youth he used to drink regularly and sometimes got senselessly drunk. However he lessened his intake of intoxicants with maturity. Up till 1578 he had a tendency to take life-threatening risks. One day, he mounted an untamable elephant called Hawai (1561). Further, he pitted this animal against another equally fierce elephant— Ran-Bhaga. The combat between the excited elephants with Akbar seated on one of them was just too dangerous. The onlookers prayed for the Baadshah's safety. Finally someone called Shamsuddin Atka to persuade Akbar to break the fight and return to safety. He refused.

---

[86]See works of Irfan Habib, Shireen Moosvi and Iqtidar Alam Khan in this regard.

In fact he threatened Atka, that if he didn't stop being protective he (Akbar) would deliberately throw himself down from the elephant's back. Poor Atka remained utterly silent after this threat. On another occasion he rushed towards a naked sword during a party with friends and associates (1573). The sword was removed by Man Singh just in time to save Akbar from serious injuries. It was immediately removed from the scene. This annoyed Akbar so much that he fought with Man Singh over his interference. Thus on many occasions Akbar had consciously imperiled his life. He seemed to test the luckiness of his destiny by such risks. However as *Sulh-i kul* unfolded, many relationships were healed. The list included Akbar's relationship with himself.

Jalaluddin Muhammad Akbar seemed like the ultimate show-stopper. He had dodged almost all the mistakes which his grandfather and father had made. Nobody from a distant clan or with vague connections to his bloodline could seriously harm him. He was let down by his very own blood. His mistakes were his own. His slip-ups were extremely personal. He believed that children are the young saplings in the garden of life. To love them is to remember the Bountiful Creator. However his sons turned out to be his greatest disappointments, disguised as his greatest desires.

Akbar's first born was a girl named Fatima Banu Begum (b. 1562). Then were born twin boys; Mirza Hasan and Mirza Husain (b. 1564). However they died in infancy. Up to 1568 his wives and concubines bore many children but none of them survived. When a Rajput wife entitled Maryam-uz Zamani (Mary of the times) became pregnant, Akbar sent her to Sikri for the duration of the pregnancy. He believed that Sufi Shaikh Salim Chishti had interceded with God to grant him an heir and this pregnancy was blessed. Anyway he had started feeling that Agra was not all that lucky as far as his progeny was concerned. Once on a Friday, Akbar was hunting with cheetas. He was informed that the fetus had not moved in its mother's womb. He was so paranoid that he immediately vowed to never ever hunt with cheetas on Fridays. Finally on 30th August 1569 a boy was born to him. Akbar was 27 years of age and thirteen years into his reign. By medieval standards it was high time that he fathered an heir. The celebrations in Agra were proverbial. It was a public feast that went on for a week. Akbar delayed a personal visit to the Prince for superstitious reasons. The baby was named Muhammad Sultan Salim. Akbar fondly called him Shaikhu Baba. Both the names were inspired by Shaikh Salim Chishti. Akbar had vowed to visit Ajmer on foot for thanksgiving. That he did in January 1570. It was a journey of about 228 miles from Agra. He went on foot to Sikri as well. After Salim many other royal children survived. In November 1569 a daughter (Shahzada Khanam) was born. In June 1570 another son, Murad was born. He was fondly called *Pahari* (belonging to the hills) after the hilly tracts of Sikri. Like Salim, Murad was also born at Shaikh Salim Chishti's residence. No wonder Akbar decided to build a grand mausoleum for the Sheikh after the latter's death in 1572. In fact the Sikri project was on such a priority that most of its buildings were completed by 1574. In September 1572 another prince, Daniyal was born. The two princesses Shakrunnisa Begum and Aram Banu Begum were born later.

Akbar was very particular about his children's education. He had missed out on formal education in his early years due to the personal and political chaos around him. Later also, he seemed disinclined towards conventional learning. However, he valued books. He knew that knowledge is power. His translation and illustration projects are in themselves a proof of that. The *Akbarnama* is the cherry on the cake. He surrounded himself with men of proven intellect and used their skills to sharpen his own wits. His son Jahangir writes in his autobiography that since his father was so intelligent and well informed no one could ever guess that he was illiterate. Lettered or unlettered, Akbar was a smart learner. This is beyond any kind of doubt. Like any parent he wanted his children to be better than him. The curriculum fixed for his children had a variety of subjects like physical sciences, mathematics, logic, astronomy, music, mechanics, theology, household matters, medicine, rules of governance and moral studies. It is important to note that he wanted them to be well versed with everything which was relevant to their times. To train his sons in matters of governance they were given formal postings at important fronts. For example in his Kabul campaign of 1581, Salim and Murad were assigned military responsibilities. In 1582 Salim was made the formal in-charge of the department of Justice and Public celebrations. Just as Babur gave responsibilities to his sons but closely supervised them, so did Akbar. However a major difference between the two was that Babur's sons had also shared his struggles. Besides, Kabul was no match for Agra as far as prosperity was concerned. Even after Babur's celebrated victory at Panipat he and his sons could hardly rest. Akbar's sons were born in opulence. They were not a generation of strugglers. Thus although Akbar tried to educate them from the best of books and tutors, they didn't get many lessons from life, on life. It is interesting that in comparison to his ancestors' love for alcohol and opium Akbar was pretty much a teetotaler. Even his brother Mirza Hakim was quite a drunkard: alcohol did have something to do with his death at 31 years. Akbar had really lived up to Babur's philosophy of not following his ancestors blindly. His sons however out did them in consuming intoxicants. Salim began drinking alcohol in 1585 and by 1594 he used to have 20 cups of doubly distilled spirits daily. By 1601 he had to limit himself to 6–7 cups daily due to his doctor's strong recommendation. Murad was an intelligent man but he too became addicted to intoxicants. His temper and arrogance were another issue. When reports of his illness became alarming Akbar dispatched Abul Fazl to escort the Prince to the court from Berar. Unfortunately Murad died hours before Abul Fazl's arrival. This was in May 1599. Like Murad, Daniyal had also seemed like a promising prince in his early years. He was married to the daughter of Abdur Rahim Khan-i Khanan; Bairam Khan's son. However, he too lost his way in the jungle of his father's riches. After Murad's death Akbar wanted to have Daniyal close to him but the prince refused to join his father. Akbar reprimanded Abdur Rahim for being unable to knock any sense in his son-in-law's head. In 1604 he dispatched Shaikh Abul Khair to escort the prince to the court. As Daniyal's health deteriorated Abdur Rahim stopped his supply of intoxicants. The latter was a shrewd man and knew that if Daniyal lived the flow of power to him would be relatively smooth. The Prince's chambers were heavily guarded so that he would not be able to procure spirits. Anyway they were smuggled to him by 'trusted' men in the greed for money or favours. Phials were concealed in clothes and armaments and brought to the dying prince. Daniyal had named one of his favourite guns *yaka-u janaza* (the same as the bier). His own couplet was engraved on it. The poem meant: In pleasure of the chase with thee (*yaka-u janaza*) my life breathes fresh and clear. But who receives thy fatal dart, sinks lifeless on his bier. One day, on the Prince's insistence Murshid Quli Khan smuggled double-distilled spirit in the barrel of this gun. The machine was full of rust and gun powder residue. All of that got dissolved in the spirit. As soon as the ailing Prince drank from it he fainted. His condition worsened and finally he died in April 1604. He was 33. The gun had indeed lived up to its name. Thus at the time of Akbar's death, Salim was his only living son.

The first signs of fissures in Akbar and Salim's relationship had occurred in 1591. Akbar had suffered an attack of colic and he somehow believed that Salim had tried to poison him. Hakim Humam, the royal physician, was supposed to have assisted the slow poisoning of the Baadshah. In a state of semi-consciousness he muttered: 'Baba Shaikhuji, since all this Sultanate will devolve on thee why hast thou made this attack on me? To take away my life there was no need for injustice. I would have given it to thee if thou hadst asked me'.[87] By late 1590s it had become quite clear that Salim was failing as a son. Or maybe Akbar had failed as a father. The Prince had often ignored his father's advice and then he increasingly ignored his orders as well. Matters came to a head in 1601 when he revolted openly. With Murad dead and Daniyal dying, Akbar was not going to win any confrontation with Salim.

---

[87]Ibid., p. 390.

Even if he killed Salim he would have still lost the game. Anyway the Prince was no match for his father. The revolt fizzled out but failure fanned the flames of insecurities. In 1602 Salim had Abul Fazl murdered by the hand of Bir Singh Deo, a Bundela Rajput. He justified himself by arguing that Abul Fazl was the mind behind Akbar's detachment from his own blood. Salim knew that Akbar was deeply attached to Abul Fazl, he wasn't just a courtier; he was his friend. Akbar had already lost his other friends, Raja Birbal had died in 1586. He was on a mission against the Yusufzais. In 1589 Raja Todar Mal and Raja Bhagwan Das passed away soon one after another. In 1593 Shaikh Mubarak died. Anyway Abul Fazl was not only killed, his dead body was dishonoured. His head was chopped off and sent to Allahabad for Salim to see. Akbar was livid. A manhunt was launched for the Bundelas involved in this act of incredible audacity. Now Salima Sultan Begum rushed to Allahabad to persuade Salim to ask for his father's forgiveness. A civil war would have ruined the Mughal household before ruining the lot of commoners. Finally Salim came to Agra in April 1603. He had sent a written apology to Akbar in advance. Hamida–Maryam Makani went out of the palace to welcome him. He resided in her apartment. Akbar came there to meet him. The hour of their meeting was fixed by astrologers. Akbar was pressurized by his family to forgive the Prince. He did. Salim was directed to resume the command of Mughal campaign against Mewar. He marched up to Fathpur Sikri but didn't proceed any further. Instead of a straight refusal to march into a challenging battle field he delayed his departure endlessly. Akbar sent princess Bakhtunnisa to persuade the Prince to restart on mission Mewar. It didn't help. Eventually Salim headed home to his *jagir*, Allahabad in November 1603. Although terribly disappointed by his son's stubbornness Akbar granted him the permission to do so. To scare his opponents Salim made a public spectacle of his reconciliation with Akbar. The celebrations were meant to reaffirm that after all, he would inherit his father's empire. However a strong section of the nobility contemplated promoting his 17-year-old son Khusroe as the heir apparent. Khusroe's mother Maan Bai–Shah Begum was a Rajput princess. Man Singh was his maternal uncle and Mirza Aziz Koka Khan Azam was his father-in-law. This grandson was very dear to Akbar as well. As the contest between Salim and Khusroe heated up Man Bai committed suicide in May 1604. In August 1604 Akbar decided to visit Salim at Allahabad. It is unclear whether this was to be a diplomatic or a military mission. Anyway he had to return midway due to his mother's serious illness. She passed away soon after his return to Agra. The whole city mourned her loss. Heads and faces were shaven to express grief. Salim arrived at Agra in November 1604 to condole his grandmother's death. Akbar took this opportunity to reprimand him about his irresponsible and arrogant ways. The Prince was put under house arrest for ten days. The only people who could access him were a physician, a barber and a personal servant. His supply of intoxicants was restricted. Ladies of the royal family interceded with Akbar on Salim's behalf although much intercession wasn't really required. With his other sons dead Akbar couldn't have done anything much to Salim. As an astute politician he knew that Khusroe's promotion as his heir would first set fire to his home and then to his empire. He became a mere spectator of the unfolding of his children's destinies. For once he was not in control. During an elephant fight in September 1605, the supporters of Salim and Khusroe clashed openly. Salim's elephant, Giranbar, was combating Khusroe's Apurva. Rantamhan, an elephant of the royal stable was on standby to step in to help the vanquished animal. Akbar was watching the combat with his grandson, Khurram (future emperor Shah Jahan). When Apurva was outmaneuvered by Giranbar it was ordered that Rantamhan should enter the arena. Salim's supporters stoned the driver of Rantamhan since they wanted their patron's elephant to have a clear victory. A great commotion ensued. Khusroe furiously rushed to Akbar complaining about his father. Khurram was sent to Salim to convey Akbar's order for restraining his supporters. It was pathetic to watch men getting violently involved in a combat between animals. Fireworks were employed to separate the battling beasts, but they didn't disengage. Finally Apurva left the fight. Rantamhan entered into the Yamuna followed by Giranbar. Boats were deployed to break the chase. That day Akbar had a glimpse of what would follow his death. A deadly combat between his son and grandson was on the cards. He fell ill. His fever was complicated by diarrhea. He was being treated by Hakim Ali Gilani. When all remedies failed, Akbar became so irritable that he even beat his doctor with blunt arrows and accused him of being an ungrateful fraud. Intrigues in the palace began even as he battled for life. However no one was able to secure his consent for bypassing Salim in Khusroe's favour. He knew that disturbing the line of succession would cost the Mughals everything. On seeing Salim near him, he asked the Prince to be handed over his personal turban and dagger. This symbolized the passage of power. Akbar died on 17th October 1605. He had himself commissioned the building of his mausoleum at Sikandra. Salim rested his father's bier on his shoulders; still unaware of the responsibilities that he was to shoulder soon. Thousands of teary eyed, bare-headed and bare, footed people accompanied Akbar's body to Sikandra.

Akbar's secularism kept his contemporaries confused about his religious beliefs. Badauni captured the confusion beautifully when he wrote:

> The fairy has her face hidden,
> But the demon is all ogles and blandishments:
> The intellect is consumed with astonishment,
> What can this miracle mean!
> In this garden no one has ever gathered
> A rose without a thorn: Nay,
> The lamp of Muhammad is ever attended
> By the mischevious sparks of Abu Lahab.'[88]

---

[88]Ibid., p. 281. Abu Lahab was one of the uncles of the Prophet. He was a bitter opponent of the latter. His name was Abd-ul-Uzza and was entitled Abu Lahab (The Father of the Flame) by the Prophet. Shocked by the Prophet's victory in the battle of Badr, he died seven days after the said war. See *Dictionary of Islam*, Thomas Patrick Hughes, Rupa & Co. , New Delhhi, 1993, p. 8.

It is extremely important to note that theologians like Shaikh Abdul Haq Muhaddis and Shaikh Nurul Haq prayed for Akbar as a Muslim ruler and opined that his motives were misunderstood by the common man. Syed Athar Abbas Rizvi asserts that Akbar had vowed only to liberate and disassociate himself (*ibra wa tabarra namuda*) from the traditional and imitative religion (*din-i majazi wa taqlidi*). There is no doubt that he did repudiate the *taqlidi* Islam but he was not hostile to Islam that found *Sulh-i kul* imperative to its body politic.[89] This assessment is important because it implies that Akbar had understood that he doesn't have to be an atheist to respect all religions. He cautioned against those rituals of every religion, which denatured religiosity and humanism. A true follower of any religion, is certain to have humanism as his basic nature. Once that position is taken, the respect for other religions and the variety of creation would follow with the involuntariness a beating heart. Humanness was the hall mark of the Mughal brand created by Akbar. His vision of *Sulh-i kul* was so modern and futuristic that it is yet to arrive.

⌘

---

[89]*Akbar and his Age*, p. 20.

FOUR

NURUDDIN MUHAMMAD JAHANGIR
BAADSHAH GHAZI

1605–1627

'In what language can I return thanks for this gift of Allah that I am engaged in the reign of such a just king in the worship of my own Deity in ease and contentment and that the dust of discomposure from any accident, settles not on the skirt of my purpose.'

—JADRUP GOSIAN, A HINDU MENDICANT
ON JAHANGIR'S REIGN[90]

On 24th October 1605, a week after Akbar's death, 36-years-old Muhammad Sultan Salim was crowned as Nuruddin Muhammad Jahangir Baadshah Ghazi. The unhurriedness of the coronation testified to his unchallenged claim over the Mughal dominions. All along Akbar had believed that Salim was the answer to his prayers for an heir. He also was Akbar's breathing will regarding Mughal-Rajput partnership. Salim was half Rajput by blood and genes. It was an inheritance of sort. Many astrological systems were employed to make horoscopic predictions of his future. The prophecy that one day he would inherit the empire was indeed true. However one wonders what the forecasts were regarding Akbar's readiness to actually bequeath his possessions to this son. Salim was wayward and whimsical and it is difficult to tame a pampered prince.

As per customary beliefs in auspiciousness, his formal education

---

[90] *The Tuzuk-i-Jahangiri or Memoirs of Jahangir*, Alexander Rogers (translation) & Henry Beveridge (edited), Munshiram Manoharlal Publishers Pvt. Ltd. Originally published 1909–14, reprint, 2003, New Delhi, vol-II, p. 53.

began when he was four years, four months and four days old. Although Maulana Mir Kalan Harari was his personal tutor, the overall supervision of his education was Akbar's privilege. A modern curriculum was prepared to help the prince understand concepts rather than just mugging facts. Languages fascinated Salim. He learned Persian, Turkish and Hindustani. He wrote both prose and poetry. His memoirs, the *Tuzuk-i Jahangiri*, display his remarkable intelligence and interest in subjects like anatomy, botany, zoology, geography, medicine and history. His elaborate vocabulary enabled him to pen picturesque descriptions.

As an emperor Salim immediately asserted individualism. He wore his crown with his own hands. Since he didn't wish to be confused with the Ottoman rulers, Selim I and Selim II, he gave up his given name—Salim. None of his royal ancestors had done this. The word Jahangir (The World Seizer) declared his aspirations. The title Nuruddin (Light of Faith) was a reflection of Akbar's spiritual ideas where light was an indicator of divine love for all. He respected Akbar's *Sulh-i kul* and hoped to brighten everything with inclusion. The various denominations of his coins were called: Nur-Shahi, Nur-Sultani, Nur-Daulat, Nur-Karam, Nur-Meher, Nur-Jahani and Nurani. Interestingly a favourite elephant was named Nur-Bakht and of course later, his more than famous consort was called Nur Jahan. In his autobiography he referred to his relatives by glorious titles. Amir Timur–Sahib Qiran, Babur–Firdaus Makani, Humayun–Jannat Aashiyani, Akbar–Arsh Aashiyani, Daniyal–Shahzada Maghfur (The pardoned prince) and Murad–Shahzada Marhum (Prince admitted to mercy). Thus he consciously maintained and enforced the Mughal brand and the aura around it.

Jahangir made it a point to note in the *Tuzuk* that he took his own decisions and he obeyed his father for his own spiritual and temporal good. No wonder he wanted to add something to *Sulh-i kul's* secularism as his personal trademark. He added Justice. His first order was the fixation of the Chain of Justice. It was made of pure gold. Its two ends were tied to the Shah Burj inside the Agra fort and a stone post fixed on the Yamuna's bank. The sound of its 30 bells ensured that no plea went unheard. Even though Jahangir himself didn't respond to every call he appointed officers to do so. The following edicts were issued to streamline governance:

1. River tolls and other oppressive taxes imposed by the jagirdars were abolished.
2. Rest-houses and wells were to be constructed at lonely spots for the convenience of travelers and deterrence of robberies.
3. Bales of merchants were not to be opened without their permission.
4. The officials were to ensure that property was inherited by rightful heirs. In case there wasn't an heir it was to be used for charity.
5. Restrictions were imposed on the manufacture and sale of intoxicants.
6. No one was allowed to usurp the property of another.
7. Mutilation was not to be used as a means of punishment.
8. Officials were disallowed from usurpation of lands of poor peasants
9. No jagirdar could marry a local in his place of posting without seeking prior permission from the Emperor.
10. Government was to fund construction of public hospitals and the employment of doctors therein.
11. Thursday and Sunday were declared as auspicious days. Slaughter of animals was banned on these days.
12. All officials were confirmed in their positions. Many political prisoners were freed.

Severity of the punishments accorded by Prince Salim sometimes shocked everyone, including his father. A news reporter fell in love with one of the eunuchs in his service and they eloped. It was suspected that perhaps they were also involved in some conspiracy against the Prince. When they were arrested with another accomplice, one of them was severely beaten, the other castrated and the third one flayed alive. However, as a Baadshah he was more restrained. Mutilation and disfigurement were not the usually accorded punishments. Forcing religious conversions was strictly prohibited. Certain cases speak of his classic sense of justice: Once a man had kidnapped a woman, killed her parents and buried them in his own house. Jahangir imprisoned him for life; also, his tongue was cut. It was reported to Jahangir that in Sylhet, Bengal people castrated their sons to convert them into eunuchs. These children were either sold for a price or given away to revenue collectors instead of cash payment of dues. Jahangir banned this practice and decreed that such parents would receive capital punishment. The merchants who indulged in this trade were to be sent to Agra to be imprisoned for life. Young eunuchs were seized from the possession of their owners. One of his officers Saád Khan had 1,200 eunuchs in his service. It was reported that they terrorized and oppressed the poor and the weak. Jahangir sent a warning to Saád Khan stating that the scale of equity didn't differentiate between the rich and the poor. He must check his eunuchs or be ready to be punished. In Gujarat, one Abdullah Khan had cut down many trees of a garden. An enquiry was set and it was revealed that he had also murdered a man. Jahangir reduced his ranks drastically and slapped such a heavy fine on him that the man would have slogged for the rest of his life to pay it. Once a gang of thieves was caught and its leader; Naval, appealed to the Baadshah to give him a chance at surviving. He requested that he may be allowed to fight an elephant and if he survived he should be set free. Jahangir agreed. He was thrown before an elephant but also provided a dagger for defence. Luckily the elephant was defeated. Naval's life was spared but he was caught trying to escape from the royal custody. Imprisoned again, he was killed this time. Once a widow complained to the Baadshah that one of his favourite officers, Muqarrab Khan, had kidnapped her daughter and now she was told that the girl was dead. An enquiry was set up and one of the attendants of Muqarrab Khan was found to be guilty. He was put to death and his master's rank was reduced to half. The woman was compensated by the state. During his stay in Gujarat, Jahangir was quite unwell. The dust had aggravated his asthma and in desperation he called Ahmedabad: *Gardabad* (abode of dust), *Bimaristan* (abode of the sick), *Zaqqumzar* (cactus-thorn bed) and *Jahannamabad* (house of hell) etc. but still tried to give judgments in as many cases as he could. Once a crane appeared to be particularly distraught, the matter was investigated. It was found that one of the royal servants had taken away her little ones. He was ordered to return them back immediately. Jahangir made arrangements for warm bathing water for elephants of the royal stable during winters. Officers were appointed to ensure that crops were not destroyed when the army moved. In case they were, then the farmers were to be compensated by the state. The general policy was to give the benefit of doubt and not make many people suffer for the crime of one. In his later years Jahangir decreed that all sentences pronounced by him would be executed only after a time lapse and review. He didn't want his own drunkenness or mood swings to become the cause of some unjust judgement. He appreciated the remark of Sharif Khan—one of his courtiers, that honesty and dishonesty are not confined to financial matters. Concealing someone's good or bad qualities is also dishonesty. All persons should be described as they are-irrespective of their being friends or enemies.

To dispel the insecurities of Akbari nobility, status quo was maintained in official positions. Even those who had inclined towards Khusroe were forgiven. Abul Fazl's son, Shaikh Abdur Rahman was entitled Afzal Khan and assigned the rank of 2000 zat and 1500 sawar. Mirza Aziz Koka and Qulich Khan (the governor of Agra fort who had refused to let him in the fort during his rebellion) were also accommodated. Man Singh was confirmed as the governor of Bengal. He was gifted a *Charqab* (sleeveless vest), a jeweled sword and a horse from the Baadshah's personal stable. Salaries were raised. Revenue-free land grants were confirmed. Shaikh Salim Chishti's family was specially patronized. Allies of his Allahabad days became the court's nuclei. The list included Sharif Khan, Khubu-Qutubuddin Khan Koka and Zamana Beg-Mahabat Khan.

Jahangir made a public display of his affection for Khusroe. It was meant to ward off vultures who feasted on family feuds. The prince was granted a lakh of rupees to refurbish Munim Khan's house—situated outside the fort as his private residence. Perhaps until that place was ready he was assigned the top most part of Agra's citadel. Since it was feared that even the embers of his ambition could set the empire on fire, he was watched. However on the night of 15 April 1606 the prince left on the pretext of visiting Akbar's tomb at Sikandra, but in fact he had fled to Punjab. In the heat of the moment Jahangir permitted Sharif Khan to do whatever it took to stop him. But he changed his mind almost immediately. He stopped Sharif Khan from the chase and sent Shaikh Farid Bakshi and Ihtimam Khan instead. He didn't want Khusroe to be killed–and certainly not by any noble. That would have damaged royal prestige and set dangerous precedents. Neither did he want to pitch one son against another. Therefore Khurram was left in charge of Agra as Jahangir decided to pursue his rebellious child himself. He visited the tombs of Nizamuddin Auliya, Humayun and Akbar for intercession with God for his victory. The Rajput blood in Khusroe's veins could have drawn Rajput nobles to his cause. The royal family which already was a mixture of Rajputs and Mughals prayed for a bloodless solution. Meanwhile all kinds of anti-state elements joined the rebel prince. Their hooliganism was uncontrollable. When Jahangir noted their criminality he clarified that Khusroe too was upset to see the dominions of his ancestors being looted, but he had lost control and chaos was driving the looters. The skull and beard of the imperial officers who failed to control the outbreak were shaved–they were dressed in female clothing, seated on asses and paraded around Agra. Husain Beg Badakshi, one of the Akbari nobles who served as the governor of Kabul joined Khusroe. Another noble Abdul Rahim of Panipat also joined the prince as his wazir. Jahangir promptly pampered the Badakshis and Kabulis in his army to stop them from defecting to the Badakshi commander. To highlight the difference between himself and Khusroe, or perhaps between a stable and unstable government, he ordered the distribution of alms and charity to subjects who were looted by the yahoo rebels.

Jahangir was playing his cards well. He sent Mir Jamaluddin Husain to negotiate peace. The mission failed. In the following battle on 27th April 1606 not only was Khusore defeated but his box of jewels was also lost. Now he had three options: to try to take Agra or to go to Bengal and seek help from Man Singh or to accompany Husain Beg Badakshi to Kabul. He chose Kabul. Anyway, Beg was supposed to finance the rebellion so the prince was bound to follow his advice and footsteps. It was a bad decision. Soldiers of the north Indian plains were not interested in going to Kabul. They deserted. Most of the Badakshis and Kabulis in his party had already been slain by Jahangir's loyal Sayyids of Barha. So Khusroe was practically forceless. Royal agencies were on a high alert. The routes—roads and rivers—were heavily guarded. Spies looked for clues which could fetch rewards. The imperial pressure ensured the closure of every door that Khusroe knocked. Despite the money that he offered, boatmen refused to ferry him across Chenab. To his utter embarrassment he was arrested while stuck in a rotten boat inside a sand bank.

Jahangir's emotions were mixed. A rebel had been captured, but he was his son. The episode had triggered memories of his own rebellion against his father. He wrote in the *Tuzuk* that anyone who rebels against his parents is avenged by the Almighty Avenger. Khusroe's rebellion, he opined was born of the prince's youth, inexperience and short-sightedness. He was being used as a tool by the Baadshah's enemies. Mahabat Khan escorted the Prince to the royal camp outside Lahore. The velvet of the fetters on Khusroe's limbs conveyed that there was still hope for him. And indeed there was. His associates however were in a hopeless jam. Husain Beg and Abdur Rahim were stripped naked and sown in fresh skins of ox and ass respectively. The horns and ears of the animals had been retained in the skin. Seated backwards on asses they were paraded around. As the hides dried and shrunk they were torturously suffocated. Husain Beg was beheaded in an unconscious state. Perhaps he had died before the beheading. Abdur Rahim was spared on the plea of some courtier. In the following days Khusroe was walked through streets where his supporters were gibbeted. Men who were still alive were hung on flesh hooks and left thus to die slowly. Sordid sarcasm lay in Mahabat Khan's comment that the prince was out to accept salute from the dead bodies of his soldiers who were fighting the winds. Jahangir's loyalists wanted Khusroe dead. It was a replay of the time when Humayun's nobility pressurized him to eliminate Kamran. But Jahangir's fatherly instincts were too strong to allow that. Like Humayun, he also decided to impair Khusore's eyes. The exact order is unknown. Some sources report that wires were inserted in his eyes; others claim that hot iron was passed over them. Some even claim that his eyes were fine but his eyelids were stitched together. Others say that small cups were fastened on his eyes. Or that he was blind folded with a napkin which was sealed by the Emperor's personal seal. However, the fact that a doctor was employed to treat his eyes indicates that something was wrong with them and that Jahangir regretted whatever he had ordered. In April 1610 an imposter faked the poor prince's identity to raise a revolt in Bihar. He had scars around his eyes which he claimed were left by bowls tied over them. This was called the Pseudo-Khusroe-Qutub's revolt. It was curbed.

Jahangir showed exceptional far-sightedness in sparing Khusroe's life. He refrained from drawing the trend line of filicide-fratricide in the Mughal family and maintained a balance of power between his sons for many years. His inexplicable love-hate relationship with Khusroe remains an enigma. It sounds kind of sweet that Khusroe called his father *shah-bhai* (royal brother) instead of addressing him as *shah-baba* (father). What destroyed this seemingly friendly father-son relationship is unknown. It is probable that Akbar had unknowingly/ knowingly triggered rivalries between them. Anyway, beyond a point he was hardly in a position to level his son's and grandson's equations. Internal dynamics of the Mughal family in 1605 were quite different from what Babur would have imagined or liked them to be.

A regretful upshot of this uprising was the assassination of the fifth Sikh guru, Arjun Dev—a highly influential man, regarded as a holy mystic by both Muslims and the Hindus. He had commissioned

the building of the holy tank at Amritsar and the compilation of
the *Adi Granth*. He blessed Khusroe when the latter visited him
in Punjab and put a saffron *tika* on the prince's forehead. It was a
simple gesture of good-will for Akbar's grandson. Unfortunately due
to misrepresentation by the mystic's rivals, a *farman* (royal order) was
issued for his assassination. For Jahangir the issue was not religion,
it was rebellion. However the Sikh reaction was silent but solid.
They began militarizing to challenge anyone who threatened their
community or its leaders in future. Shaikh Salim Chishti's grandson;
Khubu-Qutubuddin Khan Koka—Jahangir's closest friend was sent
to Bengal as a replacement for Man Singh. Mirza Aziz Koka was
humiliated more directly. A letter in which he had criticized Akbar
was brought to Jahangir's notice. Koka was made to read it before
all the courtiers. His embarrassment can be well imagined.

The north-west frontier was critical for the security of the empire.
Kabul and Qandhar were the twin gateways of Hindustan opening
into Turkestan and Persia respectively. In 1606, Shah Abbas the ruler
of Persia attempted the annexation of Qandhar. His attempts were
foiled and by March 1607, the Mughal position in the area was
reasserted. Jahangir visited Kabul to weed out local Bangash rebels
and enforce the new laws formulated by him. Jahangir the Baadshah
was turning out to be quite different from Salim the prince.

In September 1607 on way from Kabul to Agra, Jahangir was
informed that Khusroe and his allies were conspiring to assassinate
him. It was Khurram's report. This gave an immediate setback to the
little freedom that his brother had been recently granted. Apparently
the plot was engineered by Khursoe's custodian, a eunuch named Itibar
Khan. To Jahangir's dismay Itibar Khan's correspondence revealed
that Khusroe had considerable supporters in the nobility. Though
tempted otherwise, he decided to ignore their treachery. Only four of
them were executed. Amongst them was Muhammad Sharif, younger
son of Ghiyas Beg-Itimad-ud Daula. As a repercussion, Khurram's
marriage to Itimad-ud Daula's granddaughter Arjumand Bano Begum
(later Mumtaz Mahal) was put on hold. However it was destined

that, not only would he marry this girl, but would also build the unsurpassable Taj Mahal for her. In fact Jahangir himself was destined to marry Itimad-ud Daula's daughter, Meher-un Nisa. This marriage was one of the best things to have happened to him.

Meher-un Nisa had been widowed in 1607. Her husband Ali Quli Khan Istalju-Sher Afghan was killed in a combat with Khubu-Qutubuddin, the governor of Bengal. The latter also lost his life in the same confrontation. In his days as a prince, Jahangir had bestowed Ali Quli with the title of Sher Afghan (the lion slayer). However in the last phase of the succession drama before Akbar's death, Ali Quli had distanced himself from Salim. After his accession Jahangir had granted him a fief at Burdwan in Bengal. Now he had summoned Sher Afghan to Agra to question him about his role in Khusroe's rebellion. Khubu had gone to serve the *farman* personally. Sher Afghan resisted his approach and a fatal encounter followed. Widowhood brought Meher-un Nisa and her infant daughter Ladli Begum to the court. Since her father was under arrest due to the roles of his son and son-in-law in conspiracies against the Emperor, she was attached with the entourage of Ruqaiyya Sultan Begum: Hindal's daughter, Akbar's childless wife and Khurram's foster mother. Romantic renderings situate her first meeting with Jahangir in the glamorous Meena Bazaar on 20th March 1611. It is believed that the Emperor fell in love with her instantly. Such instantaneous infatuations of the royals didn't always end in marriages. But since this girl was a prominent noble's daughter, to Jahangir she could either be a wife or nobody. The marriage took place on 3rd June 1611.

Meher-un Nisa's charms monopolized the Baadshah's attention. She was intelligent, delicate and yet strong enough to ride horses and shoot tigers. She had once shot four tigers in six shots and none of them was a miss. Jahangir scattered 1000 *ashrafis* (gold coins) over her and presented her a bracelet of one lakh rupees to mark the occasion. She was entitled Nur Mahal (light of the palace) in 1611. After Salima Sultan Begum's demise in 1613, she was called Baadshah Begum (the first lady) and then Nur Jahan (light of the world) in 1616. The greatest fashionista of her times; from personal adornment and etiquettes, to housekeeping and social work, she was the best. Jahangir loved her so much that in the *Tuzuk* he noted the loss of her necklace with rubies worth Rs. 10,000 and pearls worth Rs. 1000. He considered Wednesdays unlucky and therefore hoped that it would be recovered the next day and indeed it was. When he fell ill in 1614 he informed only Nur Jahan about his state because he felt that only she loved him enough to be trusted. Even the doctors were kept in the dark for quite some time. The illness was so serious that it lasted for 22 days and Nur Jahan took great care of him. It was after this recovery that Jahangir got his ears pierced and began wearing pearls as a mark of being a thankful disciple of Shaikh Muinuddin Chishti. Following this, wearing pearls in ears became a fashion statement amongst the elite. Hakim Ruhullah had treated Nur Jahan when she fell ill. After her recovery the doctor was gifted three villages in his native place and he was weighted in silver, which also was given to him. Nur Jahan's mother, Asmat Begum, invented a perfume styled: *Itr-e-Jahangiri* (Perfume of Jahangir). Jahangir claims that just a drop of it could disperse the fragrance of countless red roses and revive withered souls. By August 1611, Nur Jahan's father became the Wazir of the Mughal Empire. Jahangir was so fond of him that once a noble was imprisoned for criticizing the man. Her elder brother Abu-al Hasan's successive titles: *Itiqad Khan-Yamin-ud Daula-Asaf Khan* displayed his constantly upward mobility. On Friday, 10th May 1612, his daughter Arjumand Banu Begum–Mumtaz Mahal was finally married to Khurram, the most dynamic of all the princes. In Asaf Khan, Khurram found a father-in-law who could push him to the throne. The former could literally steal khol from closed eyelids and count the feathers of a flying bird.

For Jahangir political ups and downs were a phenomenon in life but not life itself. Life for him was a multidimensional explorative journey. He wanted to live up the way he liked. And he liked to travel, see, find, understand, compare and experiment or may be just relax and enjoy. His curiosity was child-like—innocent and loveable. Luckily he had the means to feed this curiosity with experimentations and explanations. He was fascinated by the rare, unusual and the strange; be it humans, creatures, natural elements or things. If the *Baburnama* inspires bravery and resilience the *Tuzuk-i Jahangiri* inspires love for life and unravelling its mysteries; external and internal. When Jahangir was passing through Afghanistan, near Bamiyan he heard about the *Khwaja Tabut* (Khwaja of the coffin)—a dead body that hadn't decayed. He sent a party of surgeons to see it and report. It was a thirteenth-century mummy which was partially intact. To understand the bravery of the *Sher-i Babbar* (fierce lion) he had one of them dissected and studied its intestines. A wolf's intestines were compared with that of a tiger. He watched an elephant give birth and noted that generally they are born feet first. Servants were ordered to note the gestation period and it was found that it was a little more if a male was to be born. Red deer were brought from Nandanah for breeding purposes. Makhur and Barbary goats were cross-bred. Jahangir had heard from Akbar that antelopes that escape from the grasp of the cheeta don't survive. To check this, 426 such antelopes were kept under observation. In fact they were administered medicines in advance to help them combat trauma. However after a day or two all of them died. The Baadshah was told that tigresses' milk was very good for eyesight. When a tigress gave birth to three cubs, servants were directed to secure some of its milk. They failed and Jahangir observed that tigresses are so fierce by nature that it is difficult for them to release milk—their udders remain dry. When the Baadshah decided to have camel's milk, the camels were given a special diet to improve the flavor of their milk. He liked the taste very much and ordered that the same diet be given to the cows and buffalos as well and it should be observed whether the taste of their milk changed by it. He studied legends like that of Bikramjeet and the *Sang-i Paras* (alchemists/Philosopher's stone)–diamond mines–methods of fishing–peculiarities. Like 'Rajauri Muslim' way of observing Sati by burying widows with their dead husbands or the Maghs who according to him ate anything available on the face of the earth and could marry their half-sisters born of a different mother; superstitions about prosperity coming from wife, slave, horse, house or land; Owls and unluckiness; Direction-wise luckiest modes of travel; east—tusked elephant, west—horse of one color, north—palanquin/litter, south—carriage, cart or two-wheeler. Karnatic jugglers' games and so on. He usually found out the history of place names: For example he writes that Baramulla is derived from Varaha-Mula or Rawal Pindi was named after its founder Rawal and Pindi means a village in the Ghakkar tongue. Jahangir loved to note the strange and the weird that he witnessed: The conjoined twins of a silk seller of Kashmir; a gardener's daughter at Daulatabad who had a moustache, a thick beard and chest hair. Women were deputed to check her private parts and report to the Emperor; One Hafiz of Kashmir, who had foretold the exact moment of his death; Shujaat Khan's accidental and minor toe injury that proved fatal; the elephant who died seven days after being bitten by a mad dog; the plague that raged in Agra; goats with bezoar stones; worms in the horns of rams and sheep; a Langur (black monkey) who had been brought up by a goat as her own child; a tiger who played with an unknown jogi (mendicant) like a friend; the sighting of a *Deonak/ ban-manush* (yeti/jungle man); the talking lark; the squirrels–Snake eating goats; white cheeta, etc. Jahangir loved to keep counts and measures: number and variety of hunts, precious stones, fruits and vegetables, species of flowers, trees, animals and birds etc. He sometimes gave names to fruit trees and plucked the fruits from the gardens himself. He noted that picking fruits from one's own garden adds sweetness to them. He was much fascinated by a plant that he saw in Gujarat which contracted its leaves on being touched and then opened them again after sometime. He noted even the synonyms of its name: *Chuii-mui/Shajrat-ul haya/Lajwanti*. The Baadshah was extremely fond of collecting rarities and curios and specially mentions: A huge ruby presented by Rana Amar Singh to Khurram; An emerald and crystal box; A European carriage-Saddles of European workmanship; A see-through glass box; A fish shaped cup; A painting of Timur with 240 figures in it. Interestingly this had been stolen from the Imperial library of Persia and bought by one Khan Alam to be presented to Jahangir. The theft had been noticed and the painting was traced before Alam could leave Persia. However Shah Abbas the ruler of Persia allowed it to leave his country because he knew of Jahangir's love for rarities and assumed that it would remain in caring hands. Lashkar Khan had presented him Persian camels, Arabian dogs and 20 cups and plates from China. Jahangir's love for the Chinese crockery was unbelievable. William Hawkins reported that when a favourite plate was broken by a servant, he was whipped out of his wits and then almost as a pardon he was packed off to China to fetch its replacement. Once when someone presented him a compendium in Humayun's handwriting, Jahangir was extremely pleased. He noted that he couldn't have had anything as valuable as this. The presenter was promoted to a rank beyond his imagination. A black granite throne which he had used as a prince was brought all the way from Allahabad. A European who had made a jeweled throne for him was given the title of *Hunarmand* (talented) and was richly rewarded. *Yusuf-w-Zulaikha* in Mulla Mir Ali's handwriting and Asaf Khan's *Khsuroe-w–Shireen* entitled *Nur Nama* were some of his treasured books. Besides hunting, Jahangir enjoyed music: flutes and songs. A mandolin player Shauqi was entitled Anand Khan. Competitions like swordsmanship, puppetry, cooking and dancing etc. were regularly organized. He sometimes played casual sports with his friends and officers but ensured that people of the same age group were pitched against each other. He loved fruits and especially mangoes and tracked their varieties and seasons. He mentioned the prolongation of mango season beyond July in Muqarrab Khan's garden. It almost seems that he was competing with Babur in keeping notes. In fact he boasts that in comparison with the *Baburnama,* paintings are an additional feature of the *Tuzuk.* He could identify the painter by taking a single look at the paintings. The ones that he commissioned went beyond stopping time like photos. They carried political statements and symbolism as well. Modern historians use them to understand Jahangir and his times. Anyway paintings or no paintings, had Babur ever read the *Tuzuk* he sure would have been proud of his great-grandson.

Jahangir comes across as an emotional man when he misses his father while eating an extra sweet fruit or when he has fretters removed from Khusroe's feet so that he too could enjoy the softness of grass on his feet. Love for his children and grand children is spilled all over his memoirs. He showered them with extremely expensive gifts like precious weapons, rubies, pearls, diamonds, elephants, horses, rare curios, etc. all the time. Their marriages were celebrated on a lavish scale. When Murad's daughter was married to Parvez, he sent him gifts worth Rs. 1,30,000. When Prince Durdanish, who was born of this wedlock died, Jahangir did his best to pacify Parvez and prayed for the child's soul. However the most loved amongst his grand children was Khurram's son, Shah Shuja. Jahangir's near crazy worries during this child's illnesses are quite moving. Once, the 4-year-old prince had fainted due to a fall and become unconscious, Jahangir noted that his (the child's) senselessness was taking away his (Baadshah's) senses. Later when the same prince was afflicted by small-pox the royal astrologer, Jyotik Rai, predicted that he would live, because Jahangir's horoscope didn't show any major sorrow for the Baadshah–although there was a death on the cards. That happened to be of another grandchild. When Shah Jahan's daughter Chimni/ Chamani Begum died in June 1616, Jahangir was so upset that he couldn't get himself to record the death in the *Tuzuk* himself. Since it was a Wednesday, the day was christened *Gham-shamba* (the day of mourning). He didn't attend the court for two days and spent three days at Khurram's house to pacify him. A wall was built in front of the dead princess's house so that it couldn't be seen by the Emperor. He wanted to block her out of his memory. However William Hawkins reports of a terrifying instance of his annoyance with Shahriyar. The 7-year-old prince was asked whether he wished to accompany his father to some place. The poor kid replied that he would do as his Majesty pleased. Jahangir felt that this was an unenthusiastic reply. He slapped Shahriyar but the prince didn't cry. When asked to explain the reason for his complacence, he said that his caretakers had taught him that princes must withstand pain without crying. This made Jahangir angrier. He hit him again and had a bodkin thrust through the child's cheek. The child bled a lot but still refrained from crying.[91] It is hard to believe this side of the Baadshah but it was there, usually latent, but awakened by alcohol. It doesn't seem a coincidence that this prince suffered from psychosomatic disorders later in life. Indeed royal addiction to drinks and drugs should be formally listed as a reason for the collapse of the Mughal Empire.

On the professional front, amongst Jahangir's sons, Parvez had failed to prove his mettle in the Mewar and Deccan campaigns. Jahandar had died young. Shahryar was too young to make an impression. Khurram was bright and a tee to take at that. He had a very special place in his father's heart because in 1616 he had risked his own life to save Jahangir's during a hunt. It was remarkable that he managed to drag the Sisodia Rajputs of Mewar in the fold of the Mughal Mansabdari (1613–1615). This had been his grandfather's wish which his father had failed to fulfill. He used the numerical strength of the imperial army with wisdom and perseverance. Mirza Aziz Koka had been posted on this front before Khurram's arrival. He was sacked and imprisoned on grounds of non-cooperation with the prince's armies. The Maharana of Mewar formally surrendered before Khurram. However he didn't have to attend Jahangir's court. His eldest son and heir Karan Singh attended the Imperial court at Ajmer and was assigned the rank of 5000 in the Mughal nobility. The fort of Chittor was surrendered. It couldn't be reoccupied or rebuilt by the Sisodias. Mewar was liable to pay tribute and render military services to the Mughals. On this occasion Jahangir noted in the *Tuzuk* that he didn't want to destroy the old rulers but wished to accommodate them. It is extremely vital to note that he was clear that he didn't wish to subjugate Karan Singh, but win his

---

[91] *Beyond the Three Seas Travellers' Tales of Mughal India*, Michael H. Fisher edited, Random House India, New Delhi, 2007, p. 66.

heart. His treatment of the Sisodia prince clearly establishes that indeed Jahangir meant what he wrote. Karan was given expensive gifts right through his stay, everyday. Nur Jahan gave him a dress of honour, jeweled sword, horse, jeweled saddle and an elephant. Jahangir presented him a rosary of the most expensive pearls, hawks, falcons, elephants, swords, two rings of ruby and emerald. On the last day of Karan's visit a hundred trays of gifts were presented to him. It is not surprising that Jahangir had once said to Mu'tamid Khan that what value would worldly good have for him (Jahangir) who buys the jewel of loyalty for a high price. Khurram was promoted. The birth of his first son almost coincided with the Mewar victory. He already had daughters: Purhunar (b. 1611), Hur-un Nisa (b. 1613) and Jahanara (b. 1614). On 29th March 1615, Mumtaz Mahal gave birth to a son. He was named Dara Shikuh after the fifth century BC Persian Emperor, Darius. Another son–Shah Shuja was born to her on 3rd July 1616. The latter was brought up under Nur Jahan's personal care.

Between 1611 and 1622 Nur Jahan and people close to her became very influential. Coins minted in this phase carried this superscription: 'By order of the King Jahangir gold has a hundred splendors added to it by receiving the name of Nur Jahan the Queen Begum.'[92] Jahangir had jokingly remarked that Nur Jahan had the potential to rule and that a bottle of wine and piece of meat would suffice for him. However this shouldn't be mistaken as his resignation. Weakened by years of drunkenness, he had found a reliable assistant in Nur Jahan. The 1585 casual cup of wine changed Jahangir's lifestyle and eventually his life. From wine of grapes he shifted to finer and harder distillations to feel exhilarated. Together with potency, portions also increased. By 1594 he was a diehard drunkard. Even the ghastly deaths of his brothers didn't deter him. Hakim Human, his physician, had warned that unrestricted consumption of alcohol would kill him. In 1601 his daily allowances were capped at six cups. This was supplemented with opium. It is difficult to calculate the

---

[92]*Edicts from the Mughal Harem,*

number of fruitful years that he lost to alcohol. The agony that his addiction caused to those who loved him is of course incalculable. From August 1614 onwards his illness became recurrent: the year 1618 marked Jahangir's first encounter with Asthma. In 1619 thickness in his blood caused him a serious eye ailment and he had to undergo an operation. Healers suggested that the colder climate of Kashmir might help him. In 1620 he spent about eight months there. By 1623 he was unable to write his diary and the task was delegated to Motamad Khan. With the progressive decline in his health Nur Jahan became more than an assistant. Power could come to her only through the channel of some male member. Jahangir was happy to be that channel because she was sure to protect it. And Jahangir knew that she was a born politician. It was a case of mutual dependence. Others like Khurram and Asaf Khan were direct beneficiaries of such an arrangement due to their closeness to both Jahangir and Nur Jahan. The queen was conscious that she must build an alternate channel of power before this one collapsed. Recurrent episodes of Jahangir's illness revived that consciousness from time to time.

Threads of inexplicable affection tied Jahangir to Khusroe. This was a cause of concern for the Nur clique (Nur Jahan, Asaf Khan and Khurram). In 1613 Khusroe was allowed to attend the court sometimes. However the order was revoked on the ground that the he was so sorrowful and quiet that his presence depressed the Emperor. Raja Anup Rai Singh Dalan, a highly trusted noble was Khusroe's custodian.

Mughal forces in the Deccan were under the command of prince Parvez since 1610. It was a complex confrontation with three intertwined polities: Ahmadnagar, Bijapur and Golconda. The brave and brisk Maratha mercenaries were employed by these states to carry on an unending guerilla combat with the Mughals. Malik Ambar the Ethiopian commander of Ahmadnagar seemed particularly irrepressible. Finally in 1616 Jahangir decided to replace Parvez with Khurram. Parvez complained to his father that handing over command to his younger brother is a disgrace that he would resist.

But if his elder brother Khusroe took over he would be okay with the change. Jahangir responded that the brothers can very well fight it out amongst themselves. He would stand by the victor, which he was sure would be Khurram. Parvez's plea was an early warning that if the Mughals did not stick to the law of primogeniture, princes' rivalries would destroy them. If the law of survival of the fittest was allowed to govern palace politics, the palace was sure to witness political assassinations. Jahangir missed this important cue. The following years would prove that Parvez was right-bang on. Anyway, the fact that he raked up Khusroe's name made Khurram insecure. Now he wouldn't travel to the Deccan unless he had his elder brother's formal custody. He argued that if Khusroe caused trouble the Deccan campaign would be disrupted midway. Earlier too, the Nur clique had pressurized Jahangir to transfer Khusroe's custody to Khurram. He had disagreed. After all it hadn't been a random decision to keep his rival-son alive—all risks notwithstanding. Now both the half-Rajput princes were pitched against one another. The transfer could trigger political imbalances which might threaten the Baadshah himself. However either alcohol or his 'assistants' insistence befuddled Jahangir's mind and he actually sanctioned the shift. But Rai Singh Dalan argued that since he had received Khusroe's custody from Jahangir he would return him to the Baadshah alone. When Jahangir regained his senses, he felt strangely betrayed by the Nur clique. The order was revoked and Khusroe was saved for the time being. The clique caught the vibe and prudently dropped the matter. Jahangir's independence of expression was diminishing with each passing day and they could wait for a bit. In 1616, when Khurram was deputed to the Deccan the matter was raised again. This time it was more of a demand—a precondition that Jahangir had to fulfill if he wanted Khurram to lead the Deccan campaign. He agreed. But the custody was transferred to Asaf Khan when Khurram was already on his way to the Deccan. Now entitled Shah Sultan Khurram— Akbar's sword tucked on his waist. Khusroe wished to be killed by his father rather than by ruthless enemies. But destiny had designed the rejection of all his desires. His sisters and other ladies of the harem accused Jahangir of injustice and cursed Nur Jahan. In fact the trauma spilled over the palace walls. It was speculated that after Khusroe's elimination, Khurram might kill Jahangir as well. The probability of a war of succession seemed so immediate that the officials of the East India Company were warned to refrain from extending investments in the Mughal dominions. Its agents were advised to keep away from local politics. Although no trouble occurred at this juncture, it marked the beginning of Khurram's assertions. Nur Jahan took note and strategized accordingly. Pietro Della Valle reports that Khusroe's custody was not given to Khurram because he had begun to dominate Nur Jahan and Asaf Khan. To prepare a favourable heir to the throne they now wished to marry Ladli Begum to Khusroe. But the unfortunate prince refused to marry her. He was too loyal to his present wife the daughter of Mirza Aziz Koka who had stood by him through all the trials. Although she also counselled him to buy his freedom with this match, he refused. He knew that he would just be used as a pawn by the scheming brother-sister duo, to be eliminated when his utility diminished. Perhaps he wasn't wrong.

Khurram employed two-track tactics of war and diplomacy in dealing with the Deccani states. He broke Bijapur-Ahmednagar Alliance by favouring the former. Ibrahim Adil Shah the ruler of Bijapur switched over to the Mughal camp. Malik Ambar was isolated and forced to call for a truce. Khurram's demands were simple: To surrender lands that Mughals claimed as 'theirs' and to pay regular tribute. Given the long history of inconsequential conflicts in the area, this was a huge victory. Khurram returned triumphant. In October 1617, Jahangir bestowed the title of Shah Jahan on him. He allowed the prince to sit on a chair near the imperial throne and gave him the rich province of Gujarat. In 1618 he allowed Shah Jahan to use some insignias of royalty and presented him a precious family jewel: Hamida Banu Begum's ruby. Parvez had indifferently accepted that he was out of the race for his father's affection and of course the crown. On 3rd November 1618, Mumtaz Mahal gave birth to another son. Jahangir named this child Aurangzeb—The Throne Adorner. Given how close Shah Jahan had come to the throne, such a name was totally apt for his son. In celebration, the former presented his father with 50 elephants and gifts worth about Rs. 2 lakh. As destiny would have it, Aurangzeb, despite being the not so favourite third son of his father, actually lived up to his name.

After the successful Deccan campaign Shah Jahan had married Izz al Nisa Begum, daughter of Iraj Shahnawaz Khan and granddaughter of Abdul Rahim Khan-i Khanan. The convention of seeking the Emperor's prior permission for such high profile matches was skipped. Jahangir chose to ignore the lapse, but others noticed it and were alarmed by the prince's audacity. Further, on Shah Jahan's recommendation Khan-i Khanan and his son were given the command of the recently acquired Deccani lands. Thus Khurram was building a lobby of personal loyalists. However between 1616 and 1617 he had turned down Nur Jahan's proposal to marry Ladli Begum. He was much, too much married to her cousin—Mumtaz Mahal. Ladli could not have been accorded a secondary status like his first wife Kandhari Begum. Nur Jahan wouldn't have allowed that, and he just couldn't get himself to let Mumtaz Mahal down. Asaf Khan continued to show loyalty to his sister. However, his dislike for his arrogant son-in-law notwithstanding, he wouldn't have liked a demotion in his own daughter's status.

In 1619–1621 Jahangir and Shah Jahan's relationship became mysteriously tense. It was so puzzling that some contemporaries blamed it on the appearance of a comet in January 1619. Shah Jahan's mother, Bilqis Makani died, plague reoccurred and caused widespread misery and Shah Jahan's fourth son Umid Baksh born in this very year died in infancy. Though Shah Jahan's loyalists had won the Kangra campaign, Jahangir selected a man of his own choice for the governorship of the place. The Baadshah's whimsical display of power after this victory was also weird. Perhaps it was a measure to intimidate Shah Jahan.

By 1620 Shah Jahan's treaty with the Deccan states was eroded by Malik Ambar. Jahangir again deputed him there. He also sent a diplomatic mission to the ruler of Persia, with rich gifts. The latter reminded Shah Abbas of Mughal wealth and power. More importantly they warned him to keep out of Hindustani politics. Shah Jahan was well aware of his strengths and his father's limitations. He negotiated to have Khusroe's custody if he was to proceed to the Deccan. Nur Jahan supported this move not because she wanted to help Khurram's political rise but because she wanted him to fall in public estimation as a benevolent heir. She knew that everyone, including Jahangir would eventually condemn anyone who killed Khusroe. If Khurram killed him, two contestants would be eliminated from the fray: the murdered prince and the murderer prince. Accordingly Khusroe's custody was transferred from Asaf Khan to a commander of Shah Jahan at Burhanpur. Mughal campaign in the south was successful. Besides favourable land settlements, they were to receive tributes from Bijapur, Ahmednagar and Golconda. However the situation could become slippery if the payments were skipped. The emergence of the Marathas as an independent fifth party was a new challenge for both the Mughals and the Deccan states. Nevertheless in the immediate context, Khurram had delivered. Between January and May 1621 he successfully brought the Deccan situation under control. However Jahangir continued to be cold and distant. All that the prince received as a reward was a ruby. Clearly his authority and ambition were being curtailed. Jahangir remembered that despite being half as competent or confident as Shah Jahan was, he had revolted against Akbar. Shah Jahan would still have remained loyal to his coldish father, had he not been driven to insecurity by Nur Jahan's manipulations. Jahangir's illnesses had grown and so had his dependence on his wife.

The Nur clique was fully and finally broken with Ladli's marriage with Shahriyar on 23rd April 1621. In 1611–1621, it had seemed that Nur Jahan and Khurram would shatter the stereotype of step-mother–step-son foe-ism by being an unbreakable team. But that wasn't to be. The Mughal men's romanticism had come in their way.

Nur Jahan could surely understand that what she was to Jahangir, Mumtaz Mahal was to Shah Jahan. Ladli could never fit in the latter's life; period. So her patronage shifted to Shahriyar. The latter's ranks shot up meteorically. It is notable that there was a time when Shahriyar was called *na-shudani* (non-entity) and now he was being projected as a competitor of his super successful brother. But this was only a projection. With both siding with their respective sons-in law, Nur Jahan and Asaf Khan's relationship was put to test. Their father's death at this critical juncture (5th February 1622) made matters worse. Interestingly Nur Jahan was granted the absolute inheritance of her deceased father's wealth. She commissioned the grand building of her parents' tomb at Agra—popular now as Itimad ud Daula. It is a precursor of the Taj Mahal due to the extensive use of white marble, Italian *pietra dura* and Indian-patterned mosaic work. Her privileges were often of the category usually reserved for the Baadshah. After 1622 the responsibilities and risks that she shouldered increased dramatically. The Mughals always respected their women; the opinion of the family's ladies was counted carefully. Jahangir was no different. He was extremely respectful towards his mother, Maryam–uz Zamani and observed all formal etiquettes for honouring her. In 1613 the Portuguese had seized some ships in which his mother had business stakes. Jahangir was enraged and he sent a military force to demand compensation from them. Most of the happy occasions: marriages, weighting ceremonies, child births' celebrations, anniversaries etc. were observed at Maryam uz Zamani's palace. Jahangir was trained to adore not just his mother but motherhood in general. Once, he imposed death sentence on a man (Pahaar, son of Ghazi Khan) who had killed his mother. In the *Tuzuk* this case is noted with shock, loathing and disdain. When his foster mother (daughter of Shaikh Salim Chishti and mother of Khubu) died, he carried the foot-side of her corpse on his shoulders. He was so distraught that it took a while for people to persuade him to eat something and change his clothes. When Salima Sultan Begum (his step-mother, daughter of Gurukh Begum and Mirza Nuruddin Muhammad) died, he immediately dispatched Itimad ud Daula to arrange for a grand burial for her in accordance with her last will. He noted that despite his utter hatred for Mirza Aziz Koka, he couldn't get the man assassinated because his mother Jiji Anga (wife of Shamsuddin Muhammad Atka) had breast fed his father, Akbar. He also noted that he had been fed a drop of his half sister Shakarunnisa's milk so that he may respect her like his own mother. Shakrarunnisa's younger sister, Aaraam Banu Begum was perhaps Akbar's youngest child. Despite her whimsical and hot-headed ways she was a great favourite of her father. So Jahangir was clearly instructed by Akbar to be always kind and polite to her, and he was, especially after their father passed away. Like his forefathers Jahangir also took care of the women of his extended family. He is reported to have given a heavy allowance to Daniyal's widow for her personal expenses and taken Ruqaiyya Sultan Begum to visit Babur's tomb at Kabul with him. Ladies of the family often accompanied him on hunts and outings. In the *Tuzuk* he makes it a point to mention the gardens commissioned by the female members of his family: Afghan Aghacha, Bika Begum, Hamida Banu Begum, Shahr Banu Begum etc. However it was a first in Mughal history that a spouse's shadow was shading the royal throne. The nobility reacted in varied ways. Abdur Rahim Khan-i-Khanan prudently swam with the tide. But Mahabat Khan couldn't accept that Salim, who had challenged the indomitable Akbar, could be dominated by his wife. He cautioned the Baadshah about being mocked by other monarchs for delegating so much power to his queen. Resultantly the noble was shunted away from the court.

In 1621 the recurrent news of Jahangir's failing health made Shah Jahan paradoxically insecure and bold. He hadn't had Khusroe assassinated as he feared their father, but now he felt that perhaps he could do so. Accordingly on 22nd February 1622 on his order Khusroe was killed by Reza Ghulam Bahadur at Burhanpur. Shah Jahan was deliberately absent—far away from the town to avoid being implicated in the act. Nevertheless it was rumored that either he had his brother killed or the latter had committed suicide. The official explanation reported that it was a natural death. For his peace of mind Jahangir believed and held on to this version. He had the prince's remains buried next to his mother's at Allahabad in a garden at Khuldabad, now known as Khusroe Bagh. It became a settlement for mendicants. Shah Jahan's image was dented, all caution notwithstanding. He already had a reputation of being arrogant and now he seemed ruthlessly ambitious as well. Despite the autocracy of medieval times, public opinion did matter. The nobles including the other princes felt intimidated by him. In a way Nur Jahan got what she wanted—her hands were clean and a rival of Shahriyar had been removed. Parvez tried to be as close to Jahangir as he could, but he had neither achievements nor mentors to help him in the race for the crown. Jahangir was still powerful. Powerful enough that Shah Jahan couldn't dare tell him the truth. Though no one jumped down Shah Jahan's neck for this murder many years later his son Aurangzeb audaciously cited it to justify his own go-ahead and get-ahead attitude.

In May 1622 the Persian ruler Shah Abbas occupied Qandhar. Shah Jahan was summoned to lead the retaliatory campaign. The posting in the north-west frontier would have distanced him from the centre. Chances of a quick and clear victory were slim. Losses would have damaged his reputation of invincibility. He was a victory monster anxious about maintaining his winning streak and fearful that his step-mother might deliberately set him up for failure. He left the Deccan in obedience to his father's command. On reaching Mandu he sent a wishlist to Jahangir and requested for the governorship of Lahore and the possession of the impregnable fortress of Ranthambor to station his family. Jahangir was greatly alarmed by these demands. The prince already had the governorships of Gujarat, Malwa, Mewar, Ahmadnagar, Khandesh and Mughal-occupied tracts in Deccan. His earliest possessions in the heart of the empire were still with him. His demand for Lahore was a bit too much. The Baadshah was hurt and angered by his son's insatiability. He immediately left Kashmir for Lahore. History was repeating itself. What Salim had done to his father, his son did to him. Jahangir wrote a letter to Shah Jahan: A royal dressing down-wrapped in parental affection. He was ready to forgive his son, like Akbar had forgiven him. But Shah Jahan wasn't asking for forgiveness. Meanwhile the imperial soldiers had a dust-up with Shah Jahan's men for the occupation of Dholpur. He had applied for its allocation. In anticipation of the acceptance of his request he dispatched a force to take charge of the said area. Interestingly Dholpur had already been assigned to Shahriyar and was in his possession. The contest was interpreted as a defiance of an imperial *farman*. Jahangir was livid. Five years ago he had vowed that if Khurram's son; Shah Shuja recovered from a serious illness he would not use guns for sport. Now he broke that vow and was hardly sorry about it. Shahriyar was further promoted and assigned the command of Shah Jahan's armies as well. The latter's governorships were revoked. He was asked to settle on the southern fringes of the empire. Shah Jahan panicked and immediately dispatched a letter of apology to his father. Perhaps he also warned him against Nur Jahan's ambitious designs and reminded him of his own loyal services. To express his selflessness and helplessness he asked Jahangir to permit him to proceed to Mecca as an ascetic. His father wasn't impressed. Nor was Nur Jahan moved by his attempts of reconciliation. Nothing worked. After Jahangir's arrival in Lahore in October 1622, Hissar Firoza which was conventionally held by the heir apparent was transferred from Shah Jahan to Shahriyar. Its revenues were earmarked for the Qandhar campaign. Shah Jahan had grossly underestimated his father. Jahangir was sick but alive enough to fight for his position; even if it meant draining his own line of blood. He knew that when a father and son fight, nobody wins. But when kingdoms are at stake defeat means death. Thus both the parties had pathetically limited options.

Imperial attempts to curb Shah Jahan's power eventually backfired. Nur Jahan's accusations became self-fulfilling prophecies. The anti-queen nobility rallied around the disgruntled prince. The latter played along and acted like a Cinderella-son grappling with his step-mother's witchy ways. The Rajputs of Amber, Marwar, Kota and Bundi reached out to support the Baadshah and Mahabat Khan was won over by the quick-witted queen. She bought off commander after commander. Shah Jahan was suddenly shut out, but he was indeed his father's son. Like Salim, he too rushed towards Agra to cease it treasures and fortress. Nur Jahan sent Asaf Khan to protect the capital. This was also meant to dispel the mystery around her brother's loyalty. He was given the title of *Umdat-ul Sultanat* (best [man] of the empire) to pressurize him to stay with the imperial camp. He did stay. Perhaps he was too smart to show his cards until the endgame. Shah Jahan failed at Agra, just like Salim had failed. Jahangir summoned Parvez from Allahabad and Mahabat Khan from Kabul to tame his son who had taken his title 'Shah Jahan' (King of the world) too seriously, too soon. Parvez was quickly promoted to a higher rank and Jahangir embraced him in the open court. It was clarified to Khurram that Khusroe's elimination didn't mean that the empire was heirless. Parvez was presented a pearl-studded dress of honour and a *nadiri* of gold brocade worth rupees 41,000, an elephant named Ratan Gaj, ten female elephants, a horse and a sword valued at rupees 77,000. Nur Jahan also gave him precious gifts. An army was raised under the command of Khusroe's son, Dawar Bakhsh. The rank of this prince was raised to 8000 zat and 3000 sawar. Shah Jahan retreated southwards. He passed through the very places he had subjugated as Jahangir's commander. Maharana Karan Singh of Mewar helped him. Despite Shah Jahan's riches and reputation the morale of his army was running low. Reduced to utter desperation he contacted his father's rivals and enemies for help: Shah Abbas of Persia and Malik Ambar. He had hoped that Abdur Rahim Khan-i Khanan would stand by him in view of his earlier favours. But Khan-i Khanan was a loyalist of the Mughal brand, likely to disown anyone who threatened its glory. So he defected to Mahabat Khan's camp at the first opportunity. Shah Abbas had already sided with Nur Jahan. He advised Shah Jahan to behave himself and submit to his father. The prince left his extended family at Asirgarh and proceeded towards Deccan. This fort was considered to be invincible. Its governor Mir

Husamuddin was married to a niece of Nur Jahan. The latter had warned him to save their family's pristine lineage by remaining loyal to the centre but he sided with the rebel. Dawar Safi, husband of another niece of Nur Jahan (Asaf Khan's daughter) also joined Shah Jahan although he betrayed him later. Anyway the prince's three wives, children and personal servants travelled with him to Deccan. There he realized that without the shade of the Mughalia banner he was nobody. No one helped him for fear of Jahangir's wrath. Perhaps for the first time Shah Jahan grasped that his father's quiet patronage was a driving force behind every victory that he thought was only his own. Passing helplessly through Ahmadnagar, Bijapur and Golcunda he reached Orissa. Typically resilient and stubborn like his ancestors: both Rajputs and the Mughals, he now decided to approach Agra again-via Orissa-Bengal-Bihar and Allahabad. The first part of the plan was a success. He occupied the very fort of Allahabad where Salim the rebel had set up a court in defiance of Akbar. But this was it. Mahabat Khan and Parvez were waiting to confront him there. In August 1624, Shah Jahan was defeated by the imperial forces. Leaving his newly born son Sultan Murad Baksh (b. 8 October 1624) in the care of nurses Shah Jahan retraced his steps. His recent victories in the east were now meaningless. The local governors were too scared to associate with him. Heads of traitors were being presented to Jahangir every day. Mahabat Khan was entitled *Mutamin-ud Daula* (trusted one of the state) and Khan-i Khanan. He was made the Sipahsalar (commander-in chief) of the imperial army. By March 1626 Shah Jahan was physically exhausted and mentally depressed. He wrote to his father begging him for forgiveness. Jahangir forgave; like Akbar. However he placed two conditions: Firstly, Dara Shikuh (11 years) and Aurangzeb (8 years) would remain in his custody as guarantee for Shah Jahan's good behavior. Secondly, the forts of Rohtas and Asirgarh would be handed over to the Imperial centre. Shah Jahan agreed to these but he refused to settle in a small fief which Jahangir had offered him. He chose to wander. He had really become *be-daulat* (pauper)–exactly the way he was designated by his father in the *Tuzuk* during his rebellion. However like Babur he knew that he still had one inalienable thing which could still propel him to power; it was his blood. If Timurid-Mongol blood could feed elixir to Babar's ambitions why couldn't Mughal-Rajput blood do the same for Shah Jahan? Of course it could. But Shah Jahan would have to compete with others of the same type of blood.

Now Nur Jahan's fears shifted from Shah Jahan to Parvez. The latter had suddenly become prominent due to his role in the suppression of his brother's revolt. Unfortunately for her he had also developed a good rapport with Mahabat Khan. The latter was posted with this prince in Burhanpur. To break their partnership Nur Jahan had Mahabat Khan transferred to Bengal. Asaf Khan who was holding Bengal was recalled to the court. Khan Jahan Lodi, one of her own men, was now sent to be with Parvez. Although the prince initially resisted this change but he was easily quietened by Nur Jahan's loud insistence.

Once in Bengal, Mahabat Khan was asked to send elephants and riches which he had accumulated from Bihar and Bengal during Shah Jahan's rebellion. He understood that Nur Jahan and Asaf Khan wanted to trap him in a case of embezzlement and treason. They weren't just after his reputation, they were after his life. His remarkable contribution in quashing the rebellion was forgotten even before the flesh of his men had decayed. Anyway he marched to the royal court with an army of about five thousand Rajputs. The elephants were dispatched in advance and he was going to furnish details of the accounts in person. This was in March 1626. Jahangir had returned from Kashmir and was on his way to Kabul. The imperial camp was near Jhelum. Nur Jahan feared that the noble might actually be able to clear his name of financial fraud so she blamed him for another bluff. Mahabat Khan had engaged his daughter with Barkhurdar, son of Khwaja Umar Naqshbandi without prior permission of the Emperor. Though technically at fault, a noble of his stature could be easily forgiven for such a slip up. He wasn't. Barkhurdar was insulted and imprisoned. The gifts which he had received from Mahabat

Khan were seized. In desperation the latter wanted a word with his old friend Salim. An opportunity arose almost immediately. Jahangir and his family were to cross Jhelum a day after the rest of the royal establishment had crossed. This meant a day of thin security cover for the Baadshah. On 24th March 1626, after the establishment had crossed over, Mahabat Khan sent about two thousand soldiers to the other side to ensure that no one could re-cross to the Imperial side. He then proceeded to the royal camp and assumed its charge. With three princes of the royal bloodline around, he definitely hadn't planned to usurp the throne. Perhaps he wanted to either resurrect the robust Salim Sultan or to personally control the sickly Jahangir.

Drinks, drugs and illnesses had already killed the Salim that Mahabat Khan was looking for. Jahangir was furious. He may have understood Mahabat Khan's intention, but Nur Jahan was his best bet for survival. She loved him in a personal capacity. He played along with his old friend as if nothing much had happened. If it became public that the Baadshah had been arrested by a noble, his majesty would have been undermined forever. Luckily Nur Jahan and Shahriyar had escaped. So the hope of his eventual freedom was alive. Nur Jahan fought the battle for Jahangir's freedom in person. But she couldn't succeed and thought it prudent to join him as a detainee of Mahabat Khan. Asaf Khan fled.

Under Mahabat Khan's protection Jahangir reached Kabul in April 1626. Unwittingly the Khan had stepped into troubled waters–a terrain his Rajput soldiery was unfamiliar with. Jahangir continued to put on an act of comradeship with Mahabat Khan, while Nur Jahan bribed, threatened and convinced officers to help her. Mahabat Khan's arrogance definitely came to her aid. The coup had gone haywire; Khan himself didn't know the path ahead. Jahangir's outings and hunts were as usual. Ultimately one fine day he sent a *farman* to Mahabat Khan that he desired to personally review the cavalry. The order was indicative of the Baadshah's reassertion. Mahabat Khan's Rajput soldiery had already vaporized after a combat with the locals, so he quickly obeyed the order. Jahangir left Kabul on 22nd August

1626–Nur Jahan was again in charge. She directed Shahriyar to occupy Lahore since Shah Jahan was proceeding towards Thatta. However Dara and Aurangzeb arrived soon after. With them in her personal custody she felt quite relieved. A further relief for her was the news of Parvez's death in Burhanpur–at 36 he had died of overdrinking and epilepsy. The comatose prince was cauterized at five places on his head and forehead but couldn't be revived. His quiet obedience to his father remained unrecognized. It remains a mystery why Shah Jahan is suspected to have had a hand in his death as well. Terry reports of a sarcastic letter of Aurangzeb in which he accused Shah Jahan of eliminating Khusroe and Parvez-who were no threat to him. As the royal family drew close to the endgame, Dawar Baksh Bulaki was also brought to Nur Jahan's custody.

Mahabat Khan's position was further weakened when his treasures from Bengal were captured by Anup Rai Singh Dalan. On 13th September 1626 he was sent off to track Shah Jahan's movements and send Asaf Khan and Daniyal's sons Tahmurath and Hoshang to the court. By October, Abdur Rahim and Asaf Khan reported to Jahangir at Lahore. Although in 1624 Jahangir had got Abdur Rahim's son, Darab Khan's head severed and had sent it to him in a napkin, now the Khan was a welcomed man. He was re-entitled Khan-e Khanan; this title had been given to Mahabat Khan during Shah Jahan's rebellion. The latter's October 1626 campaign in Thatta turned out to be an absolute fiasco. Mumtaz Mahal gave birth to another son, Lutfullah at this station. Within four days of the birth Shah Jahan headed back to Junnar. Disillusioned and depressed.

In March 1627 Jahangir left for Kashmir with his family–Nur Jahan, Asaf Khan, Shahriyar and Dawar Bakhsh. His asthma was getting worse by the day. His body was tormented by the contradiction of addiction and revulsion to alcoholic substances. The only thing that he could tolerate was grape wine. His appetite had dwindled to nothing. He gave up even his favourite: opium. His stable equipped with the best steeds was of no use for him. He couldn't ride anymore. Shahriyar's illness multiplied his worries. The prince was struck by *dau-al salab* (Fox mange), a type of leprosy. He had lost hair from head and whiskers, to eyebrows and eyelashes. Healers advised him to shift to a warmer climate. Thus he left for Lahore. Jahangir's entourage followed him soon after. On the way a hunt was organized for the Baadshah which happened to be his last. A foot soldier died accidentally in the course of a chase. This death shook Jahangir. In his younger days, during a hunt his prey—a nigai had escaped due to the accidental appearance of a groom and two palanquin bearers. Jahangir was so enraged that he had the groom killed on the spot and the back tendons of the palanquin bearers' feet were cut. As he became older and sicker he was moved by deaths. Once a blacksmith named Kalyan fell in love with a widow. Both belonged to the same caste yet the woman wasn't ready to accept his advances. He appealed to Jahangir to intervene. In an effort to convince the Emperor to order the woman to be his, he said that if the Baadshah would give her to him, he would jump off the Shah Burj of Agra fort. Jahangir jokingly said that he should first jump off the building in which they presently were and prove his love. Only then would he order the girl to accept him. Even before the Baadshah could finish his sentence, Kalyan jumped. His eyes and mouth bled instantly. Jahangir regretted his words. Asaf Khan was directed to take Kalyan to his house and personally arrange for his treatment. Anyway he died and Jahangir felt that indeed irresponsible words are stuff that regrets are made of. He blamed himself and was extremely sorry. Now that his life had almost completed a full circle even the accidental death of a random soldier broke him. He believed that the angle of death had come for him. Although the soldier's mother was well compensated it did not help the Baadshah swing away from depression. His sleeplessness and restlessness wasn't helping his weak body. On his way from Rajauri to Bhimar in the middle of an asthma attack he breathed his last on the 28/29th of October 1627. He was 58 and had worn the Mughal crown for 22 years. Although he disobeyed Akbar in his youth, his father remained his ideal for a king, parent and person. He strived to conserve the magic of Akbar's magnanimity and also add his own zing to it. He was a dynamic ruler though the last five years of his life were spent grappling with disease and dissent. He did his best to keep the madness of ambition amongst his heirs in check. He was buried at the Dilkusha Garden at Shahdara near Lahore. Later Nur Jahan commissioned an elegant mausoleum to mark the spot. Nur Jahan's unshifting loyalty for him was definitely dangerous for her, but she stuck to her guns. And Jahangir never let go of the personal and political anchor of his life—his wife.

Jahangir's religious inclinations were a complex mix of many belief systems. In the estimation of Christian missionaries he wasn't any different from his father in secular liberality or his love for Christianity. Father Ridolfo Aquawiva, leader of the Jesuit mission was a friend of his. As a prince he mediated between the Christian missionaries and Akbar to facilitate building of churches and other issues. Together with the Islamic festivals and Persian Nauroz, Jahangir celebrated all the Hindu festivals like Holi, Dussehra, Diwali, Raksha-bandhan and Shivaratri. Cards were played in his presence in Diwali. On Shivratri he interacted with the jogis. Horses were decorated and paraded on Dussehra. Brahmins tied rakhis on his wrists. Once when Rakhi and Shab-e Barat fell on the same day Jahangir called it the Mubarak Shamba (Lucky day). On the day of Pitra-daan, he sent Khurram to Akbar's tomb to distribute money and food to the poor. He instructed his followers to never darken their days with religious strife but to pursue the policy of peace with all-*Sulh-i kul*. He instructed that they must not kill anything except in battle or chase. As a recruiter, patron and professional Jahangir was no different from his father. No wonder Shaikh Ahmad Sarhindi, Shaikh Ibrahim Baba and others like them who had hoped that after Akbar's demise his heir would give preferential treatment to the Muslims, were quite disappointed. Jahangir appreciated uncomplicated spirituality. He asked the Muslim ulema to collect simple appellations of God which could be easily remembered. While bidding farewell to a mystic Sayyid Muhammad, Jahangir swore on the Quran that he would give whatever the man asked for. And lo, he asked for a copy of the Quran itself. To make the gift as expensive as possible a thirteenth-century copy written by Yaqut, a famous calligrapher was gifted. It was considered to be a wonder of its age. Jahangir requested Sayyid to prepare a translation of the Quran in simple Persian, without ornamentations. He admired how Shaikh Nizamuddin Auliya respected different ways of approaching God–the Sufi said that each race has its right road of faith and its shrine and that has to be respected. Muslim officers were prohibited to force anyone to convert to Islam. He had ordered that Daniyal's sons be tutored in Christian dogma. Historians often interpret this as a political measure to eliminate their candidature from the race for the crown. Perhaps they overlook that Akbar too had given the same kind of order for his son Murad. The Christians were anyway considered *ahl-e kitaab* (people of the book) by conventional Islamic understanding of inter-religious equations. What is remarkable is that Akbar asserted that the Hindus also were *ahl-e kitaab* due to the Vedas. It is notable that Jahangir was half Rajput and amongst his sons the two who were the most serious contenders for the Mughal throne were more than half Rajputs: Khusroe and Shah Jahan.

The account of Jahangir's meetings with Jadrup Gosain, a master of Vedanta and mysticism, is a subtle presentation of the Baadshah's take on spirituality—life and death. Akbar had also called upon this mendicant in 1601. Jahangir met him first in Ujjain in 1616 and later at Mathura. He never summoned the jogi to his presence, but walked quarter of a mile to meet him. The mendicant's abode was literally a tiny hole in which only a thin person could enter. He found it important to note Jadrup's lifestyle: He lived alone. His house had practically nothing, not even a mat or straw. He bathed twice and went out once to the town, to the house of either one of the three Brahmins that he had selected to feed him. He ate just five morsels and swallowed them without chewing. The Baadshah felt that Jadrup's life style fell perfectly into the model prescribed for spiritualists by Maulana Rumi: By day their clothes are the Sun and by night the Moon's rays become their mattress and blanket. Jahangir considered his meetings with Jadrup as opportunities for learning and occasions of good fortune and pure delight. Although himself fond of luxuries he admired Jadrup who had voluntarily forsaken everything and was so content. Jahangir compared his renunciation with that of Luqman:

> Luqman's cell was small and narrow to the boot
> Like the throat of a pipe, or the breast of a lute.
> One foolish one said to the grand old man–
> What house is this–three feet and six span?
> With tears and emotions the sage made reply-
> Ample for him whose task is to die.[93]

It is fascinating that deep inside the life-loving Jahangir was a *faqir* who respected the remembrance that man's eventual destiny is death.

❧

---

93   *Tuzuk-i Jahangiri*, p. 106.

FIVE

ABUL MUZAFFAR DAWAR BAKHSH
BAADSHAH SHER SHAH

1627–1628

'Praised be God, Who with death did break the necks of tyrants, shattering with it the backs of Persia's kings, cutting short the aspirations of the Caesars, whose hearts were long averse to recalling death, until the true promise came to them and cast them into the pit. From the loftiest of palaces into the deepest of graves they passed, and from the light of the cradle into the sepulchre's gloom. From dallying with servant-girls and boys into sustaining insects and worms they passed, and from reveling in food and drink into wallowing in the earth; from the friendliness of company into the forlornness of solitude, and from the soft couch into woeful perdition. See if they had found any strength and protection from death, or taken against it a barrier and refuge. See if you can perceive a single man of them, or hear from them the slightest sound.[94]

Travelling from Rajauri to Bhimbar with her husband's dead body might have been the most excruciating journey for Nur Jahan. The entrails; intestines and internal organs of Jahangir had been separated and buried near a mosque at Chingaz Sarai.[95] Then the corpse was given the ritual last bath and was embalmed because its final place of rest in the Dilkusha Garden of Shahadra, at Lahore was quite far.

---

[94] *The Remembrance of Death And The After Life*, Al Ghazali, Translation, introduction and notes by T. J. Winter, The Islamic Texts Society, Cambridge, 1999 (reprint), p. I.
[95] Nur Jahan, Empress of Mughal India, Ellison Banks Findly, Oxford University Press, New York, 1993, p. 284.

The *nishans* (orders of royalties other than the emperor) of Nur
Jahan to Jai Singh dated 23rd October 1625 and 1st January 1626
are ample proof of her unquestioned political authority preceding
Jahangir's death:

Be it known to the prop of peers and contemporaries, pride of
grandees and nobles, fitted for favours and graces, honest and
loyal servant Raja Jai Singh, distinguished and honoured by Her
Exalted graces, that it has been learnt from the arzdasht(written
petition) of the prop of the State, Fidai Khan that in compliance
with the royal order the loyal servant (Raja Jai Singh) has
segregated himself from Mahabat Khan (Zaman Beg son of
Ghayur Beg of Kabul-the engineer of the supposed coup) and
thereby had done a meritorious act. May God bless him. He
should keep in mind the job entrusted to him by His Majesty.
He should feel rest assured of Her Majesty's daily increasing
favours and should conduct the State affairs in consultation with
Farzand Baba Khan Jahan (Pir Khan son of Daulat Khan Lodi of
ShahuKhail clan promoted to farzandi/being an adopted son by
Jahangir) the arm of sublime caliphate. This should be deemed as
his aim and he should not do anything contrary to the command.

Be it known to the prop of peers and contemporaries, pride
of grandees and nobles, fitted for favours and graces, honest and
loyal servant Raja Jai Singh, distinguished and honoured by the
sublime bounties, that out of profound favours and bounties a
special khilat (robe of honour) has been sent through the close
confidant, Khwaja Roz Bhan, who is entitled to favours and is one
of the reliable and trustworthy servants of Her Majesty. Befitting
his service, sincerity and devotion, he should be hopeful of other
favours from Her Majesty.[96]

However when Nur Jahan called a meeting of the nobles soon after
the Emperor's demise, most of them evaded her summons. Her clout

---

[96]*Edicts From The Mughal Harem*, S. A. I. Tirmizi, Idarah-I Adabiyat-I Delli, Delhi,
1978, Pp. 34–44.

seemed to have died with Jahangir. Shah Jahan's sons: Dara, Shah Shuja and Aurangzeb who were in her custody at the time of their grandfather's death were transferred to the guardianship of Sadiq Khan. Iradat Khan the Mir Bakhshi and Asaf Khan engineered their liberation. The latter finally showed the cards that he had held secretly for decades. He hated his sister. She had deprived him of his share in their father's properties–he was dominated and sidelined by her despite formally holding important postings and titles-she pressurized him terribly during Shah Jahan's rebellion–she humiliated him during Mahabat Khan's coup. He had to prove his loyalty to her every day.

Nur Jahan's son-in-law, Shahariyar was a mansabdar of 40,000 sawar at the time of Jahangir's death. He had access to the treasury of Lahore. Her brother-in-law Qasim Khan (husband of her sister Manija) was the governor of Agra. This could facilitate access to more military funds. Besides, she had massive wealth and a fan following of her own. But to her surprise the nobles' loyalties shifted towards Asaf Khan almost overnight. Nevertheless she hoped to haggle with her brother over political power. But Asaf Khan felt no need for an alliance with his widowed sister. Anyway he didn't trust her much. In fact he curbed her freedom of movement and communication. Indeed, Nur Jahan had nurtured a snake pit under her pillow.

Shahariyar's accession would have revived Nur Jahan's authority and nothing would have improved for Asaf Khan. On the other hand his son-in-law Shah Jahan's accession would have propelled him to an enviable status in the empire. So quietly and quickly he dispatched a messenger to Junnar to inform Shah Jahan about his father's death and the need for him to rush to Agra. It was a verbal message authenticated by Asaf Khan's signet ring. Writing anything was too dangerous. The messenger, Banarsi, travelled at a stupendous speed and contacted Mahabat Khan, who had recently joined Shah Jahan in just 20 days. Although the prince was saddened by the news of his father's death but anxieties about his future dwarfed his sorrows. He started for Agra on 1st December 1627.

Meanwhile Asaf Khan deputed Maqsud Khan to escort the

remains of the late Baadshah to Lahore for burial. Nur Jahan was to accompany this army till it reached its destination. Spies slithered around her tent to report everything about her activities to Asaf Khan. The latter ensured her isolation so as to render her politically ineffective. No one knows whether it was her brother's fear or the responsibility of getting Jahangir honourably buried that kept her tied to the sanctioned route. She didn't deviate from it to participate in the succession drama which was to be staged soon. Asaf Khan also started for Lahore. He took along Khusroe's young son Dawar Bakhsh alias Bulaqi with him. It seems that at some stage this prince was made to wear a *bulaaq*(ring worn by women in the septum of their nose) to protect him from evil eye or as a part of some promise made to Divinity for protecting him from misfortune. Perhaps Jahangir's regret about his mistreatment of Khusroe had made this grandson precious. Sources dispute whether he had nominated Dawar Bakhsh or Shahariyar as his successor. The man conspicuous by his absence from this race was Shah Jahan. However as a stop gap arrangement before the latter's arrival, on 29th October 1627 Asaf Khan had announced that Jahangir had chosen Dawar Bakhsh as his heir. Acting like a loyal servant of the late emperor, whose only agenda was to implement his master's will, he arranged for Dawar Bakhsh's coronation. The urgency was such that the ceremony was conducted at Bhimbar, a nondescript settlement in the Himalayan foothills. The ulema and the nobility rushed to play their respective roles in the legitimization of the new emperor. Unintentionally Asaf Khan had averted the calamity that a civil war for succession might have brought upon the empire. Dawar Bakhsh was more terrified than happy. Familiar with his father's fate, he had never coveted his grandfather's crown. Asaf Khan and Iradat Khan swore allegiance to him in a personal capacity as well to convince him of the reality of his incredible elevation. The poor prince was pushed into the political furnace at a time when it was in full blaze.

Asaf Khan's exceptional cleverness had taken even his scheming sister by surprise. All that Nur Jahan could manage from her confinement was to push Shaharyar to use the Lahore treasures to recruit an army and proclaim that the Mughal crown was his. Accordingly 70 lakh rupees was spent within a week of this proclamation to buy support. Still no one took him seriously. The veterans refused to side with him. Baisunghar (Daniyal's son) who had sought asylum with him became his commander-in chief. Asaf Khan reached the vicinity of Lahore before Nur Jahan. He wanted Shaharyar crushed in advance of her arrival. On 19th November 1627, Baisunghar bravely faced the veteran commanders of the Mughal army three miles outside the city. Shaharyar had not even come to the battle field. He was suffering from disfiguring and humiliating symptoms perhaps, triggered by venereal disease. Due to acute alopecia he had lost even his facial hair. He had no beard, moustache, eyebrows or eyelashes.[97] His freshly recruited soldiery had neither loyalty nor skills. Desertions started even before the battle began. The imperial side had the supposed Mughal Emperor Dawar Bakhsh Bulaqi, Asaf Khan, Mirza Abu Talib Shayista Khan (Asaf Khan's eldest son), Dara Shikuh and Aurangzeb. They won. Baisunghar's fate remains a mystery. No one heard of him after the battle, except for the sporadic gossip of his survival which emerged every now and then. When the news of his defeat reached the citadel Shaharyar locked himself in it, rather than fleeing to save his life. Azam Khan, a commander of the small band of cavalry which was supposed to guard the fort betrayed him. He treacherously allowed Iradat Khan and Abu Talib Shaista Khan to enter the royal tower. They dragged Shaharyar out of the harem. His hands were tied with his own cummerbund by Fairuz Khan a favourite eunuch of Jahangir.[98] The weak and sick prince was dragged, kicked and abused by his late father's officers. Anyway this violence was nothing in comparison to the fact that he was subsequently blinded. On 20th November 1627 Dawar Bakhsh was crowned again at Lahore. Thus while Shah Jahan was still unaware of Jahangir's death,

---

[97] *Shah-Jahan Rise And Fall Of The Mughal Emperor*, Fergus Nicoll, Penguin Books, Gurgaon, 2018 (reprint),p. 193.
[98] Ibid., p. 194.

Abul Muzaffar Dawar Bakhsh Baadshah-Sher Shah was declared to be the fifth emperor of the Mughal dynasty for the second time. And of course the plans of his assassination were already in place.

Shah Jahan's march from Junnar to Agra wasn't as rushed as one would imagine. On the way he won allies, punished enemies and rewarded friends. His brother-in law Mirza Safi Saif Khan (husband of Mumtaz Mahal's sister, Malika Banu) and Maharana Karan Singh the ruler of Mewar were classic examples of his treatment of enemies and friends respectively. In mid-December, at Ahmedabad he received the news of Shaharyar's defeat. Around early January he dispatched Reza Ghulam Bahadur with a message for Asaf Khan. The Baadshah seated on the throne and the princes lodged in the Lahore jail were to be assassinated. Interestingly Reza Bahadur was the same assassin who had killed Dawar Baksh's father Khusroe as well. By late January when Shah Jahan reached near Ajmer, like his grandfather he walked on foot to the Chishti shrine. Perhaps he too had some spiritual promises to keep. Meanwhile Reza Bahadur reached Lahore in the last week of January 1628. Despite all the initial doubts Dawar Bakhsh had settled into emperorship by then. Coins were minted in his name. There is a *farman* of Sher Shah the Mughal Emperor issued to Raja Jai Singh. On 29th January 1628, the unsuspecting and innocent Baadshah was suddenly imprisoned. Nawaz Khan reports that Dawar Bakhsh was with his brother Gurshasp in the prison when Reza Bahadur appeared before him. Punning on the word *Reza* (virtue), he exclaimed that *Qaza* (death) has arrived. Finally on the 2nd of February 1628 he was beheaded. Shah Jahan and Asaf Khan thought it prudent to eliminate all the other princes as well so that there could be no threat to the new Baadshah. So Shaharyar, Gurshasp (Khusore's other son), Tahmurath and Hoshang (Daniyal's sons) were also assassinated. Thomas Herbert reported that the heads of these princes were chopped in a bathing area and were sent to Agra for Shah Jahan's reassurance. Perhaps their bodies were disposed with such secrecy that rumors about Dawar Bakhsh being alive were in circulation till as late as 1657. The *Khuld-iBarin* reported that when the war of succession began amongst the sons of Shah Jahan, Dawar Bakhsh sought help of the Persian monarch to participate in it, to recover what was rightfully his. However when Murad was arrested and Aurangzeb emerged as a clearer victor, he backed off. Texts like *Zubdut Tawarikh*, *Tarikh-iJadid* and *Khuld-iBarin*, claim that he lived in Qazwin and was a great favourite of Shah Abbas-II of Persia. It is claimed that he often came from Qazwin to attend the Shah's drinking parties. It was speculated that Baisunghar had also escaped alive and was with him.[99] Anyway Reza Bahadur was honoured with the title of: *Khidmat Parast Khan* (A Khan for whom work is worship). The spiritually inclined predicted that divine justice would ensure that these murders have repercussions for the murderers. Indeed as time passed nightmares came to Shah Jahan disguised as sweet dreams.

Anyway on the same day; 2nd February 1628, when many a beloveds of Akbar and Jahangir were slaughtered, there were celebrations because Shah Jahan had re-entered Agra. Although Jahangir could not have appointed him as his heir, he might have felt right through that eventually the most competent of his progeny would manage to grab the crown.

Nur Jahan proved her intelligence yet again. She stepped aside from the path of her enemies' ascendency and stayed in a non-glamorous but safe zone in Lahore. The immediate engagement that she took up to distract herself from her unbelievably sudden downfall was the construction of Jahangir's tomb (1628–1637). The official history of Shah Jahan's reign gives the credit of this tomb to him. And given Shah Jahan's inborn interest in designing etc. it is possible that he might have actually seen through the building plan. However it is widely accepted that Nur Jahan was the real in charge of the said project and perhaps its financer as well. Even though most of her personal treasures had been frozen and were made inaccessible to her,

[99] *History of Shah Jahan of Dihli*, Banarsi Prasad Saxena, Central Book Depot, Allahabad, 1973, pp. v-xvii.

strangely, Shah Jahan had been generous enough to fix an allowance for her, which was rather lavish but peanuts in comparison with the kind of opulence she was used to. Her daughter Ladli Begum who had been widowed almost simultaneously with her was her constant companion. In fact she happens to be buried also, close to her mother. Khadija, her sister, remained her confidante. Her brother and brother-in-law (Qasim Khan) had entered such a high speed political lane that they couldn't get off it to meet her. She was to Shah Jahan what Abul Fazl had been to Jahangir. No wonder the Baadshah tried his best to erase her not just from the immediate but also from the past and future. In violation of the familial practice of royal widows living under their husband's successor's benign guardianship, Nur Jahan was left at Lahore. Although it is speculated that she was once brought to Agra to disclose the whereabouts of all the royal treasures, but that was it. Her portrayal became like that of a classically villainous step mother of a charming prince. Coins with her name were melted to kill her memory. It might have been strange to know that her brother and once favourite step son (Shah Jahan) were in town (Lahore) but didn't ever bother to spare some time to meet her. After all she had played an important role in the initial stages of their careers. But time had taught Nur Jahan to let go. The once accomplished huntress now spent her days reading in the quietness of her not so royal house. She tried to live up to her reputation of being a philanthropist. As an empress, whenever she was informed about any poor orphan girl, she would step up to take responsibility of the child. She established workshops to train them in some kind of skills to enhance their employability.

Though otherwise disconnected with the ruling Mughal family she sure would have felt something over the deaths of Mumtaz Mahal in 1631 and then of Asaf Khan in 1641. She lived through the inception and near completion of the Taj Mahal (1632–48), her niece's grand mausoleum, but never got to see it. Her death on 18th December 1645 didn't attract much attention. She knew that it wouldn't. No wonder the epitaph of her, self-commissioned tomb at Lahore reads as follows:

Bar mazaar-e gharibaan na chiraagh na gule
Na par-e parvana na sadaa-e bulbul.[100]

By the grave of the poor, neither are lamps lit nor flowers offered. There are no wings of the love lorn self-immolating moths, neither is there the call of the nightingale.[101]

❈

---

[100]*History of Mughal Architecture* vol–3, R. Nath, Abhinav Publications, New Delhi, 1994, pp. 431–32.
[101]Translation-Author's.

SIX

SHAH JAHAN ABUL MUZAFFAR SHIHABUDDIN MUHAMMAD SAHIB QIRAN SANI

1628–1658

'In the name of One who hath no name. With whatever name thou callest Him, He uplifteth His head.' Abundant praise be showered on the Incomparable One, who has manifested on His beautiful, unparalleled and matchless face the two parallel locks of Faith (Iman) and Infidelity (Kufr), and by neither of them has He covered His beautiful face. "Faith and Infidelity, both are galloping on the way towards Him, And are exclaiming (together): He is One and none shares his Kingship."——The neighbour, the companion and the co-traveller is He, In the rags of beggars and the raiments of kings is He, In the conclave on high and the secret chamber below, By God, He is all and verily by God He is all.'

—PRINCE DARA SHUKOH SHAH BULAND IQBAL
IN HIS BOOK THE *MAJMA-UL BAHRAIN*.[102]

A son was born to Salim and a Rajput princess, Manmati Jagat Gosain; daughter of Udai Singh Mota Raja of Marwar, on 5th January 1592 at Lahore. It was the 36th year of Akbar's reign. The baby was adopted by a childless queen of the Baadshah: Ruqaiyya Sultan Begum; daughter of Mirza Hindal. It was speculated whether the 'adoption' was politically motivated so that Akbar would

---

[102]Prince Muhammad Dara Shikuh, *Majma-ul Bahrain* (The Mingling Of The Oceans), edited and translated by M. Mahfu-ul-Haq, Royal Book Company, Karachi, 1929, reprint 1990, p. 37.

have a healthy heir in his custody just in case his relations with Salim deteriorated further. The name that Akbar selected for the prince meant Happiness: Khurram.

Like his father, Khurram began his education at four years, four months and four days. Amongst his tutors was Abdul Khayr; a brother of Akbar's favourite, Abul Fazl. He learned archery from Mir Murad and rifle shooting from Raja Salivahan. Being the perfect mix of his ancestors, Khurram had Babur's spirit of indefatigable adventure, Humayun's unrelenting optimism, Akbar's unfailing strategizing, and Jahangir's love for beauty and finesse. He swung between practicality and dreaminess. Jahangir proudly recalled that Akbar said that this son of his had indeed taken after his grandfather. Khurram was Akbar's favourite. The latter was terribly worried when the prince had contracted small-pox. In 1604 when the Baadshah was on his way to reprimand Salim, the news of Hamida Banu's illness arrived. He sent Khurram to check the veracity of this information. Akbar trusted him. Until his revolt Khurram remained a favourite of Jahangir as well.

His first administrative experience was as the head of the council of regency during Khusroe's rebellion. He was awarded the rank of 8000 zat and 5000 sawar after the uprising was quashed. His engagement to Arjumand Banu Begum on 28th March 1607 was a powerful link up. As a mark of exceptional blessings Jahangir had himself placed the engagement ring on Arjumand's finger. Khurram had a talent for designing: plans and buildings. Jahangir appreciated the renovations that the prince had ordered at Urtahbagh at Kabul. He granted rights over Ujjain and Hissar Firoza to Khurram and permitted him to use a red tent; a royal prerogative and the Muhr-Uzak; a royal seal.

In this already favourable scenario Khurram got two opportunities to shield Jahangir's life. Khwaja Wais Diwan informed him about a plan hatched by Khusroe's supporters to dethrone the Baadshah. Khurram alerted Jahangir about it. And then in January 1611, in a more direct way he saved his father from an enraged tiger during a hunt. The wounded animal had pounced on the royal hunting party.

Most of the entourage had fled in fright; audaciously running over even the stunned Jahangir. The two persons who risked their life to save the Baadshah were Anup Singh and Khurram. The latter had struck the leaping tiger's loins. Jahangir personally inspected his sword and gratefully raised his ranks further. Even before his first posting in Deccan, Khurram had the rank of 20,000 zat and 10,000 sawar. In 1617 when he was entitled Shah Jahan his rank was 30,000 zat and 20,000 sawar. When his mother; entitled Bilqis Makani, died in April 1619 Jahangir took special care to console him. It was clear that Jahangir felt that Khurram would be a worthy wearer of the Mughal crown. However various personal and political issues stirred a rift between them. Although Khurram had formally apologized to his father for his rebellion, he hadn't really reconciled with the circumstances. It seems likely that Jahangir's illnesses in the last five years of his reign had something to do with Shah Jahan's insecurities and resultant wanderings.

Khurram's first marriage with Qandhari Begum; daughter of Mirza Muzaffar Husain Safavi–a descendent of Shah Ismail of Persia in 1610 was a political move of Jahangir. Likewise, his third marriage with the daughter of Shahnawaz Khan-son of Abdur Rahim Khan-i Khanan in 1617 was motivated by his own political interests. His second marriage, with Arjumand Banu-Mumtaz Mahal, was different. Love was involved in it. Qandhari Begum's daughter ParhezBanu/ PurHunarBanu was perhaps Shah Jahan's first born. Another daughter, Jahan-Afroz was born of his third wife. Out of the fourteen children that Mumtaz Mahal bore him, the following seven survived: Jahan Ara-Ajmer–23rd March 1614, Dara Shukoh-Ajmer–20th March 1615, Shah Shuja-Ajmer–23rd June 1616, Roshan Ara Begum-Burhanpur–24th August 1617, Aurangzeb–Dohad–24th October 1618, Murad Bakhsh-Rohtas–29th August 1624 and Gauhar Ara Begum-Burhanpur–7th June 1631. Hurunnisa, Lutfullah, Daulat-Afroz, Umid Bakhsh,Surayya and Husan Ara were some of the other children who didn't live long enough to secure a place in the larger historical narrative.

Although the Khutba of 19th January 1628 had proclaimed Shah Jahan to be the sixth Mughal Emperor, the occasion was darkened by the shadow of his relatives' arrests and assassinations. So another declaration bright enough to gloss over the Lahore massacres was required. After he reached near Agra, Shah Jahan waited outside the city to enter at an auspicious hour. Finally on 6th February 1628 in a second Khutba he took the title of Abul Muzaffar Shihabuddin Muhammad Sahib Qiran Sani. His doting family and loyalists showered precious gifts on their hero. Limitless alms were distributed to ward off evil eye. Shah Jahan's return gifts were far in excess of what he had received. He gifted Mumtaz Mahal; entitled Nawab Aliya Begum and her children with unprecedented generosity. Next to them were Mahabat Khan, Asaf Khan and the latter's son Shaista Khan, etc. Mumtaz Mahal ensured that her father became the *Vakil-us Sultanate* and the keeper of the royal signet ring. She herself was her husband's *Muhrdaar* (seal keeper). Shah Jahan unapologetically patronized personal loyalists.

Like a replay of the earlier part of Humayun's reign, Jahangir's nobility had become dangerously vocal in the last part of his reign. Nobles held large tracts of land in their native places. Their privileges were excessive. Khusroe's assassination, rise of the Bundelas, Khurram's rebellion, Mahabat Khan's coup and Nur Jahan's endless domination were indicators of a control-breakdown waiting to happen. Khurram expedited remedial measures. Instead of testing persons of doubtful loyalty, he just cast them aside. Perhaps for someone as ill as Jahangir was, compromise and contentment were the wisest course for survival. But Shah Jahan had no reason to compromise and contentment definitely wasn't his forte.

Khan Jahan Lodi was the first noble to rebel against the new order. A Sunni Afghan inclined towards Shiism; he was patronized by Nur Jahan. After Parvez's death he was made the governor of Deccan. Even though suspected to have deliberately surrendered Mughal territories for a bribe, Shah Jahan had confirmed his governorship before leaving the Deccan to contest Dawar Bakhsh.

While Shah Jahan seemed sure of his victory, Khan Jahan wasn't so certain. Therefore Shah Jahan's messenger was cold shouldered and returned without a word of gratitude. The Khan didn't wish to take any sides until the contest was finally over. Besides, he could also have contemplated shifting loyalties from the Mughals to the NizamShahis of Ahmadnagar. By the time Shah Jahan reached Ajmer, it became rather clear that his position was very strong. Khan Jahan realised his miscalculation. He dumped his aggressive grumpiness and sent a humble note of acceptance for Shah Jahan's earlier grant. The latter accepted his apologies but placed a rider that as the governor of Berar and Khandesh he should recover the territories that he had lost in the Deccan. That was a really tough task. Having failed, he was transferred to Malwa and eventually summoned to the court. Assets of Nur Jahan's loyalists were being audited and recovered. He was scared. On a rumour of his impending doom he fled the court without the Emperor's permission in October 1629. This defiance was rebellion. He was chased. A battle ensued in which precious lives were lost. Khidmat Parast Khan and Khan Jahan's sons topped the list of 'martyrs'. But the Khan escaped and sought asylum in Ahmednagar. This gave a serious setback to the Mughal position in Deccan. The local ruler had the audacity to assign Mughal occupied territories to his men to collect tax free salaries from there. Shah Jahan reached Deccan in 1630. The Baadshah's arrival unnerved Khan Jahan's hosts. He was unwelcomed wherever he went. His spirit was broken after he lost more family members in the succeeding combats. Ultimately he was also killed and his severed head was sent to Shah Jahan in February 1631. Ahmednagar paid a heavy price for sheltering a rebellious Mughal noble. It took Shah Jahan 16 months to bring the situation under control. This was an early warning to the Mughals to move cautiously in the Deccan. They essentially needed to revise some basic lessons of governance: Firstly, conquest and consolidation had to go hand in hand. Secondly, a balance had to be struck between freedom and fetters as far as the nobility was concerned.

The empire had grown and was growing. Its administrative policies had to be revised accordingly.

The second rebellion had to do with the Bundelas. Bir Singh Deo Bundela had helped Salim eliminate Abul Fazl. He was generously rewarded for it. His son Jujhar Singh had succeeded him in 1627. Shah Jahan confirmed Jujhar in his position, but his possessions were to be audited. This triggered insecurities and so Jujhar Singh fled. An imperial army was deputed to quash the rebellion. In early January 1629, Shah Jahan himself arrived at Gwalior to supervise the military operations. Pressured by internal factionalism and imperial presence Jujhar sued for peace. Mahabat Khan interceded on his behalf. He was reinstated and thereafter remained loyal to Shah Jahan. The latter raised his ranks and also gave him the title of 'Raja'. Till 1634 he served in the Deccan and thereafter his son Jagraj replaced him at that posting. After his return Jujhar Singh invaded Churagadh. Its ruler Prem Narayan appealed to Shah Jahan for help. This move of Jujhar was a serious breach of understanding between the Mughals and their sub-imperial associates. Shah Jahan had to sustain the tributaries' code of conduct that Akbar had managed to implement after years of struggle. Laxity in a case where one tributary had oppressed another tributary could have dug the roots of the Mughal military system. Meanwhile Jagraj left the Deccan to assist his father. Confident of his military superiority Shah Jahan placed exorbitant demands before Jujhar Singh. However the latter chose to fight. His capital was stormed on 22nd November 1634. A tedious chase ensued. Finally in 1635 Jujhar and Jagraj were killed in the jungles of Golconda by a local tribe. Their heads were dispatched to Shah Jahan. Durg Bhaan and Durjansal; Jujhar's son and grandson respectively were captured. His treasures were seized by the imperialists and whatever couldn't be located by them was looted by the locals. Shah Jahan's decision to recognize Raja Debi Singh as the ruler of Bundelkhand was challenged by Champat Rai of Mahoba. The latter had adopted Prithviraj; a minor son of Jujhar Singh and wished to rule over Bundelkand in his name. In late 1639 Shah Jahan readdressed the Bundela issue.

In the following developments, Prithviraj was imprisoned at Gwalior but Champat Rai escaped. To disqualify him Shah Jahan brought Bir Singh Deo's son Pahad Singh into the fray. This worked. Champat Rai surrendered but continued to be restless. He joined the service of Dara Shukoh. Perhaps displeased with his master, he later betrayed the prince before the battle of Samugarh by helping his rival brother Aurangzeb. Later his son Chhatrasal resisted Aurangzeb's authority. Bundelkhand's case showed an early symptom of the rising regional powers in Hindustan.

Another favourite of Jahangir; Raja Basu was a powerful zamindar of Mau Nurpur. After his death, amongst his sons, Jahangir favoured Jagat Singh instead of Suraj Mal. When Shah Jahan ascended the throne he confirmed Jagat Singh's current mansab of 3,000 zat and 2,000 sawar. While Jagat Singh served on various fronts of the Mughal army, his son Rajrup managed the ancestral lands. He often defaulted on the payment of the tribute that he owed to the imperial centre. In 1640 Jagat Singh returned to Mau on the pretext of reprimanding his son and settling the dues. However instead of doing any of those things he annexed the territories of the Raja of Chamba and even built a fort there. It was called Taragarh. As a reaction, Shah Jahan reduced Rajrup's assignments. This aggravated hostilities. Eventually a substantial force was sent under the command of Murad to reinforce Mughal authority. After a few inconclusive confrontations an agreement was reached by mid of March 1642. The outer fortifications of Taragarh were demolished but Jagat Singh was allowed to retain the residential area in its interior. After this he remained loyal to Shah Jahan. The murders of Prem Narayan and Prithichand; the Rajas of Churagarh and Chamba respectively indicated that intra-tributary rivalries were going out of hand. Their containment and continuation of the aura of Mughal dominance was vital for the survival of the empire.

Besides being conscious of indigenous regional assertions Shah Jahan was always wary of foreigners who sought trade concessions and dabbled in local politics. Jahangir had granted them trade permits on the promise of payment of an annual tribute to the Mughals. Gradually they became close to the anti-Mughal Magh rulers and supplied them with arms and ammunition. Some of them indulged in piracy and illegal slave trade as well. During his rebellion Shah Jahan had noted that the Portuguese merchants of Bengal were quite aggressive. They had looted his ships and even kidnapped two female attendants of Mumtaz Mahal. In 1629 they looted a village near Dacca and perhaps even molested some noble women. In 1632 an internal quarrel amongst two of their influential merchants gave an opportunity to the Mughal governor of Dacca to initiate action them. Although some of the merchants feared the Mughal intervention and wanted to resolve the matter amicably, others were overconfident and wanted to test their arms. Eventually Hugli was occupied by the imperialists and Portuguese power in the area was liquidated. This crack-down establishes Shah Jahan's clarity about eliminating unwarranted authority of foreign traders. He almost seemed to have a premonition about the eventual growth of their power.

Tribes of the north-west were kept under check. The recurrent rumours of Dawar Bakhsh and Baisunghar's survival ensured a constant vigil on that front. In 1622 Imam Quli the ruler of Samarqand had offered Jahangir help for the recovery of Qandhar from Shah Abbas I the ruler of Persia. Anyway the succession drama after Jahangir's death emboldened his impudent brother Nazr Muhammad; the ruler of Balkh. In May 1628 Nazr Muhammad besieged Kabul, but failed to accomplish anything. However he returned with renewed forces after a couple of weeks. Lashkar Khan who had been appointed as the Mughal governor of Kabul was still on his way. He immediately geared up to defend his place of posting. In 1628 Mahabat Khan was also dispatched to help him. However Nazr Muhammad retreated in August 1628, before Mahabat Khan's arrival. Shah Jahan extended generous alms and aid to the residents of Kabul to secure their good will. He ordered the occupation of the Astrakhanid outposts of Bamiyan to warn Nazr Muhammad and at the same time continued to maintain cordial relations with Imam Quli despite his brother's audacity. In the following three years Nazr Muhammad was toned down. In February 1639 Shah Jahan visited Kabul. The speculation that perhaps he was there to explore the feasibility of an invasion of Transoxiana sent the local bigwigs into a tizzy. Anyway his uneventful departure in August 1639 relieved them. It so happened that in the following months Imam Quli was blinded by a disease. Now Nazr Muhammad coveted his brother's crown. He deputed his son Abdul Aziz for the usurpation of his brother's crown. Nazr Muhammad was so notorious for his ill temper that his son couldn't gather enough support from the nobles for this move. Finally after much bribery and threats the Khutba was read in Nazr Muhammad's name in October 1641. Like a typically villainous brother Nazr Muhammad literally threw the blind Imam Quli out of his dominions. Not content with this he even requested the Shah of Persia to ignore his brother's pleas for help. Unmoved by the advice of a proven traitor the Shah did help Imam Quli in his journey to Arabia. Meanwhile Abdul Aziz proclaimed his independence at Bokhara. After the Khutba was read in his name in April 1645 he occupied Samarqand as well. Nazr Muhammad received even greater ungratefulness than what he had shown to his patron. This father-son fall out gave Shah Jahan an opportunity to exploit the situation in his favour. He began preparations for it from March 1645 itself. Nazr Muhammad asked for Shah Jahan's help in January 1646. He readily agreed. In fact he was waiting to be asked. A chance to set foot in north-western politics with at least one major party on his side wasn't an opportunity he would have missed. Murad was sent to Badakshan on the pretext of a peace-keeping mission. The greatest commanders of the empire accompanied him. The strategy and tactics to be used were planned by Shah Jahan personally. An army divided into seven sections, started in early February of 1646 for Kabul. It was a crisp plan of brisk marches and quick occupation of Badakshan. Despite unanticipated delays the Mughals did manage to take Badakshan in June 1646. Murad was instructed to be gentle with Nazr Muhammad. Perhaps he was actually supposed to help him recover Samarqand from Abdul

Aziz. This way the Mughals would have shifted Nazr Muhammad to Samarqand and occupied Balkh as well. The locals were aided generously to facilitate the acceptance of Mughal authority. Finally by July 1646 the Mughals actually occupied Balkh as well, without providing any alternative refuge for Nazr Muhammad. The latter fled to Mashhad via Merv and Khurasan and left for Isfahan from there. Indeed he had fallen into a pit deeper than the one that he had dug for his brother. By September Mughal coins were issued from the local mints to make it known that they had come to stay.

The occupation of Balkh and Badakshan was a pride-worthy achievement for Shah Jahan. He hoped to occupy Bokhara and Samarqand as well. But his fanciful plans were interrupted when Murad sought permission to come back to Hindustan. The prince even turned down the offer of viceroyalty of Transoxiana after the conquest of Bokhara and Samarqand. Perhaps he had read the *Tuzuk-iBaburi* and knew that the Samarqand promise had a strange quality of remaining unfulfilled. Shah Jahan was in a fix. A number of senior commanders were posted in this area. Promotion of any one of them would have caused resentment to the others. In fact, like Murad they too wanted to return home. It was almost the completion of a circle. Men in Babur's army didn't wish to stay in Hindustan and men in Shah Jahan's army didn't wish to stay outside Hindustan. Anyway, true to his diplomatic finesse, even in the middle of this chaos Shah Jahan sent Jan Nisar Khan as an ambassador to the court of Shah Abbas II of Persia to congratulate the latter on his accession and relate his version of the developments in the north-west. Later Mir Aziz was sent with an explanation to Nazr Muhammad as well. Shah Jahan asserted that neither he nor Murad had any intention of troubling Nazr Muhammad. They wished to stabilize the situation in Balkh and help in the recovery of Bukhara and Samarqand from Abdul Aziz. Their officer Rustam Khan's entry into the fort of Balkh while Nazr was residing there was an on the spot decision of the concerned officer. It was a paradox that Nazr Muhammad was not offered the restoration of Balkh to him, instead he was asked that where could Shah Jahan have his family escorted. Shah Jahan moved as cautiously as he could, covering every angle of the field. However certain factors were beyond his control. The Mughals had to be constantly vigilant on the Oxus side, north of the areas that they had occupied. Fluidity and fickleness of tribal politics could never be frozen by any agreements. Uzbegs' rule was more acceptable to the locals rather than the Mughals'. A prince of pure Timurid blood may have had some appeal for them. But Mughals were known to be Hindustanis; a mixture of Mongol, Timurid and Rajput genes. When Babur had found it so very difficult to thrive in these regions what could poor Murad do? Perhaps years and years of power and prestige made Shah Jahan forget that Babur had dropped his mission Farghana-Samarqand for a reason. And he had dropped it for good. He was quite clear that Hindustan was going to be his home, forever. Kabul and Qandhar were to be its gateways and that was it. Eventually Shah Jahan realized that he had reached a dead-end: Weather was too cold, terrain was difficult and unfamiliar, Uzbeg raids at Mughal outposts were uncontainable and local production was too little to sustain the mammoth Mughal forces. The situation was like a ruptured vein. If bandaged at one place, it would bleed at another. Perhaps if the Mughals had retreated from Balkh, they might have been able to still retain Badakshan. But retreat would have felt like the belated acceptance of a defeat—which had been misunderstood as a victory. Like the scion of a well-established business house that begins to look beyond business, Shah Jahan became adamant about making this victory real irrespective of the costs involved.

In 1647 Aurangzeb was deputed to re-boot the Mughal position in the north-west. He was expected to keep all the commanders stringed together and focussed. The preparations for Balkh-Badakshan take-II were beyond grand. The prince started from Kabul in April 1647 and reached Balkh in late May. Abdul Aziz knew that if he didn't step-up to free Balkh from the Mughals, he would soon lose Bokhara and Samarqand to them. Perhaps if he had realized this while Murad was in command he could have saved a lot of effort, because

now he was dealing with the most stubborn of the Mughal princes—
stubborn and unrelenting, even to the extent of being self-destructive.
Aurangzeb was a strangely quiet man; someone who would walk over
smouldering coal to reach his goal-without a sigh. The tribal allies of
Abdul Aziz were hardly a match for his disciplined army. Gradually
their enthusiasm to beat the Mughals faded. The Turkomans who
had earlier promised to assist him sold their horses for whatever price
they got and crossed over to the other side of Oxus to save their
lives. Thus Aziz opened negotiations with Aurangzeb. He requested
that his brother Subhan Quli may be assigned Bokhara. Aurangzeb
referred the proposal to his father. In the interim cease fire, Abdul
Aziz retired to Samarqand. Meanwhile Nazr Muhammad started from
Persia to recover his lost kingdom. Some tribes joined him in the hope
of making quick gains. On reaching near Balkh he realized that this
war had become much bigger than what it was when he had fled.
Both Abdul Aziz and Aurangzeb were trying their best to stick to
their ground and compared to these egoistic enthusiasts he was only
an old and unpopular ex-ruler. The major worries on the Mughal
side were related to the approaching winters and the unavailability
of resources to sustain their massive army. Shah Jahan had to take
a quick call on this front. He realised that holding on to Balkh was
almost impossible. To make a graceful exit from there he ordered
Aurangzeb to take a formal submission from Nazr Muhammad and
then hand over the place to him. Shah Jahan pushed Subhan Quli
out of these tracts because Abdul Aziz and Quli would have united
against him. On the other hand Nazr Muhammad was alone and
far more vulnerable. Before October 1647 Aurangzeb left Balkh.
Although this was the best political choice anyone could make, it
didn't work out that favourably for Shah Jahan. Eventually Nazr
Muhammad had to abdicate in favour of his sons. They constantly
raided his territories. This deadened Nazr Muhammad's confidence
in himself–and that of his subjects' in him. He died in 1650, on
his way to Medina.

These campaigns had cost the Mughal exchequer a bomb. And

the gains were practically zero. Although successful at conquest they had failed at consolidation. Losses were incurred due to unfavourable climatic conditions, disinclination of their soldiery to stay put, traditional Uzbeg-Chaghtai rivalries and unstable local-tribal allies. Losses of the Transoxiana experiment were multiplied by the subsequent occupation of Qandhar by the Persian ruler Shah Abbas II. The latter conveyed his appreciation for Shah Jahan's 'generosity' of returning Nazr Muhammad's domains to him. In the same strain he requested the return of Qandhar to himself. Both, Shah Abbas and Shah Jahan knew that such a demand had no meaning. It was like mocking Mughal proclamations and pretensions of generosity and righteousness. Military preparations for the occupation of Qandhar were begun in Persia. Abbas reached in the vicinity of Qandhar in December 1648. In response Shah Jahan also wanted to be in Kabul close to the expected scene of action. But his officers convinced him that his presence wasn't required. They were wrong. In early February 1649, the Persian army occupied Qandhar. Almost after a month, Aurangzeb and Saadullah Khan arrived at Kabul in March 1649. Shah Jahan wisely instructed Aurangzeb to start action before the Persians could consolidate their position. The Mughals ensured that their enemies didn't get anything from the standing harvest. By May 1649 the Mughal siege of Qandhar had become stiflingly tight. The first major confrontation known as the battle of Shah Mir was won by them. But it was far from conclusive. The siege continued. The Mughals wanted to drain out water from the moat around the fort. However the execution of that plan required time. The onset of winters meant being timed out. In early September 1649 the Mughal retreat began. It was indeed wiser to leave and return prepared rather than being killed by the climate. Shah Jahan and Aurangzeb noted the loopholes in their last campaign: The Persian artillery was superior; the local production wasn't enough to support the Mughal army for an indefinite time and Qandhar definitely wasn't an easy nut to crack. However Shah Jahan wasn't used to giving up a chase and complimenting that, Aurangzeb was a man possessed by perseverance. The Baadshah arrived at Kabul in early April 1652. Aurangzeb and Sadullah Khan resumed their responsibilities. Despite all the preparations Qandhar–take II, wasn't any better than the take I. Helpless before the defending Persian artillery, Shah Jahan decided to call the siege off. Although Aurangzeb requested for permission to continue the blockade, he was turned down. On 7th July 1652 the Mughals receded and in about a month Aurangzeb joined his father at Kabul.

Subsequently Shah Jahan sanctioned a third attempt for Qandhar's recovery with Dara in command. This time the preparations were many notches above the last times. The artillery had been upgraded. The presence of personnel was unprecedented: 107 Mansabdars, 5,000 ahadis, 2,000 footmen, 6,000 snappers, 500 miners and 500 water carriers were in attendance. Dara was assigned Kabul and Multan and his ranks were raised to 30,000 zat and 20,000 sawar. Shah Jahan himself accompanied the prince up to Lahore. Dara started from here in early February 1653 and reached Qandhar in April. By late May Qandhar was besieged yet again. Bribes and threats: Methods beyond military measures were tried to crack the Persian line of defence. Nothing worked. The Mughals stared at the fort in utter despair. Rustam Khan captured and lost Bist and Zamindawar. Rumours that the Persians would run out of provisions soon didn't allow the Mughals to backtrack. The siege dragged on. With time the price of hope became higher. The Mughal stock of ammunitions diminished to a dangerous low. Finally Dara retreated from Qandhar in late September. He reached Lahore via Multan after about two months. Shah Jahan dropped the idea of pursuing Qandhar's possession. Mughal-Persian friendship which dated back to Babur's times received a set-back.

Although internal, tributary and intra-tributary tussles had taken quite a bit of Shah Jahan's time and energy he was still hopeful about effective expansion of the Empire in terms of lands or resources. Mughal efforts to occupy Deccan were not new but Ahmednagar's anti-Mughal stand throughout Khan-i Jahan Lodi's rebellion brought it under severe firing. This alarmed Bijapur and Golconda; the other two big kingdoms of Deccan. Ahmednagar was like a buffer between them and the Mughals. The Maratha mercenaries became a much sought after lot, since all the big warring parties needed their assistance. Bijapur was prepared to confront the Mughals to save Ahmednagar for the sake of its own safety. However internal conspiracies within the Ahmednagar changed the game in favour of the Mughals. Its ruler Murtaza Nizam Shah on his wife's advice, appointed her brother Fath Khan as the commander-in-chief. Muqarrab Khan who was thus replaced, felt let down and joined the Mughals. He was welcomed with open arms. Fath Khan proved to be a bad choice. He had Murtaza Nizam Shah killed and opened negotiations with the Mughals. A ten-year-old prince, Husaain Nizam Shah, was put on the throne as a puppet ruler. Meanwhile Shahji; a Maratha chieftain occupied Junnar. His power was on the rise. His loyalties shifted with his interests. Bijapur was searching for a way to revive Ahmednagar. In the middle of all this political and military chaos Mumtaz Mahal died in child birth (7–8 June 1631). The royal family was stationed at Burhanpur. It was a huge-huge personal loss for Shah Jahan. Perhaps he might have stayed there longer to settle the Ahmednagar issue once and for all, but he didn't. He just couldn't. Thus a quick settlement was drawn which brought immediate and temporary gains. Fath Khan was asked to surrender all the jewels and elephants of the royal family. Shah Jahan's name was added in the Khutba of Ahmednagar's mosques. In March 1632 he left Burhanpur. On Asaf Khan's refusal to be the viceroy of Deccan, this appointment went to Mahabat Khan. Until the latter's arrival in June 1633, his son Khan-e Zaman held the precarious position. Although the Deccan was a very slippery ground Mahabat Khan managed to send Fath Khan and Hussain Nizam Shah to the court by September 1633. The latter was imprisoned at Gwalior. Fath Khan was not only pardoned but he also received lands and allowances. Still Shah Jahan was dissatisfied with the overall situation in Deccan. Mahabat Khan struggled with both; in-house and external politics to prove his worth. He was worthy, but the field was

just too uneven for a successful run. In October 1634 he died trying
to dig the Mughal feet in the Deccan grounds. His death impacted
the political and military scenario almost immediately. Nizam Shahi
(Ahmednagar) and Adil Shahi (Bijapur) officers dared to grab lands
from the Mughals. Shahji became a mainstream player in the tug
of war for Ahmednagar. Shah Jahan reacted sharply by posting his
best men at this site. He himself left for Deccan in September 1635.
Indeed his arrival made a difference. Shahji backed off and Adil Shah
of Bijapur bended for negotiations. After a fresh settlement of the
area Shah Jahan appointed Aurangzeb as its viceroy. The terms of the
1636 treaties with Bijapur and Golconda were the most favourable
that the Mughals had so far negotiated. They received exorbitant
sums of money as war indemnity from the Deccani states. Shah
Jahan was recognized as their overlord. Boundaries of Bijapur were
redrawn keeping Mughal interests in view. Bijapur and Golconda
lost the right to formulate their foreign policies without Mughal
approval. In fact Aurangzeb actually stationed his representative at
Golconda between 1636 and 1642. Both of them had to cooperate
with the Mughals to fight Maratha insurgencies. They had to send
a fixed sum as a tribute to the Mughal sovereign.

Amongst all the princes Aurangzeb got the roughest ground
to practice his skills: both military and political. He stayed in the
Deccan for eight years–relentlessly fighting for the Mughal Empire—
trying to impress his father. Shah Jahan was indeed impressed because
Aurangzeb got a second run as the viceroy. However the financial
support that he might have expected from the centre was not
forthcoming. Thus he reformed the agrarian sector of his region.
His Diwan, Murshid Quli Khan helped him. Intermediaries were
appointed to facilitate a win-win situation for payers, collectors and
appropriators of taxes. Loans on low rates of interest were advanced
to farmers. Production of cash crops was encouraged. Villages were
rehabilitated. His efforts paid off. His dependence on the Imperial
funds decreased. Production was stabilized and tax collection became
steady. Aurangzeb was determined to make a success out of whatever

posting he had. He visits to Agra were rare. Once in 1637 he went there for his own marriage to Dilras Banu Begum and then in 1644 to see his sister Jahan Ara who had got burnt in an accident. He was doing the groundwork for the eventual addition of Bijapur and Golconda to the Mughal Empire.

When Aurangzeb returned as Deccan's viceroy in 1653 he tightened the noose around Golconda. Even in the 1636 treaty the terms were harsher for Golconda. Now the prince demanded arrears from it since the exchange rate between Huns and Rupiya had changed. Also, he challenged Golconda's occupation of the Cranatic. In November 1655 Mir Jumla; an extremely rich diamond merchant of Golconda was arrested by its ruler, Abdullah Qutub Shah. Obviously Jumla was an extremely shrewd man. He knew that the only person who could help him against his own king was the Mughal viceroy Aurangzeb. The latter immediately secured an imperial order for the release of Jumla and helped him and his family escape from Golconda. On Aurangzeb's recommendation Shah Jahan granted a mansab of 5,000 zat and 5,000 sawar to Jumla immediately. Muhammad Adil Shah's (ruler of Bijapur) death in 1656 weakened Bijapur and Aurangzeb felt that now he could easily annex these kingdoms. He sought Shah Jahan's permission to invade Golconda. He felt that instead of repeated efforts for collection of tributes, these regions should be annexed so that a steady policy could be formulated to manage the surplus production and tax appropriation in the area. His advance in these regions was fired with anticipation and enthusiasm. Accordingly, in anticipation of his father's permission to invade Golconda, Aurangzeb dispatched his son Muhammad to that front. Abdullah Qutub Shah locked himself in the fort of Golconda. He knew that Shah Jahan's grandson was only an executor, not a decision maker. That had to be either Aurangzeb or Shah Jahan himself. Aurangzeb had arrived in the vicinity of the siege around early February of 1656 and seemed determined to annex Golconda. So Qutub Shah intensified efforts to approach the Baadshah himself for relief. Meanwhile the terms that Aurangzeb dictated him were extremely favourable for the Mughals in general and for Aurangzeb in particular. If these terms were actually implemented Aurangzeb's accomplishments would have out shone his father's successes on this front. And of course his brothers' proficiency would not have measured up to even half of his. This may have worried the heir apparent Dara. After all, the Mughals didn't really have any law of succession. Shah Jahan was Jahangir's third son and he had outpaced two elder brothers to wear the Mughal crown. Thus it is possible that Dara influenced his father to order Aurangzeb to retreat from Golconda. Whether Shah Jahan acted so for personal or political reasons remains a mystery. Anyway a *farman* directing Aurangzeb to abandon a front nearing victory left the prince embarrassed and angry. He suspected that Dara held the remote control of Deccan without any hands-on experience of the region. Besides major funds for the war had been generated by Aurangzeb and he had his own logistics. Shah Jahan's abrupt intervention made no sense to him. However on March 30th 1656, Aurangzeb stepped back from Golconda. He felt let down; as if years of loyalty and hard work meant nothing to his father.

Perhaps Shah Jahan's perspective lay in his political insight. He would rather be content with a tribute which he received without undertaking administrative responsibilities that came with annexation. Besides, he too had first-hand experience of the Deccan politics. He knew that investment in consolidating lands which were wrecked by unending local feuds was just not worth it. Looking at the larger, long term interest of his empire, Shah Jahan thought it prudent to use the threat of annexation as a tool of extracting money from these kingdoms. He calculated that actual annexation might suck his resources into a deficit enterprise. It seems that Dara and Aurangzeb looked at the situation from their own perspectives. Dara felt that Aurangzeb would monopolize their father's attention and affection by procuring him new toys: Bijapur and Golconda. While Aurangzeb's anger was like that of a child who is enraged when a hazardous toy is abruptly snatched from it by his parent.

In December 1656 an epidemic broke out in Delhi. Shah Jahan

stayed at Garh Mukteshwar during this period. He came back on 31st January 1657 and soon after left for Mukhlispur-Faizabad. A grand *durbar* was held there. He was back in Delhi in April 1657. On 7th September 1657 he fell ill. The sickness began with strangury and constipation. Then his lower limbs swelled and palate and tongue became extremely dry. Eventually fever set in. It made him so weak that he stopped appearing for the Jharokha Darshan. His absence from public view triggered off all kinds of rumours including those of his death. At this point Shah Jahan might have had a lot of worries but choosing a successor wasn't one of them. He had chosen long ago. To avoid intra-princes competition and blood lust he had projected his eldest son Dara Shukoh Buland Iqbal as the heir designate. Dara was permitted to sit near the royal throne. He often interceded with Shah Jahan on behalf of various petitioners. Shah Jahan felt that the law of primogeniture did have some disadvantages but at least it saved parents from the misfortune of seeing their children fight each other. Thus he had roughly divided the empire between his sons: Dara's *jagirs* lay in the heart of the empire—Allahabad, Punjab etc. The others held *jagirs* in the radiating masses of lands: Shah Shuja—Bengal, Aurangzeb—Deccan and Murad Bakhsh—Gujarat. It was assumed that the brothers would stand by each other in case of any trouble and thus the entire structure of the empire would remain safe. All these sons were born of the same mother. Dara was expected to be like what Babur or Humayun were to their brothers. Although Shah Jahan was prepared to give it all to Dara but one wonders whether Dara was prepared enough to take and mange it. He was well-trained to handle courtly grandness and glamour but untrained for survival in the grim and grind of wars. However none of his brothers could match up to his intellectualism and sophistication. He researched philosophy and mysticism. The books authored by him are ample proof of his mystical and secular inclinations: *Safinat-ul Auliya, Sakinat-ul Auliya, Risala-i Haqnuma, Hasanaat-ul Aarifin, Majma-ul Bahrain, Sirr-i Akbar* etc. The latter is a translation of about fifty chapters of the *Upanishads*. If Akbar had commissioned the study of the religion of the majority of his subjects, Dara himself undertook that study. He felt that Hinduism didn't negate monotheism. Thus he saw Hinduism and Islam as parallel lines. Though they couldn't meet, but they could easily run next to each other. According to him the Vedic verses which spoke of monotheism had been explained in the *Upanishads*. He is also known to have translated the *Bhagvat Gita* into Persian. Besides these confirmed writings, some other rare works on Sufism have been attributed to him by contemporaries, like the *Risaala-i Ma' arif, Nadir-ul Nikaat* etc. He was a poet as well. A collection of his poems is called *Iksir-i Aazam*. The *Murakka* (introduction) of *Nigaristan-i Munir*, an Album that contains the finest paintings and calligraphic treasures from Persia, Central Asia and Hindustan was written by Dara. He had presented this work to his beloved wife Nadira Banu. In fact he was himself an accomplished calligraphist. His jottings in both Naskh and Nastaliq are examples of marvellous hand-writing. A reading of his works clearly reveals his respect for all systems of belief. Dara might have been an ideal emperor for an empire which was full of diversities of religion, language and culture. However he lacked military and administrative experience. His *jagirs* were managed by agents while he lived with Shah Jahan at the central court. He seemed to be the most loved child—like a priceless gem that Shah Jahan didn't wish to part with. Little did the Baadshah know that his gem was too delicate; susceptible to break the moment it fell off the grooves that held it in place.

Shah Jahan was sure that he had provided enough for his children to live peacefully with each other. The fact that any of these princes could feel that the world is not enough for him remained unanticipated. Shah Shuja had held the rich province of Bengal for 17 years. He was an intelligent man and an astute business entrepreneur. Aurangzeb had a quiet tongue and a sharp sword. Ever since he was 16 he had been on field duties at different fronts. As the viceroy of Deccan he had been in the centre of endless strife. Murad the youngest one held Malwa and Gujarat. The latter was a great production and business centre of the empire. Shah Jahan's open favouritism had made Shah Shuja and Aurangzeb jealous of Dara. After the second Qandhar campaign the marriage of Aurangzeb's son, Sultan Muhammad was fixed with Shah Shuja's daughter and Aurangzeb's daughter was to be married with Zain-ul Abedin, Shuja's son. These matches brought the brothers closer. When Shah Jahan's health showed no sign of improvement for a week he formally declared Dara to be his successor. The moment the news of his illness reached his sons, Shuja, Aurangzeb and Murad began communicating with each other. They feared Dara's influence at the centre. It was agreed that they would meet near Agra if a need arose. Meanwhile Dara arrested the *Wakils* (agents) of the princes at the court. This blocked their access to authentic news and developments. Their insecurity pushed them to be initially defensive and eventually offensive. Senior officers were recalled from various fronts. Dara's favourites were immediately promoted to positions of responsibility. Bihar was added to Dara's *jagirs* and rumours ran that Malwa and Berar would be taken from Murad and Aurangzeb respectively to be given to Dara. In early October, Murad murdered the Mughal Diwan Ali Naqi Khan and confiscated his wealth besides looting Surat. It seems that he was collecting funds to handle any eventuality arising out of his father's death. By mid of November 1657 Shah Jahan had recovered substantially. But it was beyond anyone's power to stop the circulation of rumours of his death. Amidst all this confusion Murad declared his independence on 5th December 1657. The khutba was read and the coins struck in his name. This step had almost collided with an imperial order which directed him to leave Gujarat and move to Berar. The latter place was in Aurangzeb's possession. The order was clearly a trick to divide these brothers. But it misfired. Now they came closer to each other and the belief that Dara was their common enemy was reinforced. Following Murad's example Shuja also declared his independence. He took the title of NasiruddinTimur III. By January 1658 he had reached Benaras on his way to Agra. Aurangzeb was quiet. Indeed he was most calm, cool, cunning and cautious. Shah Jahan's daughters had teamed up with different brothers: Jahan Ara-Dara Shukoh, Roshan Ara-Aurangzeb and Gauhar Ara-Murad. Jai Singh and Diler Khan Ruhela were dispatched to combat Shuja. Dara's son Sulaiman Shukoh was the commander-in chief of the imperial force. The two armies confronted each other at Bahadurpur near Benaras on 14th February 1658. Shuja was defeated. On Shah Jahan's orders Sulaiman Shukoh concluded a treaty with Shuja according to which the latter was to get Orissa, Bengal and territories in Bihar. Two armies were dispatched from the centre under the command of Qasim Khan and Jaswant Singh to tackle Murad and Aurangzeb respectively. Asaf Khan's son Shaista Khan was known to be close to Aurangzeb, so he was recalled from Malwa. Aurangzeb arrested Mir Jumla in Deccan and moved northwards. In fact this arrest was just a drama. In reality Mir Jumla was one of the greatest loyalists of Aurangzeb. The fake arrest saved him from reporting at the centre at such a critical hour. He could keep the Deccan provinces safe for Aurangzeb in case if he lost everything in the north and returned southward. Aurangzeb started on 20th March 1658. By 15th April he had caught up with Murad. Meanwhile Qasim Khan and Jaswant Singh also reached Ujjain and waited there to watch the princes' next action. Aurangzeb advised these commanders to give up the idea of a confrontation. That however was hardly an option for officers who were on duty in the middle of this royal showdown. Thus a battle was fought. Popular as the battle of Dharmat (1658), it marked the beginning of the end of Shah Jahan's glorious reign. The imperialists were defeated. Jaswant Singh went back to Jodhpur with his contingents and the rest of the army staggered back to Agra in utter shame. This development generated a lot of positive publicity for Aurangzeb. Although he had not declared his independence but he was acting the most independent. Dara's confidence in the efficiency of the imperial army was indeed misplaced. The extent of disillusionment can be gauged by the fact that without even waiting for the outcome of Daharmat, Shah Jahan had left the city on 11th April to avoid the discomfort of its hot weather. He was at Bilochpur when the news of the defeat reached him. Dara sent him desperate messages to return. Obviously he returned post haste. The quantum of Aurangzeb's audacity and anger had hit him like a bolt. Unfortunately for him this was just the trailer of what was to follow. It was clear that it wasn't Murad but Aurangzeb who was in-charge of their combined armies. The rebellious brothers reached Gwalior and crossed the river Chambal with the help of Champat Rai, the Bundela chieftain. After Aurangzeb had crossed the Chambal, hoping that emotions might work where force had failed Jahan Ara wrote to him. Her letter was a sensitive appeal to humanism and Quranic injunctions about unquestioned and complete respect for one's parents. It was delivered by Muhammad Faruq, her Mir Bakshi. She wrote as follows:

> Praise be to God that His Majesty the Sahib Qiran Sani is free from all bodily infirmities, which afflict the human frame, and is devoting all his attention to the improvement of the condition of his subjects and the maintenance of peace in the Empire. Being just and equitable by nature, he does not like anyone, particularly any of his sons to commit any acts of disturbance among the people and disorder in the country. Now that he is striving with all his power to dispel the confusion caused by his illness, the prevailing conflicts and dissentions which are ruinous and destructive to the country and the people will be a source of great pain and grief to him, in particular the unbecoming and improper action of this wise and prudent brother (Aurangzeb), who is endowed with an elegant disposition, a noble mind, amiable manners and mildness of temper. It is with the solicitude of his felicity that these few words are being written, so that he may be advised to keep himself away from objectionable and evil deeds. If your advance is with the object of creating disturbance and making war, you should yourself judge how impolite it is on your part to encounter and draw the sword against your own father, in whose obedience lies the pleasure of God and His Prophet and to shed the blood of innocent people. The result of such action will be nothing but disgrace and ultimate ruin. Even

if your expedition is due to antagonism to Prince Dara Shukoh it cannot be approved by the principle of wisdom, for according to Islamic law and convention the elder brother has the status of a father. His Majesty holds the same view. In short, the strife and hostile contest began by this sagacious and high minded brother (Aurangzeb), who is esteemed for his laudable demeanour, praiseworthy behaviour and generous disposition, and who has always endeavoured to fulfil the wishes of the holy and blessed Emperor, is not to be appreciated in any way or by any person; for the life of a few days in this transitory and evil world and its deceitful and deceptive enjoyments are no compensation for eternal infamy and misfortune. Don't, don't for the virtuous, do not behave like this.[103]

Aurangzeb was too obsessed with the presumption that his father discriminated against him. No spiritual-emotional logic could have penetrated the mental-block created by the recent Golconda episode. His mind was wired to feel insecure and he believed that if he didn't displace Shah Jahan he would be destroyed. There is no way of knowing whether Dara actually dominated his father or was it just an impression that was created by Shah Jahan's love for this son. It is even possible that Shah Jahan's enemies exaggerated the notion of his being dictated by the eldest prince. Given that even a relatively easy going monarch like Jahangir was also not bossed over by any of his sons, it is very unlikely that an energetic ruler like Shah Jahan could be controlled by a son who wasn't half as competent or experienced as him. Some sources claim that Shah Jahan too had written to Aurangzeb but he replied that the Baadshah's decision regarding sudden closure of the Golconda campaign could have cost him (Aurangzeb) his life. Berar was snatched away from him for no reason. And then an army was sent by the imperial centre against him. Were these not reasons enough for him to lose faith in his

---

[103]Cf. *Jahan Ara Begum A Biographical Study(1614–1681)*,NausheenJaffery, Idarah-iAdabiyatDilli, Delhi, 2011, p. 40–41.

father's sense of impartiality towards his children? He challenged Dara to combat him directly and to leave the court if he failed. He implied that Dara was threatening his life in the name of 'serving' their father and thus he would rather 'serve' his father himself.

Now a direct contest between Dara and his brothers was imminent. Dara's strategy was poor. In fact he had naively believed that his brothers would not be able to cross the Chambal. Once they did, his plan-A failed and he had no plan-B. Instead of taking advantage of his enemies' fatigue he delayed launching an offensive attack. The victorious army of the Bahadurgarh battle had been directed to join Dara at the very earliest. However it never made it in time. It is speculated that Jai Singh, who held a grudge against Dara delayed its movement. He wanted Dara to be defeated. Eventually the rival brothers came face to face at Samugarh, just ten miles from Agra. Their armies numbered over a lakh of men and in terms of region, ethnicity and religion they were equally balanced. The data in this regard nullifies the assumption that Dara was the Hindus' candidate and Aurangzeb represented the Muslims. Religion had no role to play in the war of succession amongst the sons of Shah Jahan. All that mattered to anyone was money, politics and power. However the balance of organization and enthusiasm tilted in favour of the rebels. The fateful battle began on 8th of June 1658. The Rajputs on either side fought bravely. Dara's inexperience came into play when on the advice of a noble; Khalilullah Khan he dismounted from his elephant. On horseback he wasn't visible to his soldiers and was thus presumed to be dead. Desertions began the moment it was noticed that his elephant's howdah was vacant. Aurangzeb's victory was made easier. He won; hands down. Dara fled to Agra and from there to Delhi. Ashamed of his miserable defeat, he didn't even show his face to his doting father. Vanquished by his own flesh and blood, Shah Jahan's spirit was clobbered. When his sons led the opposite sides of the warring armies there was no way that he could win. His defeat was absolutely certain. Since Aurangzeb wasn't ready for any dialogue with his father supporting Dara further was the only option he was left with. He ordered that the treasures of Delhi should be given to the defeated prince. It surely was painful to see his wealth being used by his children to destroy each other. After a short period of rest Aurangzeb and Murad marched towards Agra. By now Murad had realized that after all, his father wasn't as ill as he had imagined and perhaps the whole idea of declaring independence was a mistake. He wished to be a Baadshah but not by dethroning his own father. Thus he wrote to Shah Jahan that during his illness Dara Bhai Jiyu had perhaps acted on his own initiative and taken measures detrimental to his younger brothers' interests. Since the correspondence between the younger princes and their agents at the court had been stopped by Dara they didn't get the correct updates about the Baadshah's health. He explained that he had taken the Malwa route due to scarcity of water at Ajmer. He joined Aurangzeb because the latter was also coming to pay respects to their father. Jaswant Singh had blocked their way and thus had to be fought. Murad's correspondence conveyed that he had genuinely believed that his father was dead. As these sons neared Agra, Shah Jahan hoped to meet them and sort the matter out. To drag Murad away from falling into any kind of emotional trap in favour of Shah Jahan, Aurangzeb rubbed it in that he does not want any share in the empire. Further he reminded Murad that they could never be sure of their father's forgiveness. They could well be treated the way Khusroe was treated by Jahangir. On the other hand Aurangzeb promised to serve him all his life, like a selfless and loyal officer.

The rebel brothers reached near Agra on 12th June. Their tents were pitched in Nur-Manzil; a favourite garden of Jahangir. Officers rushed to swear allegiance to the Baadshah to be, who, according to Aurangzeb was Murad. Jai Singh was amongst them. Everyone felt that something was amiss because this gesture of Aurangzeb was too noble to be true. Of course they could never have imagined, in their wildest dreams the ignobility that this drama was going to stage. Shah Jahan was still hopeful of finding some solution. After all the people involved were his children. They had been raised under his personal care and attention. He loved all of them. He recalled the anxiety that he and Mumtaz Mahal shared when Dara and Aurangzeb were in Nur Jahan's custody. After Jahangir's death the very first worry for his supporters was the freedom of these princes. His first offer to Aurangzeb was a promise of complete pardon, and the reconfirmation of his status in the Deccan. It was rejected. He then asked Aurangzeb to visit him personally for negotiations. He reasoned that he had been so very ill and had literally got a second lease of life, the least that a son could do was to pay him a visit. Together with this letter Shah Jahan sent him jewels and a priceless family heirloom; a sword called Alamgir (Seizer of the Universe). To Shah Jahan's utter disappointment as a monarch and moreover as a parent, Aurangzeb replied that he would come only at an auspicious hour. And it was understood that such an hour would come only after a change of guards at the fort. This practically meant taking over the empire. Sadly disappointed, Shah Jahan now ordered preparations to withstand a siege. However Aurangzeb didn't even allow him the pleasure of an honourable combat. He cut off the water supply to the fort of Agra. There was no way to stop desertions from a waterless citadel. Left with no personnel to defend his home, Shah Jahan surrendered.

After this Jahan Ara went to meet Aurangzeb with Shah Jahan's proposal to partition the empire. She was treated respectfully but still felt insulted. It was promised that Aurangzeb would be declared as the heir of the entire empire. His brothers would be the viceroys: Dara-Punjab and the north-western tracts, Shah Shuja-Bengal, Murad-Gujarat and Aurangzeb's son Muazzam was to get Deccan. Shah Jahan had thought calmly like a strategist. He was ready to settle for the next best solution since the preferred first choice had failed. The unofficial division of the empire was also already in place. If Dara had failed to handle a crisis that arose out of his illness he was ready to change his heir to the central throne. He knew that Aurangzeb was suspicious, adamant and whimsical and that he would need much more of emotional intelligence to rule successfully, but he was ready to give him a chance. Earlier he had given a chance to Dara despite the latter's poor military skills. So the once arrogant Baadshah, kept his ego aside to save people and things most important to him. But his sons weren't ready to give him a chance. It was impossible to convince Aurangzeb that he actually meant to implement the proposal. On the other hand nobles of the rebels' camp feared that they would not be spared in any a case. So they didn't want any patch-up between the father and sons. Shaista Khan, Shaikh Mir and Khalilullah Khan were prominent in this category. Finally when spies reported that Shah Jahan was in touch with Dara, Aurangzeb decided against meeting his father. It was a decision that he would never change, ever. It seemed that the curse that Jahangir had given to Shah Jahan during the latter's rebellion had come true after all:

> When with a father like me, who in truth am his ostensible creator, and in my own lifetime have raised him to the great dignity of Sultanship, and denied him nothing, he acts in this manner, I appeal to the justice of Allah that He may never regard him with favour.[104]

Thus on 19th June 1658 Shah Jahan's reign ended with the classic tragedy of a parent being betrayed by his children.

Almost for the half of his reign Shah Jahan had stayed out of the capital-on the move to settle one matter or another. His itinerary's major stop overs were something like this: Agra-Gwalior-Burhanpur-Agra-Kashmir-Lahore-Agra-Delhi-Deccan-Ujjain-Mandu-Ajmer-Agra-Kabul-Lahore-Kashmir-Lahore-Agra-Ajmer-Agra-Kashmir-Kabul-Kashmir-Kabul-Lahore-Delhi-Agra-Delhi-Kabul-Kashmir-Lahore-Delhi-Agra-Ajmer-Delhi-Ajmer-Fathpur-Agra-Delhi-GadhMukteshwar-Faizabad-Delhi-Agra-Bilochpur-Agra. In the middle of all this movement he had attended to many personal commitments with exemplary care and gentleness.

The episode that displayed the most vulnerable side of the powerful Baadshah was the death of Mumtaz Mahal. In the June of 1631, she had gone into labour for the fourteenth time. It was

---

[104]Cf. *Tuzuk-i Jahangiri*, p. 256.

perhaps a pre-mature birth that went wrong. Shah Jahan rushed to the harem as soon as Jahan Ara's desperate message of her mother's condition reached him. Precious gems were distributed as sadaqa to solicit divine help by the poor princess. It goes without saying that medical caregivers were helpless and so was Shah Jahan. He surely would have felt that his title: King of the World doesn't really mean anything much. He watched in utter despair as Mumtaz Mahal sunk into slumber in the lap of death. The scene of her death and the Baadshah's immediate reaction to it would have been a very private affair. However the deep mysterious sadness that it involved inspired authors to recreate it in all kinds of imagined details. Some versions claimed that the unborn baby (later named Gauhar Ara) had cried inside her mother's womb; a rarest of the rare circumstance that forecasts the mother's immediate death. In the last few moments of her life, Mumtaz Mahal made Shah Jahan promise two things: Firstly that he would not seek any more sons from any woman. Birth of more princes would jeopardize the life of her sons who were anyway enough to run the dynasty and the empire. Secondly, Shah Jahan should make a mausoleum for her, which should be beautiful enough to leave the world mesmerized. One version attributes the conception of the design of the Taj Mahal to a mystic Bilul Shah. It says that during a hunt the royal couple happened to see a saint in a cemetery. He was shaping a building with clay. The mud structure caught their fancy and they asked him to sell the design to them. After receiving a price much more than the one that he had quoted, the mystic directed an imperial architect to gaze at his armpit and thus the design with all the detailing was transferred to the man's mind. This architect made a model of the Taj Mahal which was approved by Mumtaz Mahal herself.[105] Anyway, if promises were made, Shah Jahan kept them. It is unlikely that the request for the mausoleum would have come from Mumtaz Mahal. From wherever the idea came, it helped Shah Jahan cope with the loss of his beloved wife of 19

---

[105] *Shah-Jahan The Rise And Fall of The Mughal Emperor*, Fergus Nicoll, Penguin Books, Gurgaon, 2018 (reprint), p. 229–230 & 237.

years. The mammoth expense that he incurred for making the Taj Mahal would have given him the solace that his partner and co-sharer from the days of distress got at least a fraction from his opulence.

Mumtaz Mahal was buried the day she died. The river Tapti flowed between the Burhanpur citadel and her burial site at Zeinabad. The place was close enough to be visible to Shah Jahan from his quarters, but it took him nine days to summon the courage to visit her grave. Thereafter he went there every Friday and offered the *Fatiha* (first chapter of the Quran; popularly recited at graves) and prayers. He took almost two years to deal with this loss. Suffering from classic signs of depression, he lost interest in all the things that he used to enjoy earlier: wearing gorgeous jewels and clothes. Music, dance and other acts of festivities didn't entertain him. Earlier he was quite conscious about his looks but now his hair turned grey and he didn't seem to care. Around mid December of 1631, Mumtaz Mahal's body was carefully exhumed and sent to Agra. Her son Shah Shuja was assigned this heavy task. The late queen's personal physician Alimuddin Wazir Khan and her trusted assistant Sati al NisaKhanam accompanied the retinue. The body was quietly and quickly reburied as soon as it reached Agra. A semblance of the original place of her burial at Burhanpur was maintained. Like Tapti the river Yamuna flowed by the mausoleum and it was visible from the Emperor's residence at the Agra citadel. The blinding whiteness of the Taj Mahal was its most massive asset. Even if it didn't have precious stones from Yemen, Persia, Sri Lanka, Egypt and Hindustan twinkling on its surface, it would still have remained mesmeric. Talking about what the Taj Mahal cost, it would suffice to say that Shah Jahan actually issued blank cheques to the people involved in its construction. On record it costed about five million rupees. Finally after twelve years of unceasing efforts of an army of imaginative, creative, out-of-box thinkers and executors: ranging from the Baadshah to the architect, Ustad Ahmad-Nadir-ul Asr (rarest wonder of the age), supervisors Murshid Makramat Khan and Mir Abdul Karim to the pettiest, masons, stone cutters, rubble breakers and carriers, the Taj Mahal was ready—magical, unearthly and heavenly!

Many buildings added to the pages of the architectural autobiography of Shah Jahan, but like the Taj Mahal, the Red Fort and the Jama Masjid of Delhi constituted major chapters. The Delhi buildings were a part of a much bigger scheme, that of a capital city–a city that was truly cosmopolitan. It accommodated all sorts of business houses and governmental offices. Agra was too crammed to be redone in a planned manner, besides, Delhi had already hosted great monarchs and mystics. Therefore Shah Jahan shifted his capital. This was a master move to legitimize the Mughal rule in the psychological context of Hindustan's history. Besides, it made an addition to the many firsts that his reign had witnessed. He personally supervised this project as well. The interior of the fort had majestic buildings like the Diwan-i Aaam (the court room) and the Diwan-i Khas (hall for exclusive high profile meetings). Despite the collection of a large number of people in the court, pin drop silence was observed on the Baadshah's arrival. Officials used gold and silver sticks to maintain discipline in the public hall.[106] The Aramgaah (Baadshah's personal chamber) and the Imtiyaz Mahal (main palace of the royalty) were heavily guarded. The Mahtab Bagh and the Hayat Bakhsh Bagh were two major gardens within the fort. It also had one of the most luxurious *hammams* (bath) of its times. Equipped with provision of water of a suitable temperature it had facilities like a sauna and a perfumery as well. The wall that encircled the fort had two major gateways: Lahori Darwaza and the Dilli/Akbarabadi Darwaza. As the names suggest the former led towards the highway to Lahore and the latter to the old cities of Delhi and Agra. The nearby old fort of Salimgarh was connected with the new one. Smaller gateways opened to the river front as well. An octagonal square with a large pool in its centre became a hub of great activity in Shahjahanabad. Commissioned by Jahan Ara, it was called Chandini Chowk due to

[106]*Chandni Chowk The Mughal City of Old Delhi*, Swapna Liddle, Speaking Tiger Publishing Pvt. Ltd., New Delhi, 2017, p. 29.

the reflection of moonlight in its pond.[107] Besides Jahan Ara other ladies of the royal family like Roshan Ara Begum, Fatehpuri Begum, Sarhindi Begum and Akbarabadi Begum also spent out of their private incomes to add buildings and mosques to the city. Foundation of the Jama Masjid was laid in 1650 and its completion took six years. An elevated spot was chosen for its construction. It turned out to be the largest mosque ever commissioned in Hindustan. Shah Jahan's first formal visit to the mosque was in July 1656 to offer Eid-ul Fitr prayers. In comparison with defence, grandness had been a more serious concern for the Baadshah. Obviously then, none could have even dreamt of violating the Great Mughals' home: Shahjahanabad-Delhi.

The *TakhtMurassa* (Ornamented Throne)/*Takht-iTaaus* (Peacock Throne) was yet another marker of Shah Jahan's love for achieving the unachievable. Made with approximately 2,600 pounds of solid gold, its dimensions were: depth-eight feet, width-seven feet, length fourteen feet. It was studded with the most exquisite gems of the Mughal treasury. The throne was commissioned because Shah Jahan felt that the massive royal collection of gems was of no use if nobody got to relish their beauty. Studded in a throne they could be put on display. The *Takht Murassa* was more expensive than even the Taj Mahal. It earned the title of Be-badal Khan (Irreplaceable/Peerless) for its chief designer Said Gilani.

Shah Jahan's affection for his immediate family was an intense affair. His daughter Jahan Ara was a great favourite of her father. She held grand titles like Sahibal-uz-Zamani (Mistress of the age) and was Begum Sahib etc. On 26th March 1644, while she was on her way to the harem, her fine muslin dress caught fire from a lamp. Two of her maids who had tried to save her died after a few days of the accident due to their injuries. Shah Jahan tried every possible thing to relieve his child of sickness and pain. One thousand silver coins were placed under her pillow each night and given away to the poor in the morning. On 19th April 1644, which was her birthday

---

[107]Ibid., p. 15.

thousands of gold and silver coins were distributed amongst the poor for invoking God's mercy for her recovery. Many doctors were employed to treat her. Shah Jahan himself stayed with her at Dara Shukoh's residence for a few days so that she could have a change of place. Finally after her recovery, a grand function was held on 5th November 1644 to celebrate. The festivities lasted for eight days. Lakhs of rupees were distributed amongst the poor. The presents that the Emperor gave to the princess were selected by him with great care: pearls worth five lakhs, a tiara of a huge diamond, gems studded gold chains etc. More over the princess was granted the territory of Surat. Its revenue was approximately three crore dams equivalent to almost seven lakhs and fifty thousand rupees per annum. The duties collected at its port were also hers. These amounted to another crore of dams annually. Presents were distributed to all members of the family and officers as well.

Typical of any affectionate father, Shah Jahan took personal interest in the arrangement of his sons' weddings. In 1633 Dara's marriage with Nadira Banu, daughter of the late prince Parvez was a very grand affair. The match had been fixed by Mumtaz Mahal but since the wedding happened after her death, Jahan Ara undertook the responsibility of making all the arrangements. On this occasion the ban over court sponsored music and dance which had been in place since Mumtaz Mahal's death was lifted. In February 1633 Shah Shuja was married to the daughter of Rustam Mirza Safavi. In 1634 Aurangzeb was married to the daughter of Shah Nawaz Safavi and in 1638 Murad Bakhsh was married to a younger daughter of the same noble. Shah Jahan himself tied the *sehra* on the forehead of his sons when they dressed up for their marriages. The sehras were made of the best of pearls available in the Empire. He personally inspected the details of the preparations: jewels and clothes of the brides, gifts for her family members, fixation of the *meher* (brides' money), draft of the *nikaah* document and the fees of the people involved in it. Alms were distributed with exemplary generosity. When Aurangzeb had arrived from Deccan for his marriage he was stationed at the Nur Manzil garden. Shah Jahan had deputed officers to receive and honour him. He made extremely elaborate arrangements for the wedding of his grandson: Dara Shukoh's son, Sulaiman Shukoh with the granddaughter of Raja Gaj Singh of Marwar in 1654. The bride was also the grandniece of Raja Jai Singh of Amer. A timber fort lit with lamps served as a venue and the skyline was lit with unbelievable fireworks. He made it a point to thank and reward people who helped in the preparations and execution of these marriages. Jahan Ara was the most prominent amongst them. In fact she stood by her father and helped him not only through good times but also the testing ones.

For over seven years Shah Jahan lived in a tiny corner of the huge Mughal Empire. Agra had proven to be a place of extremes for him. It had welcomed him as a victor and also saw him off as a defeated warrior. But he fought bravely. Living through the violent-untimely deaths of sons and grandsons and losing every material thing that he held dear would have been quite an unbearable torture. It was topped up by physical discomfort from Agra's extreme heat and cold. Mir Sayyid Muhammad of Kannauj helped him tide through with his discourses on the Quran. They reminded Shah Jahan that after all there is a court where he could appeal against whoever had wronged him: The court of the true 'Shah Jahan'-King of the World-God. He planned and prepared for making that appeal. The day for that meeting came on 22nd January 1666. His last illness was triggered off by dysentery and fever. Medications weren't of much use. He gave away whatever little he now possessed. The most precious thing that he could give to his caretakers and loyalists was the reassurance that after he was gone Aurangzeb would accept them as his own people gracefully. His assessment of Aurangzeb in at least this regard was correct. Even though penniless at the time of his death, Shah Jahan still gave a parting gift to the Mughal Emperor Aurangzeb: Forgiveness.[108] Aurangzeb however was not ready to receive it. He didn't come from Shahjahanabad for his father's funeral. Therefore the aristocrats also

---

[108]*History of ShahJahan of Dihli*, Banarsi Prasad Saxena, Central Book Depot, Allahabad, 1973, p. 343.

refrained from participating in it. Mir Sayyid Muhammad, Hoshdar Khan; superintendent of Agra fort and Qazi Muhammad Qurban; Chief judge of the city were the only people around.

After the completion of the Taj Mahal, Shah Jahan's visits to it had been very few—only two major occasions of it are recorded. Aurangzeb wrote a letter to Shah Jahan in 1652 when he visited the Taj Mahal on his way to Deccan. The prince felt that his mother's tomb had been struck by some kind of an evil eye. He requested his father to boost the maintenance of the complex:

> The buildings of this shrine enclosure of holy foundation are still firm and strong...except that the dome over the fragrant sepulchre leaks during the rainy season in two places on the north side. Likewise the four arched portals, several of the recessed alcoves on the second storey, the four small domes... have become dampened. The marble-covered terrace of the large dome has leaked in two or three places during this past rainy season and has been repaired. Let us see what happens in the coming rainy season...
>
> Long–living protector! An extraordinary evil eye has struck this model of lofty buildings. If the rays of your august attention fall on the remedy to ward it off, it will be proper...
>
> May the world illuminating Sun of the Caliphate (Shah Jahan) remain shinig upon the heads of the people of the world.[109]

Perhaps the evil eye that Aurangzeb referred to had not struck just the Taj Mahal, it had also struck the Mughal family or perhaps it had touched the Mughal Empire itself. The unmarked Black twin of the Taj Mahal that Shah Jahan had hoped to construct on the opposite bank of Yamuna has become a metaphor for impossibilities. After all everything is not possible. Not even for the kings of the world.

❈

---

[109]Cf. *Shah-Jahan*, p. 254

SEVEN

ABUL MUZAFFAR MUHIUDDIN MUHAMMAD AURANGZEB BAHADUR ALAMGIR BAADSHAH GHAZI

1658–1707

'Alas, My life has been wasted in vain! This world has passed away in labour and faith has gone out of my hand. I have angered God, and people are not pleased. I have wasted a quantity of water and fodder......Do not be the architect of your own (self), lest you should ruin the houses. Be a ruin, so that upon you may be raised a new high structure.'

—AURANGZEB[110]

On the 3rd of November 1618 Mumtaz Mahal gave birth to a son at Dohad. Jahangir prayed that this grandson may be fortunate and may he bring luck to the Mughal dynasty. He named him Aurangzeb: The Throne Adorner.

According to the post-March 1626 negotiations between Jahangir and Shah Jahan, Dara and Aurangzeb were sent to Agra as a guarantee of their father's future good behaviour. This derailed the formal education of these princes. Anyway Mir Muhammad Hashim al-Gilani and his team tutored Aurangzeb. His command over Hindustani, Chaghtai Turki, Persian and Arabic was quite impressive.

Aurangzeb was a stubborn child who loved taking risks. In May 1633, Shah Jahan had ordered an elephant fight between Sudhakar (tusked) and Surat Sundar (tusk-less). The princes were at a spot

---

[110]Cf. *Structure of Politics Under Aurangzeb*, Azizuddin Husain, Kanishka, New Delhi, 2002, p. 180.

close to the site of combat. Suddenly Surat Sundar disengaged and ran past them. Sudhakar followed him, but deviated and charged towards Aurangzeb. The latter reacted with a calm mind and brisk reflexes. He struck the elephant's head with his spear and got off his horse before it was tossed by the animal's tusk. Dara rode off to safety. Shuja tried to hit it with his lance, but his horse was bewildered by a *charkhi* (fire-wheels) and it threw him off. Raja Jai Singh's horse sensed danger and refused to enter the arena. Even fireworks failed to distract Sudhakar. Luckily Surat Sundar returned and Sudhakar was reengaged. Aurangzeb was rewarded by Shah Jahan with 500 gold coins, the elephant Sudhakar and gifts worth Rs. 2 lakh for his courage. Comparisons were drawn between that day and the day when Shah Jahan had bravely killed a lion to save his father's life. The *Ahkam-i-Alamgiri* adds that after the episode Aurangzeb was admonished by Itimad Khan; an influential eunuch, for his leisurely pace while going to meet his anxious father. Responding with his signature coolness he said: 'If the elephant were here I might have walked faster.'[111] Although happy to be appreciated, he maintained that even if he had died fighting the elephant, it would not have been a reflection on his valor because death can catch up with the bravest of the brave.

In 1634 he was appointed as a Mansabdar of 10,000 zat and 4,000 sawar. In approximately twenty years of serving his father he rarely neglected his duties. But he felt that his dedication remained unappreciated.

Aurangzeb and Dara had a history of mistrust. The latter had invited his father and brothers to his newly constructed mansion at Agra in 1644. They were to be seated in a cool underground chamber. Interestingly it had a single entry-exit doorway. Aurangzeb didn't step in the room and sat at its entrance like a guard. On Dara's cue Shah Jahan asked him to come in. Instead of doing that he left the place after sometime without seeking his father's permission. Shah Jahan was miffed. He debarred Aurangzeb from royal audience for seven

---

[111]*Anecdotes of Aurangzeb* (translation of *Ahkam I Alamgiri*), Jadunath Sarkar, M. C. Sarkar & Sons Ltd., Calcutta, 1949, pp. 30–31.

months. His *jagir* and rank were also suspended. He was reinstated on Jahan Ara's intercession. He had explained that all the male members of the royal family had been gathered in one room with a single door and he feared that Dara could get them all easily assassinated.

While Dara was a learned scholar inclined towards mysticism Aurangzeb was more humble and far more practical. Anyway neither of them were religious recluses. In 1653 on his way to the Deccan, Aurangzeb stopped at Burhanpur to meet his maternal aunt Saliha Banu. At her place he saw a beautiful girl standing under a tree, holding a branch in her hand, she hummed melodiously. He fell in love with her instantly and fainted by the impact of it. This was Hira Bai–Zainabadi. Saliha Banu ran barefoot to attend to him. Offerings of *tassadduq* (propitiatory alms) and *qurbani* (sacrifice of animals for protection or thanksgiving) began. Aurangzeb was bombarded with questions about the blackout. Finally he asked Saliha whether she would help him if he told her about his ailment. The poor woman promised that she would die to see him cured.[112] Then he confessed his love. Unfortunately Saliha's husband also fancied the same girl. She feared that he would rather like to see her dead than transferred to Aurangzeb. The latter then sent Murshid Quli Khan to negotiate with his uncle. Finally Hira Bai was sent to Aurangzeb in exchange for Chattar Bai from his harem. When news of this affair reached the royal court at Agra, Dara remarked sarcastically, 'See the piety and abstinence of this hypocritical knave! He has gone to the dogs for the sake of a wench of his aunt's household.'[113] Known for his teetotalism, Aurangzeb was ready to have wine when Hira Bai pestered him to have it to prove his love for her. However she stopped him saying that her purpose was to test his love and not to embitter his mouth with the wicked and unlucky liquor.[114] Hira Bai's sudden death depressed Aurangzeb so much that he deliberately went for risky hunting expeditions. However many years later when he had

---

[112]Ibid, p. 37
[113]Ibid., p. 40.
[114]Ibid., p. 39.

embraced personal religiosity in a big way he thanked God for her early death; believing that it saved him from sins.

Aurangzeb was not born with the kind of rigid personal orthodoxy that he died with. In 1661 he had written a letter to Yogi Mahant Anand Nath to write a prescription for some ailment. He had also given him land grants in Punjab.[115] Bahktawar Khan reported that Aurangzeb had expert knowledge of the art of music. The musical treatise of Faqirullah; *Rag Darpan* dated 1666 listed the names of his favourite singers and instrumentalists.[116] In early 1690s, Chandraman had dedicated his Persian poetic retelling of the *Ramayan*; *Nargisistan* (Narcissus Garden) to Aurangzeb.[117] Princess Zebunnisa; his daughter, was a poet with the pen name *Makhfi* (the hidden one). Like Akbar, Aurangzeb also had evolved. While Akbar shifted towards liberality and Aurangzeb famously/infamously relocated to orthodoxy. Relocation notwithstanding we find that in 1705 Amar Singh dedicated his Persian prose *Ramayana*; *Amar Prakash* to him.[118] Usurers had the audacity to charge interest even from the Emperor despite the fact that Islam strictly prohibits usury. Aurangzeb paid them without a hitch. Astrologers had access to him even as late as 1707. In fact just days before his death, a court astrologer had recommended the donation of an elephant and a diamond to cure his fever.[119] The advice was rejected but an astrologer was consulted, that itself is a big deal. Mughal grants to the temples of Mathura and Vrindavan continued even during his reign. The shift in case of Aurangzeb was more personal than professional. It seemed to be driven by remorse activated by the cruel deaths of his family members.

Shah Jahan's deposition on 19th of June 1658 was not followed by the coronation of either Murad or Aurangzeb. The confused nobles

---

[115]*Aurangzeb The Man And The Myth*, Audrey Truschke, Penguin, Gurgaon, 2017, p. 53.
[116]Ibid.
[117]Ibid.
[118]Ibid., p. 60
[119]Ibid.

paid respects to both.[120] With haversacks stuffed with Shah Jahan's treasures, the brothers hurried off in pursuit of Dara who was at Lahore and had raised a fresh army. His supporters feared that without Shah Jahan as his shield Dara would not be able to withstand Aurangzeb's shrewd politicking. Indeed they were right. But at least Dara wasn't cheated by Aurangzeb. Their enmity was open. The trusting brother who was ignobly betrayed by him was Murad Bakhsh.

Murad's well-wishers suspected that Aurangzeb would sell him out at the first opportunity. So they advised him to stay in the vicinity of Agra-Delhi and depute Aurangzeb to pursue Dara. Shahbaz, Murad's faithful eunuch literally begged him to see sense, but the prince was blinded by the honeyed-screen of oaths of allegiance sworn with the Quran as a witness. Eventually Murad honoured the sanctity of the text, but died. Aurangzeb dishonoured the promises invoked on the Quran but lived to read and write it over and over again like a possessed man.

The brothers pitched camps at Mathura, near Agra. Murad was under the spell of Aurangzeb's sugar-dripping gestures and words.[121] On 15th June Aurangzeb invited him to his camp on the pretext of crowning him as the emperor. All props of the drama were in place: new tents, jewels, entertainers, caparisoned elephants and horses, lavish dishes, musicians and dancing women were waiting for Murad's arrival. But behind curtains secret confabulations with nods and metaphors were on.[122] Until the last moment Murad's loyalists tried to stop him. One of them said: 'I rejoice greatly, but what is the necessity of your highness to go to another's house, when with greater security you can carry it (crowning) out in your own.'[123] He even guided the prince's horse to take a U-turn. When Murad turned the horse again the officer shouted out: 'Your Majesty is on your way

---

[120] *Travels in the Mughal Empire*, Francois Bernier, V. A. Smith (ed.), Low Price Publications, Delhi, 1989 (reprint) p. 65.

[121] Niccolao Manucci, *Storia Do Mogor*, William Irvine (translation & notes), Editions Indian, Calcutta, 1965,p. 285.

[122] Ibid.

[123] Ibid., p. 287.

to prison'.[124] Blinded by vanity Murad touched his sword and said 'None is braver that I am'[125] and galloped away. At the entrance of Aurangzeb's camp, the Qazi who was leaving the place crossed him and murmured: 'With your feet you have come!'[126] The man was amazed to see how people walk themselves into end-game situations. Aurangzeb embraced Murad affectionately. He waved off flies and wiped off sweat and dust from his face. Rose water and perfumes, dances and songs enlivened the day and the best wines from Shiraz and Kabul were served. After the banquet Murad was escorted to a resting chamber and a beautiful woman was sent to him. Shahbaz dissuaded the prince from engaging with any enchantress at this critical hour. He kneaded his master's feet to put him off to sleep. His own eyes were wide open; searching for the danger that he sensed but couldn't see. While Murad slumbered, Shahbaz was kidnapped, strangulated and buried. The prince's personal arms were removed with the help of Aurangzeb's five years old grandson Sultan Azam. Murad woke up when his limbs were being tied with fretters. Aurangzeb gave him a dressing down: 'Oh shame and infamy! Thou a king and yet possessing so little discretion? What will the world say of thee, and even of me? Let this drunken man be bound hand and foot and removed there within to sleep away his shame.'[127] 'What a shame! What a disgrace is this! For a king as you are to be so debauched as to make himself thus drunk? Let this base man, this drunkard be bound hands and feet and shut up to digest his wine.'[128] Murad's officers were bribed or bullied into believing that they should not waste their life for a cause which was already beyond their help. Murad also would never have liked them to die in vain.[129]

Initially Murad abused Aurangzeb and his own bad luck. He

---

[124]Ibid.

[125]Ibid.

[126]Ibid.

[127]*Travels in the Mughal Empire*, p. 68.

[128]*Indian Travels of Jean De Thevenot & Gemelli Careri*, Surendranath Sen (ed.), National Archives of India, New Delhi, 1949, p. 227.

[129]*Storia Do Mogor*, p. 305.

muttered to himself: 'This is the word and oath sworn to me on the Quran.'[130] At dusk two elephants with *Ambaris* (covered litter) exited from the eastern and the western gates of his makeshift prison. They headed for Delhi and Agra respectively. Nobody knew that which one of them carried the unfortunate prince. This strategy was employed to divide Murad's loyalist just in case they thought of helping him escape. His absence in either of them was also a possibility. The intervening night gave time to Aurangzeb to settle other matters before the news of Murad's arrest became public. The cries of 'Long live Aurangzeb!' proved to Shah Jahan that after all, his third son was not an underachiever.

Murad was brought to Delhi and imprisoned in the fort of Salimgarh/Nurgarh; built by Salim Shah Sur in 1546. On Aurangzeb's orders his face was uncovered when he entered Delhi: 'his face dejected; wearing a blue turban, ill put on; behind him an executioner with a naked sword in his hand, ready upon any attempt at rescue to cut off his head. Daler Khan followed at the rear of Murad Bakhsh upon another elephant, an arrow ready in his bow—it seemed as if some criminal were being borne to the scaffold.'[131] Murad was to be fed poppy-water every day until he lost his mental and physical faculties.

Aurangzeb's first coronation took place on 31st July 1658 in the Shalimar garden at Delhi. Though he sat on the *Takht-i Taaus*; the Khutba was not read in his name. It was a deliberate omission to avoid the maze of Islamic judicial takes on his usurpation. According to the *Shariat* his assumption of power was indeed illegal and the *Qazi-ul Quzat* (priest & chief justice of Islamic courts) pointed that out. However the *Qazi-i Lashkar* (Chief Qazi of the royal army) Abdul Wahab argued that since Shah Jahan was too weak Aurangzeb's accession was legal. Abdul Wahab was promptly promoted as the Qazi-ul Quzat and Aurangzeb was crowned again on 15th June 1659. This time the Khutba had his name. Although the local ulema didn't question this manipulation, the Grand Sherif of Mecca refused to

---

[130]Ibid., p. 304.
[131]Ibid., p. 306

accept the money sent by him in the early part of his reign. Shah Sulaiman the Safavid ruler taunted him over his title 'Alamgir' (world-seizer) which was inspired by a sword gifted to him by Shah Jahan. In a scathing letter he accused Aurangzeb of mistakenly announcing his seizure of the world (alam-giri) when he had merely seized his father (pidar–giri).[132]

Dara moved from Lahore to Multan. He was his own van-guard; pre-exposed and unattended. He survived on dry bread and dirty water. The bare and hot ground was his bed. He was trying his best. Some strategists advised him to reach Kabul and seek help from the local governor. Seeking assistance from the Uzbegs and Persians was also an option. However he chose to station himself at Bhakkar, in Sindh. Although it was a strategically located military stronghold but currently it didn't offer any opportunities of military alliances. It was such an obvious misjudgment that Aurangzeb dropped the idea of personally coming to fight him. Instead he left for Agra to bulldoze his father's stratagems and deputed Mir Baba to tackle his brother. It was rumored that on Shah Jahan's behest Rajput rajas would undo the coup. Also Sulaiman Shukoh and Shuja could capture Agra or negotiate with Shah Jahan. On his way from Lahore to Agra Aurangzeb met Jai Singh. He addressed the raja with exemplary humility: 'My Lord Raja! My Lord Father! I cannot describe how impatiently I have waited to see you. The war is at an end: Dara is ruined and wanders alone. I have sent Mir Baba after the fugitive. He cannot possibly escape.'[133]He placed his own pearls around the Raja's neck and said: 'My army is fatigued. I am anxious. You should immediately proceed to Lahore, for I am apprehensive of some movement there. I appoint you governor of that city and commit all things to your hands. I shall soon join you; but before we part. I cannot avoid returning my thanks for your manner of disposing of Soliman Chekouh (Sulaiman Shukoh)'.[134] Thus Jai Singh joined Aurangzeb's camp.

---

[132]*Aurangzeb The Man*, p. 44.

[133]*Travels in the Mughal Empire*, p. 72.

[134]Ibid., p. 73.

Meanwhile Dara proceeded towards Ahmedabad. Its governor, Shahnawaz Khan was Aurangzeb's father-in-law. One of his daughters was married to Murad Bakhsh as well. He was an easygoing man. Though terrified of this dangerous war he reluctantly opened the gates of the city to welcome Dara. Now Aurangzeb had three tasks at hand: keeping his control over Shah Jahan and Agra intact, reversing Shuja's fast moving forces and dislodging Dara from Ahmedabad. Since Shuja had already reached near Allahabad and was moving towards Agra at a breakneck speed Aurangzeb prioritized his ruination. A battle was fought at Khajwa, about 30 miles west of Fatehpur Haswa. Aurangzeb's loyal officer Mir Jumla was in command of his army. Shuja fought valorously living up to his name which meant 'King of the brave'. Meanwhile Raja Jaswant Singh's men looted the rear of Aurangzeb's army. Adding to this loss the guide of Aurangzeb's elephant was killed in the middle of the combat. To remain seated on an unguided elephant was dangerous and getting off it could have conveyed the impression that he was dead. In this puzzlement Mir Jumla shouted 'Qaim-Qaim' (stand fast/hold on) to Aurangzeb[135] and instructed soldiers to cover him. The battle had almost concluded in Shuja's favour when his officer Alivardi Khan advised him to dismount from his elephant and ride a horse to bring the combat to a speedy close. Desertions began the moment his soldiers noticed that his elephant's howdah was empty. They presumed that he was dead.[136] Later Shuja killed Aliwardi Khan with his own hands.[137] A less popular version of the battle claims that Shuja's elephant had fallen into a dry well. Anyway it was an anticlimax, he lost.

Jaswant Singh was greatly flustered by Aurangzeb's victory and he immediately left for Agra. Interestingly the rumors at Agra were that Aurangzeb had been defeated and the victor Shuja was approaching the city. Shaista Khan the governor of Agra was so terrified by this tittle-tattle that he even contemplated suicide. Aurangzeb feared that

[135]Ibid., p. 76.
[136]Ibid., p. 77
[137]Storia *Do Mogor*, p. 315.

Jaswant Singh could use this confusion to design a revolution to reinstate Shah Jahan. Murtaza Khan, the weak commander of the Agra fort was no match for the Raja. But the latter didn't try any such thing. He assessed that the current political storm was too turbulent for Shah Jahan to withstand. Three of his sons were raging around. The victor was sure to dislodge the old emperor again. The gamble of investing in a sinking ship was not Jaswant Singh's idea of prudence.

Aurangzeb would have personally ensured Shuja's liquidation, but uncertainties at Agra didn't allow him that privilege. So Mir Jumla was deputed for this task. Aurangzeb's son Sultan Muhammad was the co-commander of this army. It was speculated that Aurangzeb posted two of his best men far from Agra because he felt threatened by their competence. He suspected that Muhammad's recent successes had made him over confident and contemptuous of parental control. Muhammad's favourite wife who was the daughter of the king of Golconda and Mir Jumla's son Muhammad Amir Khan were left with Aurangzeb. They were hostages retained as collateral to check these commanders from straying.

It was unsafe for Shuja to travel back to Bengal. So he reached Munger and waited for the arrival of the imperial army. Mir Jumla divided his forces. The more powerful section was sent to block the Prince's entry in Raj Mahal; his stronghold in Bengal. This was bad news for Shuja. His current design of defense wasn't strong enough to sustain any prolonged assault. Once the attacks began the entrenchments made by his men couldn't withstand the onslaught. So he fled towards Dacca. Much of his expensive baggage and artillery were lost in the run. Mir Jumla didn't follow him immediately. He feared that Shuja had feigned retreat to ambush his forces. Heavy rains set in before the imperial army started the chase. Thus between June and September 1659 Shuja rebuilt his resources. He also formed an alliance with the Portuguese.[138]

Meanwhile Muhammad's relationship with Mir Jumla soured. Subordination to a noble humiliated him. He foolishly complained

---

[138]Ibid., p. 319.

to his father regarding this issue. The prince had probably forgotten that Aurangzeb was also a competent son who had just displaced and imprisoned his own father. There was no way that he would give the command of a huge army to a competent prince of the royal blood. Driven to desperation Muhammad switched sides. He reached Shuja's stronghold and declared his loyalty for his uncle.[139] A request was made for the revival of the proposal of his marriage with Shuja's daughter Mah Khanum. Though this was an embarrassing set-back for Aurangzeb he had travelled too far on the road of ambition to go back to collect one of his lost children. Shuja treated Muhammad with his signature generosity but didn't trust him much. In a mockup wedding a girl posing as Mah Khanum was married to him and he wasn't given a big force to command. To create a misunderstanding between the two, Mir Jumla wrote a fake congratulatory letter to Muhammad and expressed happiness over the success of their plan to deceive Shuja. In the letter the prince was advised to wait for an opportune moment to fulfill the promise that he had made to Aurangzeb. This letter was meant for Shuja and was delivered to him with such trickery that he felt that he had found it accidentally. Poor Muhammad lost all credibility. Shuja threw him out. With nowhere to go he returned to Mir Jumla. Subsequently he was arrested and dispatched to Delhi in a heavily guarded palanquin. When he tried to escape he was bound with silver fetters of the type used for Murad. Aurangzeb's faithful eunuch escorted him to the prison of Gwalior fort. He was lodged in an isolated cell where all human communication was prohibited. He was not allowed even a barber. Mocking his resignation, Aurangzeb inquired whether his wife should be sent to keep him company.'[140] He was administered *posto* (opium water) until his death in 1676 in the fort of Salimgarh. He was buried in the complex of Humayun's tomb. The treatment which he got from Aurangzeb in retribution for his revolt was a warning for his brothers. Aurangzeb said to his son Muazzam: 'The art of

[139]Ibid., p. 219.
[140]Ibid., p. 338.

reigning is so delicate, that a king's jealousy should be awakened by his very shadow. Be wise or a fate similar to that which has befallen your brother awaits you. Indulge not in fatal delusion that Aurangzeb may be treated by his children as was Jahangir by his son, Shah Jahan; or that like the latter (Shah Jahan) he (Aurangzeb) will permit the scepter to fall from his hand.'[141] Aurangzeb's punishments of transgressive cruelty were in violation of Islamic laws. At this point, beyond rituals he had little to do with lived Islam.

Shuja's resources were drained. Inconclusive battles had exhausted his men. Confident that Mir Jumla would handle him, Aurangzeb turned towards Dara. Jaswant Singh had invited Dara to move towards the road to Agra. It was planned that the Rajputs would join him. Dara enthusiastically started from Ahmedabad and reached Ajmer. However Jai Singh influenced Jaswant Singh to change his mind. He wrote to the latter: 'What can be your inducement to endeavor to sustain the falling fortunes of this prince (Dara)? Perseverance in such an undertaking must inevitably bring ruin upon you and your family, without advancing the interests of the wretched Dara. From Aurangzeb you will never obtain forgiveness. I, who am also a Raja, conjure you to spare the blood of the Rajputs. Do not buoy yourself up with the hope of driving the other rajas to your party; for I have means to counteract any such attempt. This is a business which concerns all the Hindus, and you cannot be permitted to kindle a flame that would soon rage throughout the kingdom, and which no effort might be able to extinguish. If, on the other hand, you leave Dara to his own resources, Aurangzeb will bury all the past in oblivion; will not reclaim the money you obtained at Khajuha, but will nominate you to the government of Gujarat. You can easily appreciate the advantage of ruling a province so contiguous to your own territories: there you will remain in perfect quiet and security and I hereby offer you my guarantee for the exact fulfillment of all I have mentioned.'[142] Seemingly Jai Singh had suggested a general

---

[141]Travels in *The Mughal Empire*, p. 84.
[142]Ibid., p. 86.

policy for the Rajput rajas. They were to flow with the tide during the succession crisis and then be loyal to the victor. Thus the army which Dara found waiting for him was that of Aurangzeb. He was in a fix. In this grim scenario his confidant; a double crossing trickster Shahnawaz Khan betrayed him. The level of treason was such that live cartridges were exchanged with blank ones. The battle began on the 12–13th March 1659, at Deora, about six miles south of Ajmer. Jai Singh was in command and he didn't want to insult any prince of the blood. Despite the risks involved he sent word to Dara to escape if he wanted to avoid arrest. Dara fled. Right through the way back to Ahmedabad, his lot was harassed by the villagers. When he was just a day's journey away from Ahmedabad, communication was received from the Governor that he wasn't welcome there anymore. Bernier, a doctor who was treating one of Dara's wives for Erysipelas; a serious bacterial infection, notes that sheets were tied to wheels of carriages as separators to guard the privacy of the ladies of his harem. They had run out of tents. The Governor's message was a breaking point: 'The shrieks of females drew tears from every eye. We (Bernier) were all overwhelmed with confusion and despair, gazing in speechless horror at each other, at a loss what plan to recommend and ignorant of the fate which perhaps awaited us from hour to hour. We observed Dara stepping out, more dead than alive, speaking now to one, then to another; stopping and consulting even the commonest soldier. He saw consternation depicted in every countenance, and felt assured that he should be left without a single follower; but what was to become of him? Wither must he go? To delay his departure was to accelerate his ruin.'[143] Subsequently Dara's forces were reduced to just 400–500 horsemen. Resources were at such a low that he couldn't even arrange for a horse, ox or camel to carry Bernier with him. Though probably he still had a couple of elephants loaded with gold and silver. Finally with the help of Kanji Koli; a notorious robber of the territory he sought shelter with the Raja of Kutch. Bernier remarks that perhaps Dara would have been luckier if he had not survived

---

[143]Ibid., p. 90.

this perilous march. But he did. He struggled through obstacles; each one of them and lived to see much worse. The Delhi-Ahmedabad route was littered with dead bodies of men, elephants, oxen, horses and camels; the wrecks of Dara's army.[144]

Initially Dara was well received at Kutch, but later perhaps due to Aurangzeb's pressure the Raja's attitude changed. Fearful of betrayal Dara fled from there as well. Meanwhile Mir Baba; in anticipation of Dara's arrival, besieged the fortress of Bhakkar. The defenders of the fortress had hoped that Dara would engage the imperial army from outside and they would defend the fort from inside. But Dara decided to migrate to Persia instead of fighting for Bhakkar. That also entailed great risks-hostile Afghans and rajas, dangerous jungles and water scarcity etc. Besides, his wife argued that she and her daughters would have to become slaves of the Persian monarch if Dara sought asylum there. Although, Humayun's wife Hamida Banu had stayed there with absolute dignity, Nadira Banu was apprehensive. In this state of indecision Dara was tempted to take refuge with Malik Jiwan son of Ayyub a Barozai Afghan. Dara had saved Jiwan's life thrice. He assumed that the man would be grateful to him. But Nadira and her children literally fell on his feet to stop him from trusting a rebel prone to notoriety, deceit and misdemeanor. However, Dara ignored their pleas. Bernier wrote: 'He (Dara) departed not withstanding every solicitation; and soon afforded an additional and melancholy proof that the wicked feel not the weight of obligation when their interest demands the sacrifice of their benefactors.'[145]

Within two or three days of Dara's arrival in Jiwan's territory, Nadira Banu died. It was the 6th of June 1659. He had married her when he was twenty and ever since then she had been his friend and beloved. Sulaiman Shukoh and Sipihr Shukoh were her sons. She loved Hindustan so much, that even in this tragically chaotic situation her last wish was to be buried here. Typical of the Mughal style of

---

[144]Ibid., p. 91–92.
[145]Ibid., p. 96

romance, Dara honoured her wish. In the custody of a loyalist Gul Muhammad, her body was sent to Lahore for burial.

Nadira was an influential member of the Mughal family. In the initial stages of the war of succession it was planned that Sipihr Shukoh would go to Sultanpur to oppose the van of Aurangzeb's army. She didn't want her child to be exposed to such a great danger. It was very difficult for Dara to convince her. However by then Jai Singh had arrived to reinforce Aurangzeb and it was too late to implement the proposal. Thus Sipihr Shukoh was recalled and he accompanied his parents, right through their perilous journey from Lahore to Multan, Sind, Kutch, and Gujarat. Four *nishans* issued by her have survived.[146] Most of them are addressed to Jai Singh, in response to his arzdashts (petitions). In 1652 she advised Jai Singh to join the troops of the Qandhar expedition as soon as possible. In the following years (1553–54) Jai Singh was deputed with Sulaiman Shukoh and Dara Shukoh on that front. In the beginning of the war of succession in 1657, Sulaiman Shukoh was dispatched against Shuja. Raja Jai Singh was to accompany him. On this occasion she directed him to collect rupees 50,000 from the imperial treasury. He was urged to make all efforts for victory. It was rumored that in the battle of Bahadurpur Jai Singh and his friend Diler Khan's efforts were lukewarm and that is why Shuja was not completely destroyed. Jai Singh was highly appreciated by Shah Jahan. Thus Nadira sent a *nishan* to Jai Singh in which she praised his sincerity. She assured him that he should entertain no fears in his mind on the score of rumors about his alleged disloyalty:

> Be it known to the best of the Rajas of the illustrious lineage, exemplar for the sincere servants of blessed character, leader of the zealous warriors, pillar of the devoted, sincere and faithful followers, Mirza Raja Jai Singh, exalted, privileged and comforted by the manifold and various bounties and favours of her Exalted

---

[146]S. I. A. Trimizi, Edicts from the Mughal Harem, Idara-I Adabiyat-i Dilli, New Delhi, 1979, p. xxvi.

Highness, that the *arzdasht* which he had transmitted to Her Highness expressing therein the sincerity of devotion, purity of purpose and firmness of faith, was perused by Her Highness and brought to the notice of His Majesty who went through it from the beginning to the end...if the selfish people misrepresented to His Majesty about him (Jai Singh), he hoped that His Majesty would not pay any heed or give credence to what they said and he had also made a request regarding the promotion of his sons. All these facts have come to the knowledge of His Majesty in details.... Trusting him to utmost His Majesty has honoured him with this high assignment and made him an advance guard of the army. Under the circumstances the devotion, reverence and respect of that noble, entitled to abundant favours, for this sublime court are not of such a degree as to allow any heed and credence to the words of the selfish. Who has the power and courage to give over and plunge himself in peril? It is proper for that noble of high rank not to entertain any fears in his mind on this score and not to worry at all about his sons and family in as much as they will be recipients of favours and patronage in all respects and will be well looked after.[147]

Nadira had died in a state of tiredness and vexation; such was the trickery of fate. A relatively simple affliction like Dysentery had gone untreated. In this mournful situation Sipihr Shukoh's arrest by Jiwan shocked Dara. When he saw his captivated son-hands bound behind his back, he roared at Jiwan: 'Finish, finish! Ungrateful and infamous wretch that thou art, finish that which thou hast commenced; we are the victims of evil fortune and the unjust passion of Aurangzeb, but remember that I do not merit death except for having saved thy life, and remember that a prince of the royal blood never had his, hands tied behind his back.'[148] It is unknown whether Jiwan

---

[147]Ibid., p. 78
[148]cf. *Travels in India* (2nd edition), Jean Baptiste Tavernier, V. Ball (tr.), London, 1925, Vol I, pp. 351–52.

was driven by threats or greed. He delivered the father and son
to Aurangzeb. Dara was tied to the back of an elephant. A public
executioner sat behind him, with the order to slice off his head
at the least indication of resistance. As the entourage advanced it
was debated in the royal court whether he should be brought to
Delhi or sent to the Gwalior prison straight away. Many nobles felt
that disgracing Dara was equivalent to disgracing the royal family
itself. Besides, his sight could move people in his favour. The other
argument was that presenting the pauperized prince would establish
the finality of Aurangzeb's ascent. The last outlook was approved.
Accordingly on 29th August 1659 Dara and Siphir Shukoh were
seated on an elephant, guarded by executioners with naked swords.
Deliberately a miserable and worn-out animal was employed for the
ride. That day the clothes of Shah Jahan's beloved son resembled those
of the poorest of his subjects.[149] Dara was paraded in every street
of Shahjahanabad. The citizenry condemned Aurangzeb's 'unnatural
conduct'.[150] Jiwan was now entitled Bakhtiyar Khan–rode next to
Dara's elephant. The crowd abused and stoned the dastardly betrayer.
Dara was imprisoned at Khizrabad. Instead of being impressed by
Aurangzeb's power people had shown disgust. Jiwan had become
a popular villain. So Dara's execution was had to be expedited. It
was so shocking an idea that even some of Dara's enemies opposed
it. But Aurangzeb was obstinate. To curtain the ruthlessness of his
ambition, Aurangzeb craftily mixed religion in it. Dara was declared
a heretic. In his book *Majma-ul Bahrain*, in a search for common
threads of monotheism and humanism he had analyzed concepts of
Hinduism and Islam. In a disclaimer about the book being written
for personal research and not for public preaching, Dara had written:
'Now thus sayeth this unaffiliated unsorrowing 'fakir', Muhammad
Dara Shukoh, that after knowing the Truth of truths and ascertaining
the secrets and subtleties of the true religion of the Sufis and having
been endowed with this great gift (Sufistic inspiration), he thirsted

---

[149]Bernier, op. cit. , p. 98.
[150]Ibid.

to know the tenets of the religion of the Indian monotheists; and having had repeated intercourse and discussion with the doctors and perfect divines of this religion, who had attained the highest pitch of perfection in religious exercises, comprehension (of God), intelligence and (religious) insight, he did not find any difference except verbal, in the way in which they sought and comprehend Truth. Consequently, having collected the views of the two parties and having brought together the points—a knowledge of which is absolutely essential and useful for the seekers of Truth—he has compiled a tract and entitled it—*Majma-ul-Bahrain* as it is a collection of the truth and wisdom of two Truth-knowing groups (Hindus and Muslims)... So, one who is just and discerning will at once understand that in ascertaining these points how deeply I had to think. It is certain that discerning, intelligent persons will derive much pleasure from this tract, while persons of blunt intelligence, of either side (Hindu or Muslim) will get no share of its benefits. I have put down these researches of mine, according to my own intuition and taste, for the benefit of the members of my family and I have no concern with the common folk of either community.'[151] Another amplifier was the ring which Dara wore; it had the word *Prabhu* (Lord) inscribed on it in the ancient Devanagri script.[152] Aurangzeb said that: 'If it be sinful to shed the blood of such a person (as Dara was), may the sin be visited upon my own head!'[153]It is reported that Dara wrote to him: 'My brother and my king. I think not of sovereignty. I wish it may be auspicious to you and your descendants. The idea of my execution in your lofty mind is unnecessary. If I am allowed a residential place and one of my maids to attend me, I would pray for Your Majesty from my peaceful corner.'[154] The European travelers

---

[151]Cf. *Majma-ul-Bahrain*, Dara Shikuh, M. Mahfuz-ul Haq (edited and translated), Royal Book Company, Karachi, 1990 (reprint) pp. 37–38.

[152]*Shah-Jahan The Rise And Fall Of The Mughal Emperor*, Fergus Nicoll, Penguin Books, Gurgaon, 2018, p. 316.

[153]*Travels in the Mughal Empire*, p. 101.

[154]*Shah-Jahan The Rise and Fall of the Mughal Emperor*, p. 316.

claim that in his last hours, Dara had converted to Christianity.[155] A few hours before the execution Aurangzeb asked Dara: 'What would you have done to the Emperor (Aurangzeb) had he fallen into your hands as you have fallen into his?' Dara replied: 'He is a rebel and a parricide, let him judge of the treatment he has merited by reflecting upon his crimes and such desserts he would have received with the utmost rigor at my hands.' Dara said that he would have had Aurangzeb's body cut into four halves and displayed the pieces at the four gates of Delhi.[156]

Dara was decapitated by Nazar Beg Chelah. The latter had been raised by Shah Jahan but he held some grudge against this prince. Sipihr Shukoh was drawn aside to avoid the gruesome sight of his father's barbaric decapitation. Some accounts claim that he was imprisoned elsewhere. The exact date of the execution is also debated 30th August 1659/22th October 1659. Accounts of Aurangzeb's reaction over the sight of his severed head are varied but uniformly indicative of his hatred for Dara. The head was placed in a dish and washed with water before him so that he could be assured that, indeed it was Dara's.[157] Then he tearfully exclaimed: '*Ai Bad-Bakht* (Ah! wretched one!)—Let his shocking sight no more offend my eyes, but take away the head and let it be buried in Humayun's tomb'.[158] Another account says that Aurangzeb examined it with an air of satisfaction; he touched it with the point of his sword; opened the eyes to observe a speck. Yet another account claims that he looked for some mark on the forehead for confirmation and remarked sarcastically: 'Behold the face of a would be king and emperor of all the Mogul realms! Take him out of my sight.'[159] Another account claims that on Raushan Ara's advice the head was embalmed and sent to Shah Jahan. It was brought to him at his dining table at

[155] *Travels in the Mughal Empire*, p. 103.
[156] *Storia Do Mogor*, p. 339.
[157] Travels in the Mughal Empire, p. 102.
[158] Ibid., 103.
[159] *Storia Do Mogor*, p. 340.

dinner time. The accompanying message said that: this is a token to say that 'he (Aurangzeb) does not forget him (Shah Jahan)'.[160] Shah Jahan believed that it was indeed some gift from his son. He said: 'It is at least a consolation for an unhappy father to find that the usurper has, not wholly forgotten me.'[161] However, when the 'gift' was opened he fainted. He fell–face first–and his teeth struck the vessels and chipped off. Jahan Ara also fainted. Women wailed with their hair and garments disheveled. When he regained consciousness he nervously plucked hair of his beard till his face bled. He raised his hand heavens ward and exclaimed: *Khuda teri riza* (God! Thy will be done). The head was buried in the Taj Mahal. A eunuch, Itibar Khan reported every detail to Aurangzeb.[162] He finally got what he had fancied for a long time.[163]

Sipihr Shukoh was imprisoned at Gwalior. Dara's daughter Jani Begum was sent to Agra on Jahan Ara's insistent requests. The young girl was suffering from depression. Her arrival gave some happiness to Shah Jahan. Amongst the two prominent wives of Dara, Bai Udaipuri was married to Aurangzeb. She gave birth to his son Kam Bakhsh on 6th March 1667 and remained loyal to him. The other, Rana-dil rejected his proposal. It is believed that she asked Aurangzeb the reason for his attraction towards her. When he replied that he loved her hair, she cut all of it and sent it to him. Later, she mutilated and disfigured her face with a knife so that the Emperor would lose interest in her. Ultimately Aurangzeb's solicitations ceased.[164]

When Jiwan was on his way back, an express imperial order reached the governor of Sirhind that he and his associates should be killed in route. Accordingly they were stoned to death. Their corpses; about 15 in number, lay outside the city gate of Sirhind,

---

[160]Ibid., p. 341.
[161]Travels in the Mughal Empire, p. 103.
[162]*Storia Do Mogor*, p. 341.
[163]*Shah-Jahan The Rise and Fall of the Mughal Emperor*, p. 310.
[164]*Storia Do Mogor*, p. 343.

just a few leagues away from his home.[165] Bernier observed: 'This barbarian (Malik Jiwan) had not sufficiently reflected, that though tyrants appear to countenance the blackest crimes while they conduce to their interest or promote a favourite object, they yet hold the perpetrators in abhorrence and will not scruple to punish them when they can no longer be rendered subservient to any iniquitous project.'[166] Nazar Beg Chelah who had beheaded Dara was stabbed and killed on Aurangzeb's orders.

Sulaiman Shukoh was still alive. He was at Srinagar (Garhwal). Jai Singh tried to make the local raja Prithvi Singh agreeable to throw him out from his dominions. Dara's death and the hostility of his neighbours were a challenge to his resolve. However he replied to Jai Singh that he would never betray someone who had sought shelter with him.[167] However the Raja's son secretly opened negotiations with Aurangzeb.[168] Aware that his position was slipping Sulaiman tried to flee to Tibet but was pursued by the local prince and imprisoned. When he was presented before Aurangzeb in the court the extremely handsome Prince stood in a hall full of onlookers; hands tied behind his back. The foot fetters had been taken off just before his entry in the public area. The teary eyed ladies seated behind lattice work were shocked by the unfathomably tragic scene. Aurangzeb was surprisingly polite. This occasion was used to publicly reaffirm that he wasn't all that cruel. He said: 'Be comforted, no harm shall befall you. You shall be treated with tenderness. God is great and you should put your trust in Him. Dara, your father was not permitted to live only because had become a *kafir*, a man devoid of all religion.'[169] The Prince requested that instead of being subjected to slow death with poppy concoction, he may be executed immediately. But eventually he was killed by the very means he dreaded. The story of Dara's

---

[165]Ibid.
[166]*Travels in the Mughal Empire*, p. 104.
[167]*Storia Do Mogor*, p. 359.
[168]*Travels in the Mughal Empire*, p. 93.
[169]*Storia Do Mogor*, p. 106.

family evoked such emotion in the commoners that a song about the power of fate became popular in those days. It highlighted the temporariness in the nature of glory and good fortune. A flip of fate had made Shah Jahan a prisoner, had his heir Dara decapitated and made Aurangzeb, the Emperor: 'In turn it changed the *faqir's* (mendicant's) cowl and beheaded the prince in passing.'[170] Aurangzeb banned it. Anyone who sang it would lose his to tongue. However the truth in the ballad was too dark and deep to be dusted away by an imperial order. It was sung in concealment until time faded the memory of this tragedy and new challenges emerged.

Lyrics composed in honour of Murad Bakhsh were another issue for Aurangzeb. His victimization had made him popular. To smash his tragic-hero image criminal charges were pinned on him. Murad had killed and looted Syed Mir Ali Naqi the Diwan of Gujarat at Ahmedabad when he needed funding for the 1657 rebellion. Now one of Ali Naqi's sons was pressurized to press charges against him. In a following mock-trial he was found guilty and was killed in Gwalior on 4th December 1661. Poisonous snakes were let loose in his cell to bite him to death. Paradoxically Aurangzeb rewarded that son of Ali Naqi who had refused to sue Murad. The latter's debts were paid off by the Emperor.

Now only Shuja remained. He had put up a remarkable resistance. However every assassination of the princes of blood weakened his resolve. Ultimately he fled to Dacca. He sent his son Sultan Banque to the court of the king of Arakan / Magh with the request for a temporary asylum and a subsequent safe passage. The king responded well and he was accorded a descent reception. However no arrangements were made for his onward journey. Perhaps Shuja's wealth had tempted the king to invite him over. Letting the prince leave safely was never a part of his plan. When Shuja's demands for onwards transportation intensified, the Raja took offense. He made a case that Shuja had not visited him personally. It is unknown whether Shuja considered it below his dignity to go there or was

---

[170]Ibid., p. 343.

he just scared of being arrested and looted if he went. However he sent his son again. Sultan Banque distributed gold and silver coins as he approached the court. The Raja was gifted many precious gems. Apologies were presented for Shuja's inability to come due to sickness. Then the king was humbly reminded about his promise regarding the vessels. Now the Raja demanded the hand of one of Shuja's daughters in marriage. This was turned down. Shuja even explored the possibility of overthrowing this king by an internal coup. Unfortunately the plan was leaked, further adding to his troubles. Eventually he managed to jailbreak but the Raja's forces caught up with him. Sultan Banque who was a few leagues behind him, was ambushed and literally bathed in his own blood. Shuja got away but his family was arrested. Whatever happened to him was never known. His sword and dagger were recovered from the battle ground, but his body was not found. Every now and then rumors emerged that he was seen in different places; Masulipatnam, Surat, Kabul, Qandhar and Persia. His fate remains a mystery.

Initially Sultan Banque and his relatives were imprisoned and treated very harshly. Later, the Raja actually married the eldest daughter of Shuja and his attitude towards the family became relatively mild. In this situation Sultan Banque was drawn into a plot against his host. Unfortunately the latter got a wind of it. In retaliation every member of the Mughal clan, in his custody was assassinated. Even the princess married to him, pregnant with his child, was not spared. Sultan Banque and his brothers were decapitated with horrifying looking axes, whose bluntness would have made their death even more painful. The females were closely confined in their apartments. They died of starvation.

Aurangzeb might have hoped to find peace after the elimination of all his rivals. He was wrong. His head spun with the weight of a crown dripping with familial blood. His personal space was crammed with guilt. He had betrayed so many, that he found it very difficult to trust. His own children topped the list of suspects. There was a marked shift in his personal ways. He abstained from lavish foods, and other indulgences of emperors of his stature. But no matter how orthodoxly religious he posed to be or maybe he really was–he took enough decisions in a secular manner to prove that he didn't want to mix religion with politics once his position on the throne was secure. He is often hated as a hater of Non-Muslims. But the people whom he destroyed with the most ruthless resolution were in fact Muslims— exactly of his own type and his own belief—his own blood. Religion didn't guide the path of his armies. Uncountable non-Muslims worked for him and served in his army. Even during the war of succession out of Rajput nobles above the rank of 1000, 23 were supporting Aurangzeb and 24 were in support of Dara. Many Muslims were supporting Dara, just as they had, supported Akbar, their super liberal policies, notwithstanding. Aurangzeb asserted that he was the Baadshah of both, Muslims and Non-Muslims and he acted like one. A Hindu astrologer Ishvardas, writing in Sanskrit in 1663 said that Aurangzeb was *dharmya* (righteous) and his policies were *vivdhivat* (lawful).[171]

Some problematic issues which had been sedated by Shah Jahan were suddenly awakened: rise of locality based-small power groups, the failing *Mansabdari* system, shortfall of *jagirs*, a poor and indifferent peasantry, corrupt and unreliable officers and an army that craved luxury instead of war. Aurangzeb thought that perhaps feeding more lands would keep the empire alive. The mirage of Deccan looked like a solution to him. But in fact it smashed Aurangzeb's pride, scraped his shining crown and punctured the bubble of Mughal invincibility. Roads of damage control cut through the heart of Mughal-Rajput alliance. The recruitment of Marathas in the imperial army and the absence of the Emperor from north India drove the last nail in the coffin.

As the governor of Bengal, Mir Jumla recovered the territories which had been lost in the wake of the civil war. Later he invaded Assam. After his death on 10th April 1663 Shaista Khan was appointed in his place. However the Mughal victories in this region never really crystallized. Conflict with the local rajas continued and borders were redefined often enough to keep the Mughals on their toes. Shaista

---

[171]Aurangzeb The Man, p. 50.

Khan tried to control piracy on the Bengal coast.

Aurangzeb tried to settle the north-western frontier. The tribe men of this area often robbed the highways to loot traders carrying goods to and from Afghanistan. They had to be bribed to allow peaceful traffic. Sometimes up to rupees 6 lakh were spent annually on bribes and yet it was not a fool proof arrangement. In 1667 Bhagu—a leader of the Yusufzai clan of the Swat and Bajaur districts, north of Peshawar crossed the Indus and invaded a district which was under Mughal control. Other bands of the Yusufzais plundered the Attock and Peshawar districts and attempted to hold the ferry on the Indus to stop the Mughal army from reaching their base. They were defeated by Kamil Khan the commandant of Attock in April 1667. After this episode they remained low for a couple of years. In 1672 the Afridis revolted. Their chief Akmal Khan summoned the Pathans to join him in a crusade against the Mughals. Thereafter this area became an open wound. Aurangzeb himself proceeded to close it. Bribes and threats tamed some of the rebels while others like Ghorais, Ghilzais, Shiranis and Yusufzais fought back, but were eventually defeated. The resources of the tribes were very small in comparison with the Mughals, but they cost the Mughals dear in terms of money and time. Specially time because while Aurangzeb was busy on this front the Maratha power was consolidated unchecked.

The Jat Rebellion (1668–89) caused a big disturbance in the heart of the Empire. In 1669, the Mughal officer Abdul Nabi was killed by Gokula Jat. Gokula was finally defeated in the battle of Tilpat. He was brought to Agra and killed. But uprisings continued under the leadership of Raja Ram of Sinsani and Ramchera of Soghar. The rebels used guerilla tactics. Their equipment was light and their horses fast. Even flimsy forts and forests were enough to keep them going. A shocked Manucci reports that Akbar's tomb at Sikandra was looted. The damage caused to the building was nothing in comparison with fact that the rebels dug Akbar's bones out of his grave and burnt them. No surprise that Aurangzeb was livid. In 1688, his grandson Bidar Bakht, was able to suppress the uprising with the help of

Bishan Singh of Amber the then in-charge of Mathura. Raja Ram was succeeded by his nephew Churaman. The latter founded the state of Bharatpur. Thus Aurangzeb couldn't really close the Jat Chapter. The Satnami Rebellion was another uprising which weakened the fabric of the Empire. Aurangzeb was so disturbed by these uprisings that he himself tied charms and spells to the flags of his army to solicit victory. Every rebellion left a dent in his crown.

The most formidable of all the adversaries that Aurangzeb faced were the Sikhs and the Marathas. Aurangzeb's contemporary Guru Tegh Bahadur was settled at Anandpur. The constant movement of the Mughal armies in Punjab caused economic losses to these people. Thus resistance began. Ultimately Guru Tegh Bahadur was arrested and brought to Delhi. Here he was killed in December 1675. Now the Sikhs improved their military organization. Guru Govind Singh; Guru Tegh Bahadur's son swore to avenge his father and thus emerged the *Khalsa* (literally–pure). To solidify a distinctive sense of identity the members of the *Khalsa* were instructed to essentially carry the following with them at all times: *Kesh* (they didn't trim their hair), *Kripan* (dagger), *Kachcha* (underwear), *Kanghi* (comb) and *Kara* (single bangle). Local ideas of purity and impurity based on birth were discouraged to further the unity of the group. The confrontation wasn't easy for either the Mughals or the *Khalsa*. Guru Govind Singh lost four sons in this struggle. He was chased from place to place and could finally return to north India only after Aurangzeb's death.

The Mughal fall-out with the Rajputs was a political tragedy of sorts. They shared the royal state, the royal family and the royal blood. By Akbar's arrangement the Rajputs were left undisturbed in their home territories called *watan jagir*s. The Mughals emperor retained a symbolic supremacy by his entitlement to sanction the succession of a new ruler in the event of death / removal of the previous one. This was formally called granting the *Tika* (making an auspicious mark with sacred substances on the forehead). To save embroilment in the local politics of the rajas, Akbar broadly insisted on predictable successions based on the law of primogeniture. However, if the succession became complicated the Mughal emperors steered the process. Jaswant Singh had come to occupy the throne of Marwar because his father Gaj Singh had bypassed the claims of his first born Amar Singh. When he was accused of looting the rear of Aurangzeb's army in the battle of Khajwa (1658) Aurangzeb decreed that Rai Singh son of his elder brother Amar Singh would be recognized as the new king of Marwar. Although later he patched up with Jaswant Singh but the interim order revived an old rivalry between the children of Gaj Singh. This flicker became a fire when Jaswant Singh died without leaving any male heir. However two of his queens were pregnant. The Emperor was bound to wait for the deliveries before taking any decision. He ordered that for the time being Marwar be brought under *Khalisa* (literally pure–territory directly administered by the imperial centre). This was resisted by the local clans' chieftains. They feared that once a territory went into central control it would be difficult to retrieve it. While the plea that the imperial court took was that a *watan jagir* could not be conferred on either *naukaran* (servants) or *masturat* (women). To apply an immediate balm on the wounded Rajput pride Aurangzeb ordered that status quo would be maintained in case of all appointments as left by Jaswant Singh. This development satisfied only those who didn't want a change in Marwar. But there were many who wanted a change. Taking advantage of the vacant throne of Marwar they regrouped and reasserted themselves. Two sons were born to the widows of Jaswant Singh in February 1679. One of them died within a week and the other-Ajit Singh survived. But rumors floated that an imposter was being presented as the prince. Suspicious, Aurangzeb became reluctant about giving the *tika* to him. Also the Rathor chieftains would have had a free run if their raja was a newborn. Eventually three parties emerged in the fray. Firstly Rani Hadi; Jaswant Singh's chief queen, Ajit Singh's advocate, though not his mother. Secondly, Inder Singh, a grandson of Amar Singh and thirdly, Anup Singh, a Rathore with a distant relationship with the royal bloodline of Marwar. A situation of intra-Rathor conflict had built up. Aurangzeb's assertion of authority in this volatile atmosphere didn't help. In the meantime Mewar was also drawn into this struggle. By September 1680 one section was pacified because Rani Hadi was assigned a *jagir*. Other groups of Rathors and Sisodias were defeated or reconciled. Eventually in 1699 Ajit Singh was granted a *mansab* and a *jagir*. Durga Das a prominent Rathor chieftain joined Mughal service. The Rathor uprising of 1669 unmasked the rotting face of Mughal-Rajput partnership. It emboldened non-imperial Rajputs and others who ran down old barriers of subservience. It is often labelled as a Hindu-Muslim conflict, which it wasn't. The Rathors were divided into three parties and all of them wanted to secure their respective interests. In his 1657 *nishan* to Rana Raj Singh Aurangzeb had written that an emperor who discriminates on religious grounds is a rebel against God. The Rajputs of Marwar had been in such a state of tandem with Muslims that Jaswant Singh had built three big mosques in Jodhpur and maintained them. While the Mughals' grants which were extended to the Vaishnava temples of Mathura-Vrindavan in Akbar's reign continued down to Aurangzeb's. Even though the earlier Mughal emperors had also steered the choice of recipients of *tika* there hadn't been any uprisings. Aurangzeb's reign was different. There was a simultaneous rise of many types of power groups. However he knew that allowing anyone to ravage the secular character of the Mughal government would be a poor compromise with a big price.

The most remarkable conflict that Aurangzeb faced in terms of longevity was with Shivaji. He was the son of Shahji, who was an influential Maratha commander who took advantage of the indefinite state of power shifts in the Deccan. Shivaji was raised with exceptional care by his mother Jijabai. She instilled self respect and self-reliance in him. He learned to respect women. Religion did not color his professional choices. Using Poona as a base of operations Shivaji recruited many Kolis and Marathas into his service. By the mid of seventeenth-century he had captured many important forts. He first brushed with Aurangzeb when the latter was the viceroy of Deccan. When Aurangzeb left Deccan in 1657, Shivaji expand his territories further. His activities alarmed Bijapur. Abdullah Bhatari popularly known as Afzal Khan, was commissioned to handle him but he was killed by Shivaji in September 1659. This emboldened Shivaji even more. His confrontations with Bijapur continued.

Meanwhile Aurangzeb appointed Shaista Khan his maternal uncle to cap the growing Maratha power. However on 15th April 1663 the Mughal press down was reversed by Shaista Khan's miserable failure. In January 1664 Shivaji raided Surat the richest port of the Empire. As a reaction Shaista Khan was transferred to Bengal and Prince Muazzam was posted as the governor in his place. Jaswant Singh was sent to Poona. However it was only when Jai Singh was posted in Deccan that the situation seemed to brighten for the Mughals. He was an expert at preparing just the right concoction of diplomacy and diehard action to dissolve enemies. Bijapur was lured into an anti Shivaji alliance by promise of leniency in the tributes they owed to the Mughal court. Other disgruntled elements; Portuguese, zamindars and the local sub clans who had been displaced by Shivaji all pitched in with Jai Singh. Consequently important forts and towns fell under the Mughal sway. Finally Shivaji opened negotiations with Jai Singh. Their meeting took place on the 24th of June 1665. A broad understanding was reached whereby Shivaji was to help the Mughal forces against Bijapur. This was a win-win situation for the Mughals. Two of their enemies; Marathas and Bijapur had been pitched against each other. Besides, the Mughals were to receive tributes from both of them. But this delicately balanced victory didn't stand for long. Jai Singh wanted to have a more firm agreement with the Marathas. With this agenda he arranged for Shivaji's meeting with Aurangzeb. Unfortunately his rivals at the court created a hostile environment for Shivaji's reception. Shivaji reached Agra in late May 1666. Despite the best efforts of Jai Singh' son Ram Singh the meeting turned out to be a fiasco. The intra Rajput rivalry between the Kachchwahas and Rathors was active and the Rathor lobby led by Jaswant Singh didn't want the Deccan issue to be resolved by Jai Singh. Thus Shivaji was literally put under arrest at Agra. Anyway soon enough he escaped. Unrecognizably disguised he reached back to Raigarh in September 1666. Aurangzeb suspected that Ram Singh had assisted in this incredible getaway. As a penalty he banned him from royal presence and transferred Jai Singh from Deccan. This was a mistake.

On the Deccan front Jai Singh had done the best that could be done. His assessment of Shivaji's abilities was bang on correct. On 7 September 1667, he died at Burhanpur on his way to Agra. After a short truce (1667–1670) the Mughals and the Marathas resumed hostilities. Shivaji had built an impressive kingdom. His coronation marked yet another victory, of the social type. He was not of the Kshatriya caste and the orthodox Brahmins of Maharashtra were deeply skeptical about performing rituals for crowning him. So he summoned the most learned and renowned Brahmin of Benaras to conduct the ceremony. This was Vishweshwara Gaga Bhatta, master of all Vedas, scriptures and philosophies of Hinduism. Finally he was crowned just as Kshatriyas were. He broke the stereotype that the reputation of being baffling battlefield players was anyone's monopoly. Marathas emerged as contenders of Rajputs. This hammered fissures in the Mughal-Rajput partnership as well.

Shivaji's son Shambhuji's could not match his father's gritty courage. Shivaji resented this. Alienated and unsure Shambhuji joined hands with the Mughal governor Diler Khan. Later he took shelter with the Bijapur court. However the fear of betrayal drove him back to his father's keeping. Although happy about his return, Shivaji was vexed at the prospect of a succession crisis. Soyra Bai, the mother of his younger son Raja Ram, wanted her 10-year-old son to succeed him. Besides, two powerful ministers, More Pant Pingle and Annaji Datto were fighting each other. In this situation Shivaji died on 13th April 1680. He left an inheritance of pride to enthuse one Maratha leader or another. His conflict with Aurangzeb was a purely political affair and not a religious war; from either side.

An unpredictable twist in the Mughal–Maratha relations was Shambhuji's alliance with Aurangzeb's rebel son; Akbar. Unfortunately their affiliation turned out to be a tragedy greater than the infamous meeting of their fathers. The immediate reason for Akbar's rebellion was his transfer from Chittor in 1680. With the support of some anti-Aurangzeb Rajput clans he declared independence on the 11th of January 1681. It is interesting that just like Aurangzeb had got a *Fatwa* issued against Dara, so did Akbar against Aurangzeb. This audacity triggered a bitter war between the father and son. Eventually Akbar escaped to Deccan and sought asylum at Shambhuji's court. This changed the course of Aurangzeb's journey forever. He closed the Rajasthan front. His mission now was to punish Akbar. After all, Aurangzeb himself had been a dangerously ambitious son. He, out of all the people, would have never risked ignoring a disobedient child.

Aurangzeb's arrival at Burhanpur on 1st April 1682 was a new beginning and also an end. In the following years he faced hardships, losses and betrayals of a new pitch; a much higher one. He never returned to the glamour and pleasures of Shahjahanabad. The vibrancy that his arrival brought to Deccan was short lived. On the other hand the northern part of the empire faded away in the chaos kicked off by his departure. Cracks in the Mughal-Rajput partnership became increasingly pronounced. The Rathors, Sisodias, Haras, Gaurs etc; clans chipped off one after another. Aurangzeb had neither the time and perhaps nor the inclination to fix the wreckage. Or probably he knew that he would fail even if he tried. War; consistently his nemesis, held him back, until death. The empire was too vast and the fluidity of political and social parameters was beyond his control. It was beyond anyone's control. The basic algorithm was lost.

Soon Akbar realized that Shambhuji didn't quite fit the bill as a confederate. Maratha court politics were in a mess. So he left for Persia in 1686 and reached there in 1688. Shambhuji was arrested in 1689. Aware of his weak political position Aurangzeb didn't bother to negotiate anything with him. He was assassinated. Durgadas delivered Akbar's daughter Safiyat-un-Nisa and son Buland Akhtar to Aurangzeb.

The Marathas, Bijapur and Golconda formed a flexible alliance against the Mughals. As a cocktail of enemies they diluted the Mughal potency. Aurangzeb planned to first annex Bijapur and Golconda and to then contain the Marathas. He reached Bijapur on 13th July 1686.

The supply line of the resisting Bijapur forces was cut off. Finally they surrendered on 22nd September 1686. Prince Shah Alam was deputed against Golconda. After Hyderabad fell, the Sultan took shelter in the fort of Golconda. Despite diminishing resources and incessant rains both the parties stuck to their positions. Soldiers were dying of wounds and starvation. But the siege continued. Aurangzeb issued an official statement that the kingdom of Golconda had seized to exist. Thus, anyone who sent supplies for the fugitive Sultan of Golconda would be a traitor of the Mughal Empire. This and many more threats were floated but to no avail. Finally Mohammad Ibrahim the commander-in-chief of the fort was bribed and Golconda was captured on 3rd October 1687. The comatose Mughal Empire edged towards expansion and death.

The Marathas' guerilla forces disrupted and looted the Mughal supply lines. Absence of a single Head of State of the Marathas made any decisive confrontation or agreement with them impossible. This war was not going to end-definitely not in Aurangzeb's lifetime. Thus Aurangzeb 'ornament of the throne' spent years without a throne. He marched in fields of endless battles. So much so that it was speculated that he deliberately continued with the wars because if he abandoned the command of his staggering army, his sons would depose him just as he had deposed his father. Involuntarily the option of normal court life was bulldozed.[172] Aurangzeb advised his son: 'It is bad for both emperors and water to remain at same place. The water grows putrid and the kings' power slips out of his control'.[173] Gascoigne assesses: 'Where any other man summons his sons to his death bed Aurangzeb like a dying animal snapping at the vultures, deliberately sent them away.'[174] The Mughal officers and armies were exhausted, but Aurangzeb wasn't. As a frail old man, reading feverishly from the Quran even when on the move for a military inspection, he was

---

[172]*Indian Travels*, p. 239.

[173]*Structure of Politics*, p. 178.

[174]*A Brief History Of The Great Moghuls*, Bamber Gascoigne, Robinson, London, 2002 (reprint), p. 239.

quite an inspiring sight even without his throne.

Due to tensions triggered by financial insufficiency and revolts he banned the official and public celebration of many festivities. The controversial *Jaziya* was re-imposed in 1679. Aurangzeb's orders to remedy the desperate situation in the agrarian sector are documented in his *farmans* to Rasik Das and Muhammad Hashim. The state was faced with a situation where peasants were demoralized by heavy taxation and corrupt officials. Aurangzeb wrote to Muhammad Hashim that the tax collectors should be benevolent towards the peasants. So that the cultivators are motivated to enthusiastically try to increase the cultivation. This way every arable tract could be brought under tillage.[175] His instructions to Rasik Das Karori mirrored his concern for his subjects. He barred his officers from meeting powerful intermediaries privately so that bribes couldn't be exchanged. They were directed to hear the petitions of even the poorest of the farmers and try their best to help them. The abolition of illegal taxes which impaired the welfare of his subjects was to be implemented with strictness. Names of the corrupt officials were to be reported to him, so that they could be dismissed and punished. Likewise the honest and hardworking ones were also to be reported for rewards and promotions.[176] He ordered the writing of the *Fatwa-i Alamgiri* with a view to codify laws.

Aurangzeb's simplicity in the later part of his reign was puzzling. Careri analyzed: 'Aurangzeb considering the heinousness of the crimes he had committed for the compassing of his ends; voluntarily imposed on himself a rigorous abstinence, not to eat for the future any wheaten-bread, fish or flesh; and to live upon barley-bread, rice, herbs and sweet meats and such things; nor to drink any sort of liquor but water.[177] Besides this his table was not maintained out of the revenue of the crown. He said that every man ought to work for his living. So he

---

[175] *The Agrarian System of Mughal India*, Irfan Habib, Oxford University Press, New Delhi, 1999, pp. 271–283.
[176] Ibid.
[177] *Indian Travels*, p. 231.

made caps and presented them to the governors of his provinces, who in return sent him presents worth several thousands of rupees. In his decrepit old age, when he couldn't work anymore revenue of four towns was reserved for his table. His expense was small, a vest of his did not cost above Rs. 8 and the sash and cap cost lesser.[178] He had lost interest in sexual activity.[179] Aurangzeb was hard working. He bathed before dawn and began working thereafter. He reportedly gave two hours to his family each day. The eunuchs in his service reported that he slept for just two hours. Some claimed that Aurangzeb was skilled in necromancy. He was a sorcerer who drew power from the black realm. There was no other way for him to harness that kind of energy at his age.[180] Towards the last years of his life he had become strangely mild and resigned. He was disillusioned by the rampant corruption and disloyalty of his officers. A contemporary describes him as an old man; who was white all over, from his beard to his immaculately white clothes. When being carried in an open litter people gathered to see him; they stared. However he used to be so engaged in reading a book that he always carried (The Quran), that he never noticed them.[181] In the beginning of his career he used to act like a mendicant; and towards the end of it he had actually become one. So much so that he was called *Zinda Pir* (The living saint). Following is a mystical advice from him: 'Untie little by little the knot that has bound your heart to earthly things. Or else death will snatch away this string all at once and unawares.'[182] And 'Do justice as the folly of these bad men, is better than a thousand brains of the fox-natured.' 'Every wise man who enters into a dispute with a worthless man. Only strikes his own lustrous jewel on a hard stone.' Speaking about the lasting impact of corruption he wrote: 'Even after his death the tyrant does not cease to oppress. The plumes of the dead eagle become in the end the feathers

[178]Ibid., p. 237.

[179]Ibid., 236–237.

[180]Ibid., 236.

[181]*A Brief History,* p. 236.

[182]*Structure of Politics,* p. 179.

of arrows.'[183] In his old age he often recalled the 'good old times'. In 1700 he shared a memory of prince Azam's childhood with him and wrote that the prince imitated the beating of drums and called out to his father: 'Babaji, dhum, dhum'.[184]

The withdrawal from Deccan began in 1705 when his body began failing. He was being carried back in a palanquin. He was much bereaved by Gauhar Ara's death and repeated that only he and she were left amongst Shah Jahan's children.[185] On Friday, 20th February 1707 he breathed his last. He had willed that only the money earned by his selling caps should be used for his funeral. The money which he had earned by selling Qurans copied by him was to be distributed in charity on the day of his death. His grave at Khuldabad near Daulatabad was a simple structure.

Aurangzeb was victorious and vanquished at the same time. It is unknown whether he felt like king or a pauper. He is arrested in the paradox of having friends and foes even in the present times. Indeed all prisons are not made of stones and steel some are made of abstracts. The key to Aurangzeb's prison was lost way back in 1657 and is still missing.

❈

---

[183]Ibid.
[184]*Aurangzeb the Man*, p. 123.
[185]*A Brief History*, p. 239.

EIGHT

ABU ZAFAR SIRAJUDDIN MOHAMMAD BAHADUR SHAH II

1837–1858

'Abu Zafar Mohammad Bahadur Shah died in the morning at 5 today. He was buried the same evening at a spot behind the Main Guard since all prior arrangements had been made during the day. After the burial the grave was covered properly with mud, levelling it with the surrounding ground, an enclosure of bamboos was erected nearby with the idea that once the bamboos would wither, the grass would grow all over the grave with no visible trace to identify the spot where the last remains of the last Mughal emperor were buried.'

—7th NOVEMBER 1862,
DAIRY ENTRY OF CAPTAIN NELSON DAVIS[186]

'In this turquoise palace of ancient foundation,
The son of man is wonderfully apt to err:
Gratitude is not his habit,
His business is only neglect of worship.
Although he passes his whole life amid mercies,
He never knows their value until they be lost.'[187]

The equiangular spiral of the Mughal edifice chipped off gradually with the passage of time. Exploitation, corruption, rebellions, in-house tensions and investment in deficit enterprises were junctures that made tiny perforations until the Mughal power leaked away into

---

[186] *The Life & Poetry of Bahadur Shah Zafar*, Aslam Parvez, translation by Ather Farouqui, Hay House India, New Delhi, 2017, pp. 99–100.
[187] Cf. *Muntakhab-ut Tawarikh*, p. 141.

nothingness. On their way up the ladder of sovereignty the Mughals had military skills at the bottom of the bars and then in ascending rungs came surplus appropriation, law and order, dispensation of justice, committed officialdom, diplomacy, socio-cultural integration, etc. On the chaotic downward slip, the steps broke successively until all things that signified Mughal greatness were devastated and there was no going back.

Aurangzeb saw the collapse of all that he had inherited. The Mansabdari system was under siege by the very people who ran it. Taxes leaked on their way to the treasury. While the farmers were being 'bled white' by exploitation the centre wasn't getting any richer either. The intermediaries who were the connecting link between the two were probably having the best time. They made money off the record and revolted if checked. Officialdom was so saturated, that there were no lands available to be assigned in lieu of military service. This was called *be-jagiri* or the Jagirdari Crisis as per the classical description. Since the Mughal bureaucracy was personalized, thus it came under tremendous stress when the central government became weak. The pressure of constant military success drove Shah Jahan and Aurangzeb to invest in deficit enterprises. Their successors inherited losses.

The clash of interest between the central government and its officers was aggravated by regular transfers of the latter. Transfers were meant to keep officers out of the loop of neighbourhood networks. Their over familiarity with locally influential elements was known to be a formula for rebellions. However due to this impermanence the officers lost interest in the long term development of their place of posting. The peasantry was squeezed dry. As exploitation increased production decreased. The Mughal emperors like Akbar and Aurangzeb were conscious of this fall out and had tried to ensure the protection of the poorest of the cultivators. However when the empire expanded beyond a limit numerous agencies became untameable. The merchants, moneylenders, castes-community and region based non-political groups became important influencers in power politics. Thus business entrepreneurs became powerful in the urban sector, the rural sector was dominated by the zamindars—the hereditary, largely caste bound bigwigs of the villages. The already fractured Mughal machinery disintegrated under their weight. The result was a maze of relationships where every party was driven by short sighted greed. Numerous small and localized processes of change led to one big change: the death of an empire.

Scholars understand this death through various perspectives. Some blame individuals and others institutions. The angle of economic exploitation with emphasis on the collapse of the tri-polar arrangement which balanced the zamindars, jagirdars and the peasants, professed by Irfan Habib seems the most convincing way to understand the decline. Many theories are spun around the base of economics built by Irfan Habib and Shireen Moosvi.

The rise of European merchants as stake holders in land ownership in Hindustan was a big change. The Industrial Revolution and the resultant surge in the power of the industrialized countries put Hindustan and other non-industrialized regions at a serious disadvantage. Due to mechanized processing the demand for raw materials in the industrialized countries rose very high. To ensure a smooth and cheap supply of raw materials they began controlling their suppliers politically and militarily. The suppliers were also forced to buy their finished products. It was a win-win situation for the industrialized investors.

The new regional centres of authority which had emerged in the 18th century tried to clone the Mughals. But none of them could withstand the challenge that the British East India Company posed in its political and military avatar. The land mark battles of Plassey (1757) and Buxar (1764) sealed the deal. Wealth would be drained out of Hindustan. Like the poor farmers of its villages, the whole of Hindustan was going to bleed away autonomy, dignity and wealth.

Abu Zafar, the last ruler of the Mughal line was the eldest son of Akbar Shah II and his non-Muslim wife Lalbai. He wasn't his father's choice of an heir but had been chosen by the British East India Company. From the time of Shah Alam II, the heirs of the Mughal dynasty had become pensioners of the British. When he ascended the throne Zafar was entitled to a monthly pension of rupees one lakh. His limitations can be gauged by the fact that as a punishment for not offering a seat to their governor-general, the British had disallowed him from using the *Takht-e Huma*; a silver-gold throne that he had enthusiastically commissioned for himself.[188] Despite all the inadequacies he tried his best to maintain as luxurious a life style as he could. The legacy of his ancestors' majesty was indeed hard to forget. He was generous by nature and was sometimes so even at a very high price. Heavily in debt, he didn't refrain from asking for more loans. He issued promissory notes and mortgaged properties so that the show may go on. The once inaccessible Mughal *darbar*, became accessible to anybody in return for payment of small sums of money. Corrupt officials didn't miss an opportunity of misspending and misappropriating the 'poor' Baadshah's limited resources.

Zafar's value lay in the fact that he was a symbol of the Mughal brand. Although the brand itself had become bankrupt but the label was still very precious. The tussles between his sons, when compared with the earlier grand and grotesque succession dramas of the family, were impotent. Zafar wanted Mirza Jawan Bakht, a son born of his favourite wife Begum Zeenat Mahal to succeed him. The Begum was obsessed with the idea of her son's succession. However the East India Company had its own choices. It had initially chosen Mirza Fakhru and after his death in 1852, it had decided up on Mirza Quwesh. The infirmness of the Mughals can be gauged by the fact that neither the Baadshah had the power to appoint his heir and nor did the princes have the strength to rough it out amongst themselves. The British, a third party were selecting the inheritor of Shah Jahan's Red Fort. The possession of the fort by the Mughal family was itself in jeopardy. However a violent revolt against the British in 1857 derailed everyone's schemes and plans.

This revolt was one of the first major confrontations that the imperialists faced in Asia. It is understood differently by different

---

[188] *The Life & Poetry of Bahadur Shah Zafar*, p. 33

scholars: as a mutiny of the sepoys against the use of greased cartridges or an assertion of introductory prototype of patriotic nationalism or an uprising of feudal system against commercial system or a peasant revolt against oppressive taxation or a design of the working classes against the bourgeoisie or one religion's war against another religion in context of their historical rivalry or a war of all indigenous agencies put together against the octopus of imperialism which had tentacles of socio-economic, political-religious, cultural, ethical, emotional and psychological exploitation. The fact that the 'mutiny' had spread out far and beyond the barracks and cantonments and that it involved many anti-British groups goes to prove that it was more than just soldiers' reaction over greased cartridges. Anyway whether the revolt was one or all of these, its impact on the story of the Mughal dynasty was quick and lasting. It drove the last nail in its coffin.

In his first meeting with the rebels, the eighty plus Zafar could not even understand the quantum of their resolution and the revolution. The maximum role that he had hoped to play was that of a mediator to reconcile the warring parties. However before he could make any choice, the rebels selected him to be their leader. He was a symbol of the pre-British times when the colonial dagger hadn't punctured Hindustan's heart. For him, the time to pay for the classy Mughal brand label had come. Surprisingly Zafar didn't back off from paying that price. He remained loyal to the anti-British movement and was even ready to delegate his symbolic authority to the leaders of the rebellion to strengthen it. It was ironical that a weak pensioner of the British could boost a rebellion against them. This was the magic of the Mughal legacy.

On 14th September 1857, almost four months after the break out of the revolt the British reoccupied Delhi. Zafar left the Red Fort and took shelter in Humayun's tomb. The rebels wanted to shift him to Lucknow so that the Mughal tag could still be pinned on to their banner. Therefore the British had to expedite his arrest. Finally on 21st September Zafar and his family were arrested by Major William Hodson. All the personal jewels of the royal family were handed over to the latter by Begum Zeenat Mahal. She was naïve enough to have still imagined that the British would approve the inheritance of her son after Zafar's death. While the son, Jawan Bakht himself tried to impress Hodson by informing him about secret treasures of the family. Perhaps he was clueless that the game was now too big and he was too small to even be placed as a pawn on the board. After 22 sittings of a trial that began on 27th January 1858 and ended on 9th March 1858 Zafar was found guilty of all charges levied against him by the British. A death sentence would have made him a hero of 1857 in popular memory so he was exiled to Rangoon with his family. Three princes: Mirza Mughal, Mirza Khizar Sultan and Mirza Abu Bakr were shot dead by Major Hodson at point blank range. Indeed the British had sensed the magical magnetism of the Mughal brand

Unlike the earlier Muslim rulers who sought legitimacy to rule from the Caliph of Baghdad, the Mughals sought that legitimacy from their subjects–the people of Hindustan. Seeds of democratic governance were at the bottom of the Mughal tree. They enthusiastically adopted local customs like tuladan, pitrdan and jharokha darshan. They implemented bans on the killing of birds and animals revered by their subjects in all seriousness. The study of Vrindavan Documents by Tarapad Mukherjee and Irfan Habib has proven that financial support was extended to all kinds of religious institutions. All festivals were celebrated at the Mughal court.

The Mughal governance was a mosaic of many minds. A common wire that ran through the brains of all the emperors from Babur to Aurangzeb was love for Hindustan and an eagerness to connect with all of their subjects. Once Babur saw Hindustan, Hindustan owned him. He left people who were important reference points of his life's journey but he didn't leave his new residence. Humayun struggled for years to come back home. As a child Akbar waited eagerly for his father to take him there. As an emperor Akbar set such a high standard of connection with his subjects that even modern politicians might difficult to copy. Abul Fazl wrote that translation projects were commissioned so that he and his officers could understand the people they were dealing with and empathise with them. Numerous marriage alliances with the non-Muslim royalties changed the genetic make-up of the imperial family. Jahangir appreciated variations of florae that the Hindustani soil could sustain. He wrote that Hindustan has the best flowers in the whole world. Shah Jahan didn't want to learn Turki. Not a wonder though; he wasn't a Turk and had no time to learn a foreign language. Murad wasn't interested in staying in Balkh and Badakshan; not even as a viceroy. Nadira Banu Begum's last wish was that she be buried in Hindustan. Dara honoured it despite his own miserable condition. Bahadur Shah Zafar lamented that he was not fortunate enough to be wrapped in the soil of his land for his final rest. He wrote:

'*Lagta nahin hai ji mera ujde dayar mein*
Kis ki bani hai aalam-e-naa payedaar mein
Umar daraaz maang ke laaye the chaar din
Do aarzo mein kat gaye do intezaar mein
Keh do yeh hasratoon se kahin aur jaa basen
Itni jagah kahan hai dil-e-daaghdaar mein
Kitna hai bad-nasseb Zafar dafan ke liye
Do gaz zamin bhi na mili ku-e-yaar mein.'

(I feel restless in this ruined wasteland
Who has ever had his way with times' unpredictability
The much begged for longevity (has) turned out to be just four days
Two were spent in longing and two in the wait up
Ask wistful pining to settle elsewhere
Where is the space for it in my sullied-sorrowful heart?
How very unfortunate is Zafar that for (his) burial
(He) couldn't get even two yards of land in his beloved's lane).[189]

---

[189]Urdu version from the *Diwan* of Bahadur Shah Zafar and translation by Jawaid Hassan.

In the Empire's story, the Great Mughals were not the only stars. There were many other heroes and heroines. After all, the granary is but grain upon grain. The Rajputs, as both partners and opponents, were a source of inspiration. To imitate Rajput heroics, Akbar fastened the hilt of his sword to a wall. Its pointed end faced his chest. Then he rushed towards it. Man Singh quickly came between the Baadshah and the sword. Chattarapati Shivaji was an exemplar of intelligence and courage. Many a taboo places in the socio-religious field were visited and redesigned by him.

The Great Mughals were capable of being as cruel as they could be kind, as resigned as they could be ambitious and as forgiving as they could be revengeful. The same Akbar who built the Khairpura, Dharmapura and Jogipura to feed needy Muslims, Hindus and Jogis respectively, could not be generous enough to forgive his wife/concubine Anarkali for her audacious affair with his son, Sultan Salim. She was enclosed in airtight walls, alive. According to William Finch, a remorseful Akbar later commissioned a tomb and a garden for her. The Baadshahs loved their wives immensely but didn't hesitate in snubbing them if they came in the way of their commitments towards their mothers or elders. They tried to keep up with idealism with the same panache with which they kept up with humanness. While the Taj Mahal testifies to the love of Mumtaz Mahal, Anarkali's nondescript death keeps the story of her love alive. Sanjeev Kumar Singh's frantic search for Dara's grave in 2020, confirms that indeed, every visit to the Great Mughals brings out something new- a fantastic point of view.

BIBLIOGRAPHY

Abbas Khan Sarwani, *Tarikh-i Sher Shahi*, vol-II, S. M. Imam al-Din (edited and translated), University of Dacca, Dacca, 1964.

Abdul Qadir Badaoni, *Muntakhab-utTawarikh*, vols. 1–2, G.S.A. Ranking (translation), Saeed International/Atlantic Publishers and Distributors, New Delhi, 1990.

Abraham Eraly, *The Mughal World Life in India's Last Golden Age*, Penguin Books India, New Delhi, 2007.

Abul Fazl, *Ain-i Akbari* vols. 1–3, H. Blochmann and H. S. Jarret (translation), Calcutta, 1873–94.

AbulFazl, *Akbarnama* vols. 1–3, H. Beveridge (translation), Calcutta (Asiatic Society Bibliotheca Indica), 1907–1929.

Al Ghazali, *The Remembrance of Death And The After Life,,* Translation, introduction and notes by T. J. Winter, The Islamic Texts Society, Cambridge, reprint 1999.

Alam Muzaffar and Sanjay Subramanyam, *Indo-Persian Travels in the Age of Discoveries 1400–1800*, Delhi, Cambridge University Press, 2007.

Andre Wink, Land *and Sovereignty in India: Agrarian Society and Politics under the Eighteenth Century Maratha Swarajya*, Cambridge, 1986.

Aquil Raziuddin, *Sufism, Culture and Politics: Afghans and Islam in Medieval North India*, Delhi, Oxford University Press, 2007.

Ashirbadilal Shrivastava, *The Mughal Empire*, Shiva Lal Agarwala & Company, Agra, 1977.

Aslam Parvez, *The Life & Poetry of Bahaur Shah Zafar*, Ather Farouqui (translation), Hay House India, New Delhi, 2017.

Audrey Truschke, *Aurangzeb The Man And The Myth*, Penguin, Gurgaon, 2017.

Azizuddin Husain, *Structure of Politics Under Aurangzeb*, Kanishka, New Delhi, 2002.

Babur, *Baburnama*, Wheeler M. Thackston translated, edited & annotated, introduction by Salman Rushdie: *The Baburnama: memoirs of Babur, prince and emperor*, The Modern Library, New York, 2002.

Bamber Gascoigne, *A Brief History Of The Great Moghuls India's Most Flamboyant Rulers*, Robinson, London, 2002.

Banarsi Prasad Saxena, *History of Shah Jahan of Dihli*, Central Book Depot, Allahabad, 1973.

Beni Prasad, *History of Jahangir*, Bharatiya Kala Prakashan, reprint 2013.

Ellison Banks Findly, *Nur Jahan Empress of Mughal India*, Oxford University Press, New York, 1993.

Fergus Nicoll, *Shah-Jahan Rise And Fall Of The Mughal Emperor*, Penguin Books, Gurgaon, reprint 2018 .

Francois Bernier, *Travels in the Mughal Empire*, V.A. Smith (ed.), Low Price Publications, Delhi, reprint 1989.

Gulbadan Begum *Humayun Namah*, Annette S. Beveridge (translation & notes), Sang-e-Meel Publications, Lahore, 1974.

H. M. Elliot & J. Dowson, *The History of India as told by its own Historians*, Vols 1–7, London, 1867–77.

Harbans Mukhia, *Historians and Historiography During the Reign of Akbar*, Aakar Books, New Delhi, reprint 2017.

Iqtidar Alam Khan (edited), *Akbar And His Age*, Northern Book Centre, New Delhi, 1999.

Iqtidar Alam Khan, *India's polity in the age of Akbar*, Permanent Black, and Ashoka University, Ranikhet, 2016.

Iqtidar Alam Khan, *The Mughal Nobility Two Political Biographies*, Permanent Black in association with Ashoka University, Ranikhet, 2016.

Irfan Habib, *Essays in Indian History Towards a Marxist Perception*, Tulika Books, New Delhi, reprint 2010.

Irfan Habib, *The Agrarian System of Mughal India 1556–1707*, Second Revised Edition, Oxford University Press, 1999.

Jadunath Sarkar, *Anecdotes of Aurangzeb* (translation of *Ahkam I Alamgiri*), M. C. Sarkar & Sons Ltd., Calcutta, 1949

Jahangir, *Tuzuk-i Jahangiri*, *The Tuzuk-i-Jahangiri Memoirs of Jahangir* vols. 1–2, Alexander Rogers (translation) & Henry Beveridge (edited), Munshiram Manoharlal Publishers Pvt. Ltd. New Delhi, reprint, 2003.

Jean Baptiste Tavernier, *Travels in India* (2nd edition), Vol. I, V. Ball (tr.), London, 1925.

Jauhar Aftabchi, *Tazkirat-ul Vaqiyat*, translation Major Charles Stewart, *Tazkereh Al Vakiat*, Idarah-i Adabiyat-i Delli, Delhi, 1972.

Khwandmir, *Qanun-i Humayuni*, Baini Prashad translation, The Royal Asiatic Society of Bengal, Calcutta, 1940.

Meena Bhargava (edited), *Exploring Medieval India Sixteenth to Eighteenth Centuries*,Vol-II, Orient Black Swan, New Delhi, 2010.

Michael H. Fisher (edited), *Beyond the Three Seas, Travellers' Tales of Mughal India*, Random House, New Delhi, 2007.

Mohammad Athar Ali, *Mughal India Studies in Polity, Ideas, Society and Culture*, Oxford University Press, New Delhi, 2006.

Mohammad Athar Ali, *The Mughal Nobility Under Aurangzeb*, Asia Publishing House, New Delhi, 1970.

Nausheen Jaffery, *Jahan Ara Begum A Biographical Study (1614–1681)*, Idarah-i Adabiyat Dilli, Delhi, 2011.

Niccolao Manucci, *Storia Do Mogor*, William Irvine (translation & notes), Editions Indian, Calcutta, 1965.

Nizamuddin Ahmad, *Tabaqat-i Akbari*, vols 1–3, B. De (translation), Calcutta (Bibliotheca Indica No. 225), 1927–39.

P. N. Chopra, *Society And Culture during The Mughal Age*, Agam Prakashan, Delhi, 1988.

Parvati Sharma, *Jahangir An Intimate Portrait of a Great Mughal*, Juggernaut, New Delhi, 2018.

Prince Muhammad Dara Shikuh, *Majma-ul Bahrain* (The Mingling Of The Oceans), edited and translated by M. Mahfuz –ul –Haq, Royal Book Company, Karachi, 1929, reprint 1990.

R. Nath (edited), *India as Seen by William Finch*, Historical Research Documentation, Jaipur, 1990.

R. Nath, *History of Mughal Architecture* vol–3, Abhinav Publications, New Delhi, 1994.

R. P. Tripathi, *Rise and Fall of the Mughal Empire*, Central Book Depot, Allahabad, 1974.

Rumer Godden, *Gulbadan Portrait of a Rose Princess at the Mughal Court*, The Viking Press, New York, 1981.

S. A. I. Tirmizi, *Edicts from the Mughal Harem*, Idarah-I Adabiyat-I Delli, Delhi, 1978.

Satish Chandra, *Medieval India from Sultanate to the Mughals*, Part-I, Har-Anand Publications, Pvt. Ltd. New Delhi, 2001.

Satish Chandra, *Parties and Politics at the Mughal Court 1707–1740*, Aligarh Muslim University, 1959.

Satish Chandra, *State, Society and Culture in Indian History*, Oxford University Press, New Delhi, 2012.

Shaikh Rizqullah Mushtaqui, *Waqiat-i Mushtaqi*, Iqtidar Husain Siddiqui (translated and edited), Indian Council of Historical Research and Northern Book Centre, New Delhi, 1992.

Shireen Moosvi , *Episodes in the Life of Akbar Contemporary Records and Reminiscences,*, National Book Trust, New Delhi, 1994.

Shireen Moosvi, 'Medieval Indo-Persian Historiography' in Bharti Ray ed. *Different Types of History*, Pearson Longman, 2009.

Shireen Moosvi, *People, Taxation And Trade in Mughal India*, Oxford University Press, New Delhi, reprint 2010.

Stanley Lane-Poole, *Babur*, Low Price Publications, New Delhi, reprint 1997.

Stephen Frederic Dale, *Babur Timurid Prince and Mughal Emperor 1483–1530*, Cambridge University Press, New Delhi, 2018.

Sudha Sharma, *The Status of Muslim Women in Medieval India*, Sage Publications India Pvt. Ltd., New Delhi, 2016.

Surendranath Sen (edited), *Indian Travels of Jean De Thevenot & Gemelli Careri*, National Archives of India, New Delhi, 1949.

Swapna Liddle, *Chandni Chowk The Mughal City of Old Delhi*, Speaking Tiger Publishing Pvt. Ltd., New Delhi, 2017.

T.C.A. Raghavan, *Attendant Lords Bairam Khan and Abdur Rahim Courtiers & Poets in Mughal India*, Harper Collins Publishers India, Noida, 2017.

Tapan Raychaudhuri & Irfan Habib, *The Cambridge Economic History of India, Vol-I: c. 1200-c. 1750*, Orient Longman in association with Cambridge University Press, New Delhi, reprint 1984.

Velcheru Narayan Rao, David Shulman and Sanjay Subramanyam, *Textures of Time: Writing History in South India 1600–1800*, Permanent Black, 2001.

William Erskine, *A History of India Under the Two First Sovereigns of the House of Timur, Baber and Humayun*, Vols 1–2, London, 1854.

Yusuf Husain, *Two Studies in Early Mughal History*, Indian Institute of Advanced Study, Shimla, 1976.

Ziauddin Barani, *Tarikh-i Firoz Shahi*, Ishtiyaq Ahmad Zilli (translation), Primus Books, Delhi, 2015.

ACKNOWLEDGEMENTS

I am evermore grateful to Al-Mujeeb for each and every thing and I thank Him.

I am thankful to the team at Rupa Publications for the publication of this book.

My thankfulness to Emeritus Professor Irfan Habib has multiplied multi-fold. I thank him for the encouraging foreword that he wrote for *If History has Taught Us Anything*. He is a constant source of inspiration. I thank Professor Shireen Moosvi for her patronage. I thank Professors Dwijendra Narayan Jha and Harbans Mukhia. I am indebted to Late Professors Satish Chandra and Iqtidar Husain Siddiqui. I thank Professor Ishtiyaq Ahmad Zilli for his generous support. I thank my M. Phil and Ph D supervisors; Professors Iqtidar Alam Khan and S. M. Azizuddin Husain. I am indebted to all scholars, from medieval to current times who have written on this subject. Their works are pillars on which this text stands.

I thank Mr Anwar Jafri, Mr Najeeb Jung and Mr Farrukh Ali Shah Miyan Sahib for extending kind encouragement. I thank all my friends and colleagues and especially Mr Rajneesh Kumar.

I loved my parents and I still love my parents: Mohammad Wahajuddin and Sharf-un nisa.

I thank my family: Bade-bhaijaan, Chote-bhaijaan, Apa, Baby, Bhaiya, Didi, Sonu, Shazo, Sharu, Butun, Sana, Aribu and Lolo. I thank my husband, Asif.

My daughter Zoya-Yusuf Rana is my window to viewing everything cool, calm and creative. May God bless her always and forever.